Man
Grand Symbol
of the
Mysteries

Manly P. Hall

Must Have Books
503 Deerfield Place
Victoria, BC
V9B 6G5
Canada

ISBN 9781773239699

"I had rather believe all the fables in the *Legend,* and the *Talmud,* and the *Alcoran,* than that this universal Frame is without a Mind.

"For it is a thousand times more credible that four mutable Elements and one immutable First Essence duly and eternally placed need no God than that an army of infinite small portions, or seeds unplaced, should have produced this Order and Beauty, without a Divine Marshal.

"They that deny a God destroy man's nobility, for certainly man is of kin to the beasts by his body; and if he be not of kin to God by his spirit, he is a base and ignoble creature.

"Read not to contradict and confute; nor to believe and take for granted; nor to find talk and discourse, but to weigh and consider."

—*Sir Francis Bacon.*

PREFACE TO THE SIXTH EDITION OF
MAN, THE GRAND SYMBOL OF THE MYSTERIES

IT would be natural to assume that in the forty years since the first publication of this volume, a wealth of further material would have become available. Actually, this has not been the case, and amendments do not appear to be necessary. It is only in the last decade that Western science has "discovered" Oriental concepts bearing upon the human body and its functions. Recent emphasis has been upon physiology rather than anatomy, and it is now obvious that Asiatic healers were aware of the theory of psychosomatic medicine.

The translation of *The Edwin Smith Surgical Papyrus* by Professor James Breasted of the University of Chicago cast a new light on the Egyptian science of healing. Professor Breasted told me that an Egyptian physician writing over 4,000 years ago had a knowledge of the circulation of the blood equal to that known in the West at the beginning of the 20th century.

The last ten years have brought a sudden and spectacular interest in Chinese healing procedures. Although the mysterious book, *The Yellow Emperor's Classic of Internal Medicine* (translated by Ilza Veith), is of uncertain date and origin, there is no doubt that elaborate speculations involving pathology and therapy were current more than 2,000 years ago. The study of the pulse as a means of diagnosis was so refined that over 200 diseases were successfully classified from the strength and rhythm of the heartbeat. This obviously required an advanced knowledge of the heart, made possible by dissecting the bodies of executed criminals. The Chinese also evolved a system of diagnosis based upon physiognomy. The life expectancy of patients was calculated with extreme accuracy, and native doctors were almost infallible in determining pregnancy from folds of skin around the eyes.

The latest contribution from China has been acupuncture, in which needles of various metals, ivory, or jade are inserted into the body in one or more of 365 points. The actual points are very small and are usually discovered by the pressure of the finger. Acupuncture charts are extremely complex and show a general knowledge of anatomy, although many details are incomplete. Acupuncture has found favor in a number of European countries, and for many years has been researched in France. It is also under study in the Soviet Union and has been revived with marked success in the Peoples' Republic of China, and Hong Kong. Several American physicians have become aware of the practical usage of acupuncture, especially in the field of anesthesia. It has proved successful in treating migraines, bursitis, asthma, arthritis, rheumatic problems, and general difficulties arising from inadequate circulation.

As yet, there are no scientific explanations for the results that are achieved. The Chinese themselves assume that health results from the equilibrium of the *yin* and *yang* principles of the human body. If the balance of these two (yin, female; yang, male) is disturbed, normal functions are impaired. In modern practice, elements of Western science, yoga, and vedanta are combined with an advanced skill in the manipulation of nerve centers, reminiscent of the researches of Dr. Kano in his development of modern Judo.

Acupuncture and moxacautry, or moxibustion, reached Japan from China, where the burning of cones of moxa was involved in the initiation rites of Buddhist priests. Treatment by the use of needles is called *Hari-ryoji* among the Japanese, who recognize 660 spots in which needles can be inserted. Acupuncture is a recognized profession, and practitioners must be licensed. It was long regarded as a "compassionate" art, practiced principally by the blind. The first schools for the blind in Japan were devoted to acupuncture. I have seen a textbook on the subject, showing the needles being inserted into the eyeball. Patients are warned that such treatments are habit-forming!

We also have in our collection a work on the Japanese science of osteopathy. It was published in Bunka-5 (1808), Tokyo, and the title in Japanese is *Seikotsu-han* (*A Textbook of Osteopathy*). The book, which is profusely illustrated with woodcut figures showing adjustments for the spine and for various dislocations and lesions, indicates that the technique was similar to that now used in the West. The book was written twenty years prior to the birth of Dr. Still, generally regarded as the discoverer of osteopathy.

We may look forward, therefore, to the day when our knowledge of man— both his physical body and the invisible spirit which inhabits it—will be advanced by a cooperative effort of both Eastern and Western scientists and physicians. By this partnership of effort, it is possible that preventive medicine will help us all to preserve health rather than to struggle desperately against the inroads of disease.

MANLY P. HALL

TABLE OF CONTENTS

LIST OF ILLUSTRATIONS

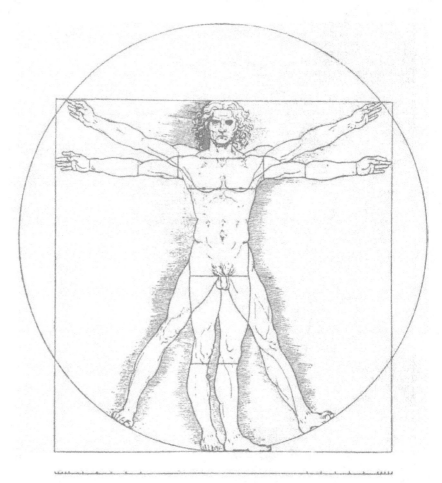

THE SQUARING OF THE CIRCLE

In this drawing Leonardo Da Vinci combines the two figures from the architectural canons of Vitruvius, thereby revealing man to be the perfect measure and pattern of all things. The commentary of the great Roman COLLEGIAN *is as follows: "For if a man be placed flat on his back, with his hands and feet extended, and a pair of compasses centered at his navel, the fingers and toes of his two hands and feet will touch the circumference of a circle described therefrom. And just as the human body yields a circular outline, so, too, a square figure may be found from it. For if we measure the distance from the soles of the feet to the top of the head, and then apply that measure to the outstretched arms, the breadth will be found to be the same as the height, as in the case of plane surfaces which are perfectly square."*

CHAPTER I

RESTATING THE THEORY OF EDUCATION

N publishing this treatise on the subject of occult anatomy, we fully realize the gantlet it must run at the hands of science. Though painfully aware of our own shortcomings in matters of treatment, we are convinced of the fundamental integrity and reasonableness of the doctrines which we have sought to defend. Plato was enriched by his philosophic vision; the modern thinker is impoverished by his unbelief. Compare the noble head of the Herculaneum bust of Aristotle with the victim of modern intellectual inbreeding. Gone from our earth, it seems, is the rugged grandeur personified by this old Peripatetic. The hair lies in curls upon the broad forehead, the eyes of the dreamer gaze out from under the brows of the sage, there is a kindly humor about the corners of the mouth, the short beard gives added strength, the head might be that of Zeus or Asclepius—divine rather than mortal. There were gods, indeed, upon the earth in those days. Professor Howard W. Haggard might well have been thinking of Aristotle when he penned the significant words: "Only the highest types of men have the intelligence, the independence, the honesty, and the courage to admit their errors and to seek without bias for truth."

To gaze upon the wreckage of our present civilization is to realize that when beauty is sacrificed to utility in the hearts of men, existence becomes but a ghastly travesty. Not to kill out idealism but to make the world safe for ideals is the true purpose of education. High above the broad proscenium of a great university is deeply carved this proud legend of enlightenment: "Education is learning to use the tools which the race has found indispensable." Is life but a battle of wits? Are these tools merely scholastic rapiers and is education but a coaching in the thrust and parry of opinion? Education obviously should fit youth for something better than a knight-errantry of notions or a lancing of windmills. True education is learning how to build an adequate foundation under the ideals of the race. In the Dark Ages, education was liberation from bondage to superstition. In this still darker age, education must liberate itself from materialism—the most miserable superstition of all. The tools indispensable to the race are the higher aspects of philosophy— æsthetics, ethics, and metaphysics. For what shall it profit a man to become the most skilled of artisans, if his hand is not apprentice to a creative vision? Education means the release of ideals and the determination of spiritual values. To the degree it falls short of this legitimate end, education fails to educate.

By facts are reasonably inferred dynamic, working truths—a knowledge of causes and principles. The fact of a matter is the reason for its existence. All facts must be answers to the question *why*, not how, when or what but *why* in no other sense than why. Until why has been established, science is not based upon facts but upon observation, experimentation, logic, reason, and opinion. These are all worthy instruments of the intellect, and far be it from us to depreciate their significance or their contributory power. We are simply questioning an imperialism of science which, through insinuation at least, professes to an infallibility not supported by the evidence at hand. Science has been neither fair, just nor equitable in its examination of metaphysics. In other words, it has not been "scientific" in its examinations. It has neither experimented nor observed. It has not reasoned from available data but from prejudices, and has dismissed the whole matter of superphysical causation with a supercilious gesture of utter contempt.

Our primary purpose is not to deal with particulars but with principles. An example, however, will not be amiss. Spiritualism is a field of research which has engaged the attention of several eminent scientific men. The existence of spiritualistic phenomena is indisputable and far more susceptible of repeated confirmation than many extremely abstract premises now enthusiastically sponsored by science. But when psychic phenomena are produced under test conditions—and even when a man like Professor Einstein is bewildered—there is only a ominous silence pregnant with subdued animosity and chagrin. If, on the other hand, it is proved that the old lady pushed the Ouija board or the medium made the raps with his big toe, then a wild outburst of scornful condemnation follows and the air is filled with "I-told-you-sos."

In a recent article Professor Edgar James Swift, Head of the Department of Psychology, Washington University, gives an amazing exhibition of the ease with which science "explains" the superphysical. He begins by setting forth the scientific requirements for a theory or belief when reduced to lowest terms. "First, the 'facts' of a mysterious phenomenon must be demonstrable to unbelievers as well as to believers; secondly, the new theory must be the simplest that will explain the mystery; and thirdly, the explanation should be consistent with established knowledge: To be sure, new facts may be discovered which are inconsistent with accepted views but they should not be accepted until the inconsistency has been eliminated and a place found for them in the recognized knowledge." It is not quite evident why these requirements are of such fundamental importance. As to the first, little, if anything, is ever demonstrable to an unbeliever. Facts have little meaning when arrayed against prejudice. A fact is a fact though never demonstrated, and, to be brutally frank, humanity is still looking for its first "fact." As to the second, we see no reason why a theory must be the simplest to explain the mystery, for if that were true the naive conclusions of childhood would be comparatively infallible. Eureka! The simplest explanation for the phenomenon of darkness is that the sun goes out every night! As to the third, the statement is positively inquisitional and would rejoice the souls of those pious bigots who steeped the world in perverted forms of Aristotelianism and Augustinianism and precipitated the Dark Ages. "Of course," says Professor Swift, "our present knowledge is admittedly incomplete. Many things which we now think untrue may later be proved true, but until they are we had better stick pretty close to the teachings of science." Noble advice for scientific Columbuses and reminiscent of that age when men were warned not to venture far from shore lest they reach the ends of the earth and fall off! The closing thought is overwhelming. If new facts are discovered inconsistent with our present views, so much the worse for the new facts. They must accustom themselves to our codes or else perish miserably. Finding a place for a "fact" in our recognized knowledge may prove a heavy strain upon the learned.

"Only geniuses," continues the learned psychologist, "can leap into the unknown and bring back knowledge which they alone have glimpsed." But since geniuses cannot prove their vision to fools, they are outlawed under Requirement 1. How does the Doctor know that such of the old masters as Pythagoras and Apollonius, who were deeply versed in transcendental magic, were not "geniuses"? To bolster up his "scientific" conclusions Professor Swift then explains that in superphysical matters "the integrity of the witness is valueless." (!!!) This is presumably because they believe the evidence of their senses and the Professor turns Vedantist long enough to declare that "modern man—if well read on the subject—knows that nothing is more unreliable." But, then, man cannot become well read without his senses; and as these are "unreliable," why read? we ask. It looks very much as though the testimony of the senses is very accurate when it agrees with our foregone conclusions but very "unreliable" when it convicts us of inconsistency. The Professor then proceeds to prejudice the minds of his readers by subjecting the whole field of psychical phenomena to the most absurd comparison imaginable. His elegant parallel is "let us admit that the supernatural theory may be true, just as there may be monkeys in Africa that speak the English language." While not prepared to demonstrate that the African simians descend to the use of our mother tongue, it is undeniably evident that tens of thousands of English-speaking monkeys are graduated annually from our institutions of higher learning.

That there is a goodly percentage of fraud in the field of psychic phenomena is quite probable. Yet if in the thousands of years during which such phenomena have been recorded but one materialization, one example of telepathy, or one message has passed between the two worlds, the genuineness of spiritualistic phenomena is scientifically proved and established. Since the scientific world is impelled to action only on "facts," it follows that any savant who categorically denies the possibility of metaphysical forces in Nature must necessarily be in position to prove beyond reasonable doubt that every claim in scriptural and classical antiquity, in the Middle Ages as well as in modern times is a 100 per cent fabrication. We would like to advance the opinion that the accumulation of such proof is utterly beyond the ability of any man or group of men. Therefore, while they may disbelieve, they are not qualified to unconditionally condemn. We would not swerve science from its course of ministering to the common good nor would we have scientists believe anything inconsistent with their intelligence. However, since science has chosen to divorce itself from superstition and opinion, and the foibles of the unenlightened, we would recommend that it pursue a course consistent with its own premise. Blind condemnation is as superstitious as blind acceptance.

We would humbly remind the scientist that astrology, for example, has not been scientifically *dis*proved. We can find no record of any scientific body examining and analyzing the premises of the starry science. On the other hand, we have plentiful evidence of so-called learned men who, scarcely knowing one astrological symbol from another, are so "unscientific" as to base their judgment not upon examination and observation but upon the bigotry of their colleagues. Incidentally, there is no man alive actually qualified to *dis*prove the existence of God, and yet the more materialistic in the realms of science depart so far from the trestleboard of their craft that they begrudge Deity the meagre benefit of a doubt! The presence of Supreme Intelligence directing creation may not be demonstrable to the physical sense perceptions or to a mind firmly grounded in the mechanistic theory. Yet it is not a scientific "fact" that God does not exist, nor is it a scientific "fact" that Cabalism is a superstition, nor is it a scientific "fact" that alchemists were mad, nor is it a scientific "fact" that the ancients suffered from a common benightedness, nor is it a scientific "fact" that miracles are frauds. These are *opinions* held by certain groups, but while opinions may be very intriguing to those who chance to hold them, they demonstrate nothing; they neither prove nor disprove anything, and for the most part clutter up the field of learning. Opinion is the antipode of wisdom, and the fewer the opinions the greater the likelihood of intelligence. Mysticism is not a vag   to amuse superannuated midwives. It is a distinct department of learning which, if given proper consideration and opportunity, could make a definite contribution to world normalcy and well-being.

A recent publication, DEVILS, DRUGS AND DOCTORS, by a prominent scientific man, contains the following comparison which, though directed by its author to the healing arts, is representative of an attitude prevalent in the field of scholarship: "There are two philosophies of medicine: the primitive or superstitious, and the modern or rational." Here is a very broad, unqualified statement. The inference is unavoidable. Previous to the Renaissance, there was nothing but superstition; subsequent to the Renaissance, nothing but rationality! While most will probably grant (for lack of knowledge) that "primitive" is synonymous with "superstitious," we are living too uncomfortably to be quite certain that "modern" is a synonym for "rational." It seems a grave mistake to implant in the minds of the present generation such an attitude of utter superiority over the past and complete self-sufficiency towards the present. Under such conditions there is no future; and where there is no future, there is no reason for life. The wisest men of all time lived before the dawn of the modern era. In the field of art there was Pericles, in medicine Hippocrates, in mathematics Euclid, in philosophy Aristotle, in poetry Homer, in theology Plato. This in Greece alone, to say nothing of Zarathustra, Buddha, Confucius, and a score of others, whose minds so changed the course of human life that foolish men today can be intolerant in comparative safety.

Now for the crux of our problem—the relationship between science and religion. A curious phenomenon can be observed in most of our large universities. Prominent among the campus buildings will be seen one or more chapels, often several. Rich men, it appears, have a penchant for building churches. It is interesting to observe the high-flung spires and belfries which at certain hours of the day may even cast their shadows upon the massive buildings devoted to the sciences. In one university there are several chapels of different denominations; in fact, we are told that from an educational standpoint such bequests are a drug upon the market. Here, indeed, is a concourse of incompatibles. Religion is dedicated to the presence of a God which education (in some cases possibly unknowingly) is constantly undermining. Scientifically speaking, it is beyond either possibility or presumption that Jesus Christ could have been the Son of God by an immaculate or any other conception—except the conceptions of superstition. In the light of physics, his birth is a myth, his life either a delusion or an imposture, his miracles idle gossip, his religion only a superstition, his death—if he died—a martyrdom to hallucination, his resurrection impossible, and his church an impediment to progress. The situation is grotesque, to say the least. Yet side by side they stand—the hall of science and the house of God!

In our present analysis of religion we are not concerned with perverted forms of theology but rather with those principles upon which the faiths of men have been founded. Our thought is equally applicable to any of the great religions which have existed in the past or which have survived to the present. God-loving philosophers as well as God-fearing theologians are included within the scope of our consideration. We are speaking not of frauds or charlatans, nor again of fanatics or misanthropes, but of "good men and just," those who have supplied the moral impulse to mankind. Dreamers, yes; but doers also. Many of these great men studied science at the feet of the gods. They found in learning the perfection of spiritual things. Science does not teach men veneration for beauty, love of good, faith in right or strength in virtue. We will not say that science directly attacks integrity. It certainly depreciates integrity, however, when it contemptuously brands every idealistic impulse as superstition. Everything that is not fact is fancy, and science alone is the privileged criterion of facts. Many scientific men are religious, but this is in spite of rather than because of the scientific aspects of their training. To the degree that a man is consistent with present-day concepts of biology and physics, to that extent he is agnostic, if not atheistic. To the degree that he believes in spiritual and mystical agencies, to that extent he is inconsistent and irreconcilable with the present trend of the "exact" sciences.

Most religions are founded upon three primary tenets: (1) the existence of God; (2) the immortality of the human soul; (3) the ultimate victory of right over wrong. How many scientifically trained men are in a position to affirm that their education supports their acceptance of these tenets? These three fundamentals of religious belief are scientifically unsound, to put it mildly, not because they have been disproved but because they conflict with the materialistic theory of existence. Let us see that we have not over-stated ourselves. Dr. Julius L. Salinger, Professor of Clinical Medicine, Jefferson Medical College, Physician to the Philadelphia General Hospital, etc., translated from the original German the conclusions of Professor Dr. Hugo Magnus. "Religious teaching," the latter says, "of whatever character, has fostered medical superstition more than any other factor of civilization." When the Herr Doctor sweeps clean with his statement, "of whatever character," he makes every religious instruction or impulse which one man has sought to communicate to another a detriment to medical learning. His words are absolute and irrevocable. So this is a scientific "fact." And may we ask for adequate proof? Remember though Dr. Magnus may bring forward a million examples of religious intolerance toward science, he is not consistent. Scientifically speaking, his statement calls for absolute proof that never in the history of mankind has there been a single example of religious instruction which has not been detrimental to medical progress. It is a large order, Doctor, for the first doctors were initiated priests of the Mysteries, without whose consecration to the furtherance of knowledge there would be no doctors of materia medica, professors of clinical medicine or physicians and surgeons. Dr. Magnus makes no distinction between priestly perversions and moral virtues. He attacks the whole body of religious teaching, i.e., the concepts of honesty, friendship, justice, and truth as first revealed to mankind by the evangelists of the old rites. It was a mystic—not a scientist—who gave to the world the Golden Rule. But to Professor Magnus it seems that everything is superstition but science. We hope that after his remarks, the Doctor does not have the bad taste to be "nominally" Christian and that he has taken the necessary steps to have torn down any chapel that might face his campus.

Apollonius of Tyana, a Pythagorean philosopher of the highest personal integrity, is a pet aversion of Dr. Magnus, who thinks the high esteem in which this sage was held by his contemporaries "to be perfectly absurd." Apollonius more than once demonstrated his medical skill, and so great were his powers that a Roman Emperor erected an image to him in his private chapel. The superlative skill of the physician of Tyana has proved irritating to the learned of modern times. According to Dr. Magnus, Apollonius "was accorded a triumph which no legitimate practitioner of any age has ever enjoyed." This is strongly reminiscent of Æsop's well-known fable concerning the sour grapes.

But the unkindest cut of all is provoked by the account of Apollonius raising a young girl from the dead. The patience of Herr Doctor reaches the saturation point. It was bad enough when the sage cured lameness by merely stroking the injured member. It was worse when he practiced obstetrics without the benefit of present technique. But when he commanded grim death to depart, Dr. Magnus calls upon even the layman to support science. "Nobody will probably accuse us," he says, "of an unjust opinion if we pronounce this philosopher, who was revered as a god by the heathen, a magician of the worst kind." He also tells us that a magician of the worst kind is a common charlatan, crafty in conjuring tricks. The Professor did not attack Apollonius as a man. His reasoning is apparently somewhat as follows. Apollonius performed miracles. Miracles are impossible. Therefore, Apollonius is an impostor. The reasoning is simple and logical, but the conclusion is not necessarily true.

The miracles of Apollonius closely parallel those of Christ. According to the Gospels, Jesus healed the sick, opened the eyes of the blind, cast out demons, and raised the dead. If Dr. Magnus's reasoning be accepted as correct, then Jesus Christ was the worst of knaves and his masters—the Essenes—taught him nothing but sleight of hand. Science is squarely confronted with the question, Are miracles possible? It cannot answer the question either in the affirmative or the negative. It is in no position to demonstrate the impossibility of miracles and unwilling also to accept the validity of any evidence favorable to transcendentalism. So it must straddle the fence, a most undignified and unscientific position. Being unable either to prove or disprove the proposition, science always has the privilege of remaining generous—and by that we mean an open, whole-hearted generosity. If science can recover from its "infallibility" complex and realize that scientists are just a group of human beings, and like all other mortals subject to error, all such difficulties will be cleared up. An old Indian medicine man was once talking to a product of our higher educational training. The college man drew a small circle in the sand and said, "This is what an Indian knows." The red man nodded gravely. The conceited white man then drew a larger circle around the smaller one, saying, "And this, my fellow, is what the white man knows." The Indian was silent for a moment. Then taking a stick, drew a still larger circle around the other two and expressed his feelings thus: "And in this third circle red man and white man both fools."

In the Socratic dialogue knowledge is presumed to bring men to agreement. Opinions may differ, but facts must agree. Men who have enjoyed the training bestowed by science, however, are apparently just as subject to "opinions" as their less educated brethren. Take the case of Paracelsus, for example. We respectfully appeal to science to provide the fine discrimination necessary to separate the false from the true in the following commentaries, complimentary and otherwise. Sir William Osler, Bart., M.D., F.R.S., in THE EVOLUTION OF MODERN MEDICINE, a series of lectures delivered at Yale

University, says: "He [Paracelsus] made important discoveries in chemistry: zinc, the various compounds of mercury, calomel, flowers of sulphur, among others, and he was a strong advocate of the use of preparations of iron and antimony. * * * Through Paracelsus a great stimulus was given to the study of chemistry and pharmacy, and he is the first of the modern Iathrochemists." Our problem now is to reconcile this tribute by a scientist to the following condemnations by scientists. Daniel W. Hering, Ph.D., LL.D., calls Paracelsus "another mediæval fraud." Dr. R. M. Lawrence says, "Paracelsus was a very prince among quacks" and that "his system was founded upon mysticism and fanaticism of the grossest kind."

We return to our original premise. Human nature still underlies man's thoughts and actions. We all love to have opinions, we all like to be suspected of intelligent opinions, and we all have a fiendish desire to force our opinions upon other men. We are superstitious enough sometimes to believe that some of our opinions are more than opinions. The result is a congeries of facts so-called, facts which have no real existence but which only future ages can ultimately disprove. Since the whole universe is encircled by the incomprehensible and we are only permitted to have our opinions concerning it, let us have only such opinions as will contribute to the common good. Since we must have beliefs, let us have only constructive beliefs. Man will be forgiven for believing in God if his belief can make this world a better place in which to live. On the other hand, unbelief is inexcusable if it produces war, destruction and death, and perverts the harmony of Nature. When opinions are over-emphasized and their value sense raised to that of facts, persecution inevitably follows. Religion had its opinions, resulting in the Inquisition. Science is now having its opinions, and an intellectual Inquisition no less unreasonable than its forbear subjects its victims to the tortures of ridicule and ostracism.

The question is asked, Should a child receive religious education in school? We would answer certainly not sectarian instruction. Teaching religion to children at home is the general suggestion. There are disadvantages, however, in the latter idea. The average parent has neither the knowledge nor the ability to overbalance the materialism inculcated in the minds of our youth. Again, the father and mother often did not enjoy the benefits of higher education and the children, schooled beyond their capacities, consequently develop overwhelming superiority complexes. When the parent, therefore, tries to modify the extreme materialism of present scientific attitudes or to tincture statistics with ideals, he may be accused of simple-mindedness by his own children. Parental advice is listened to with a pitying tolerance by the mind already converted to materialism by those who recognize life's noblest expression in the play of chemical forces rather than in the practice of idealism. Science should not attempt to overshadow the spiritual life of the race. It is utterly unqualified to provide man with a substitute for morality.

There is a popular concept that ancient learning was founded upon "opinion," and modern learning upon observation. Such a point of view is incompatible with the facts. If anything, the priest-philosophers of pre-Christian times were greater observationalists than the moderns. Their learning was accumulated through direct contact with Nature and time was such an inconsequential element that several millenia would be devoted to the verification of a single premise. Cicero states that the Chaldeans expended thousands of years in the observation and classification of astrological data. No other branch of learning can claim a more adequate background in first-hand research. No favored hypothesis of this century is raised upon a more substantial footing. The practical value which may result from attention to earlier tradition is suggested by Buchan in his SYMPTOMATOLOGY. This worthy physician wrote: "Medicine was originally considered and studied as a branch of philosophy. The medical philosophy of the present day rejects the opinion that there is any connection between the paroxysms of the maniac, and the phases of the Moon. It is difficult, however, to comprehend why the term *selenitikoi*, equivalent to moonstruck, or lunatic, should have been applied to persons thus affected, from the most remote antiquity, unless there existed some foundation for the opinion. I have found a certain degree of attention (to these ancient rules) a useful practical guide to myself, and would recommend an attentive observation of them to every student of medicine, more especially to those whose duty may call them to exercise their profession in tropical climates; in such climates these doctrines originated; and as we approach the equator, the influence of the planetary bodies will certainly be found to augment."

To attempt a reconciliation between science and mysticism is to be convicted of mediævalism. We have outgrown theurgy and are wedded to new theories of life and death which are advanced with a note of staggering finality. We believe that learning had its beginning in the sixteenth century and its ending in the twentieth. Every great scientist realizes the utter ridiculousness of such contentions, but great scientists are few. Mediocrity is the rule, genius the exception. The most dangerous of fools is the educated fool, for wise in his own conceits he is an ever-present obstacle to progress. Materialism is a fad of the mob, not a fact demonstrable by scientific procedure. The dictum of the "enlightened" to the contrary, every person of sound mind and body has within himself some small measure of idealism. He will naturally love the beautiful, venerate the good, and be moved to the recognition of a Supreme Intelligence directing universal procedure. If these natural emotions be nurtured and encouraged, the individual will become a useful citizen and a constructive factor in the progress of civilization. But something is amiss in the world. The adolescent mind is diverted from the pursuit of ethics and æsthetics. A subtle force seems at work in educational circles. By innuendo and inference spiritual values are depreciated to the vanishing point. Youth is being impressed with the dangers of a "sickly mysticism." Is it necessary, we ask, for the millions of young men and women of this country to leave our universities and colleges as apostles, yes, evangelists of scientific atheism? "All scientific discoveries depend for their value on what use mankind makes of them" declared Sir Oliver Lodge, one of the world's most eminent scientists, in a recent interview. This venerable thinker stated further that the time has come "to stop betraying science by using for mutual destruction those benefits meant for the corporate good." To teach a man all the classified phenomena within the bulging archives of science and then send him forth devoid of grace and human kindliness is to launch a monster of Frankenstein upon the world.

Universally revered by the learned of antiquity, the human body was accepted as a miniature of the universe and the most proper subject for mortal contemplation. While the sacrosanct nature of the "divine form" prohibited dissection among some ancient nations, the philosophy of anatomy reached a high degree of perfection in China and India, from whence it spread to Chaldea, Egypt, and Greece. Clinics for the observation of the sick were established in many communities and Asia introduced hospitals for the treatment of animals. The Pythagoreans—and after them the Platonists, Neo-Platonists, and Gnostics—defined the physical body as the house or domicile of the soul, even going so far as to declare that the corporeal fabric was modified into varying shapes and appearances by the geometrical activities resident in the soul. The word *soul* has no meaning in the biological systems of today. Dissection does not sustain the presumption of an *anima* in man.

At this point occult anatomy breaks with material science. Occultism does not dispute the results of scientific investigation, but maintains that the physicist has failed to demonstrate the chemical origin of life and is arbitrarily asserting an opinion irreconcilable with the facts of life. Occultism does not deny the findings of physics, but maintains that so-called physical causes are secondary to superphysical causes. The body of the world is ensouled, the mechanism of the world is directed. The phenomenal aspects of life are suspended from adequate causes, these causes belonging to a world beyond the estimation of physics as it is now defined—a world which is the peculiar province of metaphysics. The mechanists and the vitalists have been dead-locked for years. First one seems to gain the ascendancy, then the other. However, the high-flown wordiness of each contestant does little more than reconvert its own constituency. The only facts relating to First Cause possessed by materialistic learning have been "legislated" into existence without benefit of proof, and the great structure of observationalism is composed of men incapable of observing the substance of their own premises. Physics would elevate matter to the chief place in the universe, bestowing upon it most of the attributes by which theology adorns the Godhead. Metaphysics, enriched by the wisdom of fifty millenia, is not wedded to theological controversies, but does perceive dimly through the veil of substance the working of vast forces only discoverable when intellect is quickened by the understanding.

Baron von Leibnitz seems to have derived his theories of monadology from the Pythagoreans and other early atomists. The dissemination of the heliocentric system of astronomy, it is presumed, invalidated the correspondences between man and the universe promulgated in antiquity by the initiated philosophers. Again a popular conceit has been left uncorrected. The so-called Copernican system was known and accepted by those very masters who first taught the great Hermetic axiom of knowledge that the above is like unto the below and the greatest is like unto the least. It is both dangerous and questionable for modern learning to seek its own aggrandizement by discrediting the thinkers of the past, inasmuch as science is indebted to these ancient authorities for its very existence. Needless to say, however, the doctrine of macrocosms and microcosms has been banished from the house of knowledge with appropriate anathemas. "The idea of a close parallelism between the structure of man and of the wider universe," writes Charles Singer, "was gradually abandoned by the scientific, while among the unscientific it degenerated and became little better than an insane obsession. As such it appears in the ingenious ravings of the English follower of Paracelsus, the Rosicrucian, Robert Fludd, who reproduced, often with fidelity, the systems which had some novelty five centuries before his time. As a similar fantastic obsession this once fruithful hypothesis still occasionally appears in modern works of perverted learning." (See FROM MAGIC TO SCIENCE.) The most, then, which we can hope for our present writing is a modest corner in the *Index Expurgatorius scientiae.* But we shall be in good company for the congregation of the elect is gathered there. If Mr. Singer is not extremely careful, he may join us, too, for in writing of Paracelsus in the above quoted work, this gentleman remarks: "He [Paracelsus] believed still in a relation of microcosm and macrocosm—*as in a residual sense we all do* [!]." (Italics mine. M. P. H.) One is reminded of the college professor who, waxing violent in a controversy over the immortality of the soul, climaxed his argument with these exquisite words: "There is no such thing as the immortality of the soul, and when I die I shall come back and prove it to you!"

Haeckel's first principle of biogenesis verges also on this heresy, for this worthy professor declares the fundamental law of organic evolution to be expressed in the proposition "that the history of the germ is an epitome of the history of the descent," or more explicitly, "that the series of forms through which the individual organism passes during this progress from the egg cell to its fully developed state, is a brief, compressed reproduction of the long series of forms through which the animal ancestors of that organism (or the ancestral forms of its species) have passed from the earliest periods of so-called organic creation down to the present time." (See THE EVOLUTION OF MAN.)

That the greater is revealed through the lesser, that the past is epitomized in the present, and that the universe through which man evolved has, therefore, impressed itself upon him so that he is an epitome of its infinite ramifications— these are the ancient theories elsewhere denied, disparaged, defamed, and yet here restated in different language as a vital scientific "principle." If it be admitted that the unicellular ancestor of the human race gradually evolved through inconceivable ages, being constantly modified to the environmental circumstances of those ages until the comparative complexity of his present state was reached, wherein lies the heresy of presuming that, in one sense at least, he is an embodiment of these ages, bearing faithful witness in his minor constitution to the sidereal processes which precipitated him? Man is not a little universe by some arbitrary dictate of a divine tyranny, but rather the product of universal law releasing itself through a concatenation of evolving organisms. Man is a microcosm by heredity. He is the progeny of substance and motion. The universe is the cause of man, and if like produces like, man cannot be other than a universe. Biologically, heredity has precedence over environment. Environment may modify but cannot destroy the universal aspect of man. We might even invoke Mendel to support our contention that a strain of the macrocosm is transmitted and survives in each of its microcosms. But this would be stigmatized "perverted learning" and relegated to the *Index!*

Admitting the importance of environment in qualifying hereditary elements, it should not be forgotten that man's own body is his most immanent environment. Radiating into the phenomenal state, the noumenon finds body the inevitable mediator. While "no body, no phenomenon" is a scientific truism, "no tangible body, no noumenon" is less susceptible of demonstration. Health and disease are states which prove the environmental importance of body. When learning dedicates itself to the improvement of man's environmental condition, it must recognize in temperament the factor which deflects energy to constructive or destructive ends. When mental, physical or moral unbalance disturbs the organism, infecting it with the numerous phobia the flesh is heir to, the world is put at hazard. When we speak of environment, the first thought that comes ordinarily to mind is the home, the school, the playground, and the church. To the ancients, however, environment was primarily the body; the conquest of environment, self-discipline. When a man wisely directs the forces of life to a legitimate end, he best protects the commonwealth and preserves his own integrity.

Experience results from contact with environment, whether it be the primary environment of the body or that vaster environment of the world. We must depend upon our sensory equipment for the accumulation of those impressions from which knowledge is distilled and for the enrichment of the inner life. Why is it, then, that the average so-called educated person seldom associates bodily improvement with the problem of sensory extension?

Scientific research demands constant improvement in scientific instruments but no æsthetic refinement in the scientist himself. Is this not a possible clue to the bankruptcy of learning? Furthermore, mind has a saturation point. There is but one answer: Increase the capacity of the mind. That which a man takes in does not necessarily nourish him. Gluttons may die of anemia. This is also true of the mind. Only that which the intellect is capable of assimilating contributes to its well-being. If science is to ripen, the scientist must mature.

Science and mysticism may be contrasted from their own premises. Science would achieve through schooling, mysticism through becoming. The secret of the supremacy of the "golden age" of Greece lay in a now ignored and forgotten factor—the philosophic life. The average person today is not only ignorant of the higher ideals of life but in his present state incapable of learning them. Before the seed can be planted, the ground must be tilled. Here, then, is the *raison d'etre* for the Mysteries—those secret institutions now ridiculed but, in point of fact, indispensable to the upbuilding and maintenance of higher education. The old initiates were termed narrow, exclusive, auto-cratic, and unscientific, because they demanded a certain standard of excellence in those to whom they imparted the priceless secrets of life and Nature. Our age has tried to reverse the ancient rule. Instead of bringing man up to learning, it has brought learning down to man. The result is the tragic narrowness of modern vision. "He who merely sees the external appearance of things is not a philosopher," wrote Paracelsus. "The true philosopher sees the reality, not merely the outward appearance."

Science chose to depart from the old traditions. Learning, divided from itself, entered upon a course of competitive speculation. The "divine autopsies" were no longer celebrated by the Mysteries. The "blessed" rites ceased as national institutions, to be perpetuated in secret by those who remained true to the original vision. The Cabalists and later the Hermetists, alchemists, Rosicrucians, and Templars derived their occultism from the surviving adepts of the older school. As the gulf between material and spiritual science widened with the ages, certainties vanished and uncertainties multiplied until only theories remained. Science cannot be perfected until the reunion of the several departments of knowledge has been consummated. Learning has been divided into provinces and distributed among the nobility of letters. Each part flouts its independence in the face of the broader claims of universal interdependence. If the hands and feet of man, for example, were as irreconcilable in their functions as the members of the body educational, concerted action would be impossible. So long as science, religion, and philosophy find no common ground, human effort can never be coordinated to the perfection of the race.

Savants of today, be not too proud to incline your minds to the wisdom of yester-year. The Pyramid builders were also men enriched with high learning and noble vision. Be grateful to the past; respect the dreams of those who came before you. Be gentle of their memories, and if in some things the measure of your knowledge seems to be fuller than theirs, feel not contempt but rather admiration for those qualities in which they did excel. As you judge, so shall it be judged unto you. Tomorrow you rest with the ages, your works become the property of the race, and would you have the science of the future descend as a pack of hungry wolves upon your dreams? Generosity is the criterion of true greatness, tolerance the measure of true vision. Be not of those who, seating themselves in high position, pass unjust sentence upon other men. Find joy not in condemnation but in vindication. Increase the concept of science to include all learning, not just the meagre learning of a chosen few. Remember Paracelsus: "Things that are considered now to be impossible will be accomplished; that which is unexpected will in future prove to be true, and that which is looked upon as superstition in one century will be the basis of the approved science of the next." (See PHILOSOPHICA OCCULTA.)

Gaze upon the tomes of centuries gone by—scientific books in noble vellum, grand old type, curious drawings by hands long dead, and for frontispieces the quaint stilted portraits of the authors. This one stands with his left hand upon his heart, while with the right he clasps an astrolabe. His broad ruffed collar is properly Elizabethan; his crest and Latin motto are evidence of his honorable name. Within his book are locked his dreams, his aspirations, his hope of immortality in the hearts of man. These fragments of an age forgotten, how pathetic is their state! Give attention to the crude picture of the man. Examine the eyes; how tired they seem. Note the lines of the brow, the pathos of the mouth. Grave sad faces from across the years, pioneers in human well-being, pathfinders of progress, heroes who blazed trails and contributed to a progress they never lived to see. Here is Bruno, his noble face framed with the fiery tongues of the Inquisition, and in this smaller book, Paracelsus, holding mortar and pestle—murdered by hired assassins. This modest appearing little man is Petrus De Abano, "a scientist inspired with a universal thirst for knowledge," who was burned in effigy and only escaped the stake by dying before sentence could be passed upon him. Have we no word in defense of these immortals? Have we ever examined into that which they knew? Have we ever analyzed the true measure of their intellect or discovered the substance of that knowledge by which they were able to overturn the thought of the world? Martyrs and seers, as little understood now as then, your bodies sleep in the peaceful bosom of the Magna Mater; your souls have returned to the *empyrean*, there to be reunited with the stars that lighted your way while you walked the earth!

In the pages that follow we have attempted to gather a few crumbs from the banquet of the sages. We have no controversy with science, for that aspect of man to which we have limited ourselves is essentially superphysical —accordingly, outside the scope of scientific observation. We would simply introduce metaphysics to that realm where physics cannot tread. The doctrines herein set forth are not our own. They belong to the ages, part of a noble heritage from a prehistoric time. Some will say that knowledge came down from the heavens, others that it came up from the Pre-Cambrian slime. The pathway of wisdom is well marked. It winds as a golden thread through civilization—the one reality in a world of unrealities. As a ray of heavenly light it touched the buds of empire, and warmed by its glory, the ages blossomed and bore their fruit.

Those who have envisioned the true splendor of wisdom have closed their books forever. The human body is witness to a hidden majesty. Man, gazing into his own eyes, beholds therein a "new testament." Blood courses through the veins and arteries; the heart sounds the drumbeats of progress; the mind soars upward to explore the reaches of eternity; the hand reaches across the interval of bodies to touch the hand of another. It is not enough for science to teach that man is born, suffers, and dies. Such propositions are unworthy of a rational creature. Man is the symbol of a nobler purpose, the evidence of a higher destiny. The mortality of the intellect, if touched by the radiant finger of true enlightenment, is transformed. By the alchemy of realization humanity achieves immortality. Life goes on, soul goes on, purpose goes on, reality goes on. Immortality is inevitable. It is only the intellect, turned by false doctrines from its natural course, that can think itself into the belief of extinction. Sprinkle, therefore, the alchemical "powder" of idealism upon the cold facts of today and they will be transformed in a single instant into the purest gold.

ANDREAE VESALII.

—From De Humani Corporis Fabrica

ANDREAS VESALIUS, THE FATHER OF MODERN ANATOMY
(1493-1541)

CHAPTER II

OCCULT FOUNDATIONS OF SCIENCE

O amount of schooling can preserve modern civilization if man's appreciation for the higher values of life is destroyed by materialism. Learning has been turned from its ancient course and threatens to lose the name of action. Metaphysics, the first and most glorious of the sciences, has fallen into bad repute and evil times. The mentors of the Golden Age were men of heroic vision and high purpose. Now fat endowments from the bourgeoise and smug professorships, distributed among the conservatives, breed the commonplace. Learning is eclipsed by a schooling which too often is but bondage to opinion and serfdom to authority. Rejoicing in their pseudo-enlightenment, the intelligentsia of today, like the Pharisees of old, give thanks that they are not as other men. The altars of an ancient learning built to gentle spirits have crumbled in the dust. Transcendentalism has given place to materialism; the worship of Lares and Penates to the adoration of the great god, Doubt. Even flame-belching Baal was never served by a priesthood more fanatic than now grovels before the altars of mechanistic realism.

Although Nature abounds in principles which may be adapted to mechanical purposes, Nature herself is not mechanical. The world is not a machine nor was it spontaneously produced. It is an organism, not an organization. The universe is life escaping into manifestation through generation. Consciousness and intelligence are growing up through matter like tiny plants breaking through the dark earth. Among the drawings left by the great Leonardo da Vinci is one in which he compares the heart and the vessels branching from it to a sprouting seed; and Boehme compares the human soul to a seedling growing upward through the material nature of man in quest of light. The wise man will not forget the alchemical axiom that art may complement Nature but must never violate her edicts. To venerate realities is to be wise; to recognize the simple dignity of divine procedure is to establish the mind in essential truth. The first instructors of humanity—the hierophants of the elder rites—those of whom it is written that they gazed upon the gods unafraid, transmitted to succeeding ages those doctrines which have proved necessary to the survival of the human soul. Thabion, the founder of the Mysteries of the Phœnicians, concealed the secrets of generation under the figure of the World Egg, and upon the authority of Sanchoniathon prepared fables and allegories relating thereto so profound in their substance, so magnificent in their daring, and so ennobling in their application that for many ages they excited the astonishment and admiration of mortals.

Modern educators, if accused of promulgating an economic theory, would vigorously protest that their first concern was to fit youth for life. The only kind of life for which they fit youth, however, is utterly lacking in perspective. The value sense is bankrupt at the very start. Modern learning has for its chief aim the perpetuation of the social order. Ancient learning, on the other hand, sought the perfection of the individual. In our efforts to make the world fit for man, we have neglected to make man fit for the world. Æsthetics may be regarded as incidental by the realist, yet knowledge had its beginnings among those peoples enriched by highly developed metaphysical systems, as the Hindus, Chinese, Egyptians, and Greeks. It was to the hierophants of the old Mysteries that the splendid vision "of a reasonable universe" was revealed. The initiated priests were the first scientists. Adepts in an ageless wisdom, these "divine" men set for themselves the task of dissecting the body of God. These first sages to whom we are indebted for the fundamentals of science found spirituality and idealism neither detrimental to learning nor incompatible with the premises of scientific thought. These fathers of learning practiced secret rites, communed with spirits, and were not above pondering the words of oracles. A far cry, indeed, from the hoary patriarchs of elder days to the pompous professors of this enlightened age! Many a tuck in Plato's ample toga would be necessary to make it fit the sciolist of today.

Embodiment of the virtues and personification of dignity and grace, Pythagoras was a prodigy of erudition. The matchless quality of his mind lifted him far above comparison. His intellect rose like a blazing sun upon the horizon of learning, its far-flung rays illumining every corner of the world. It is exceedingly difficult to summarize his achievements, so great is their diversity. He excelled in mathematics, astronomy, music, and healing. "He was a profound geometrician." At least two of the important theorems accredited to Euclid—including the universally known 47th Proposition— were actually devised by Pythagoras, according to Diogenes Laertius. "Pythagoras is the first person, who is known to have taught the spherical figure of the earth, and that we have antipodes; and he propagated the doctrine that the earth is a planet, and that the sun is the center round which the earth and other planets move, now known by the name of the Copernican system." (For details consult Bailly's HISTOIRE DE L'ASTRONOMIE.) His discovery of the harmonic ratios and the law of octaves in music is described by Iamblichus, Nicomachus, Boetius, Macrobius, and others. He also divided the diatonic from the chromatic and enharmonic scales, thus earning for himself a chief place in the world of music. He practiced suggestive thera- peutics and healed also with music, charms, colors, herbs, and poultices. He was able to cure not only the diseases of the body but also the intemperances of the soul. He wrote considerably on herbs and is said to have prepared a complete volume concerning the medicinal properties of the sea-onion, a work mentioned by Pliny.

Let us see how the good name of this glorious thinker has been traduced by critics unworthy to loose his sandals. "It is difficult to imagine anything more instructive   *   *   *   than the contrast presented to us by the character and system of action of Pythagoras on the one hand, and those of the great enquirers of the last two centuries, for example, Bacon, Newton and Locke, on the other. Pythagoras probably does not yield to any one of these in the evidence of true intellectual greatness   *   *   *   His discoveries of various propositions in geometry, of the earth as a planet, and of the solar system as now universally recognized, clearly stamp him a genius of the highest order. Yet this man, thus enlightened and philanthropical, established his system of proceeding upon narrow and exclusive principles, and conducted it by methods of artifice, quackery and delusion." (See William Godwin.) When this author further states that "delusion and falsehood were main features of his instruction," he takes it for granted that all claims to supernatural power made by or for Pythagoras were false and that the sage of Samos was a mere charlatan and pretender. It is the old, old story: Mystics must be epileptics and saints neurotics. Pythagoras suffered from a "divinity" complex, Socrates was a degenerate, St. Paul was subject to fits, Paracelsus was a quack, and for God—in the spirit of Laplace—"there is no need for that hypothesis." Pythagoras, moreover, believed in reincarnation. He had a golden thigh bone. He tamed a wild bear so that it became a vegetarian; caused an eagle to stop in its flight and descend upon his hand; was seen in two places at once; declared that he had visited the underworld; and taught his disciples astrology. Ergo, he is the worst of knaves, a liar from the beginning. At least, these are the conclusions of very wise men who, knowing absolutely nothing about any of the things they judge, are, therefore, "peculiarly" qualified to pass final judgment upon them.

It is sometimes easier to deny a man's existence than to attempt an explanation of his life. Consider the "embarrassing" case of Numa Pompilius, second king of Rome, who ascended the throne after Romulus had been taken up to heaven in a cloud of light. Numa has the distinction of being the "mythological" character who established the cultural system of Rome and, although "non-existent," left several important books which are referred to and quoted by subsequent Latin writers. Numa Pompilus gave himself over entirely to mysticism and esoteric philosophy and, having renounced the ambitions of the world, dedicated his life to the civilizing of the Romans. He was certainly one of the great physicists of the West, although that science had already been cultivated for thousands of years in the Orient. On the authority of Livius, Numa was of most venerable appearance, his person was regarded as sacred, and he communed with the gods. All this sounds very unscientific, but it must be remembered that in those days science was as yet undivorced from sacred orders and hence education was a balanced instruction in both physical and spiritual values. Numa built a laboratory, equipping it with instruments theretofore unknown to the Romans and, possibly instructed by the same Eastern sages who later imparted their learning to Alexander, began experimenting with electricity. From the fragments that have descended to us, it seems that he must have constructed some kind of battery, for he captured Jupiter Elicius in bottles and could control the lightning by creating it at will. "Salvertes is of the opinion that before Franklin discovered his refined electricity, Numa had experimented with it most successfully." (See ISIS UNVEILED.) The prince, Tullus Hostilius, is said to have discovered the secret books placed in a hidden recess before Numa's death, and resolved to experiment with the electrical god. As the result of some mistake due to his imperfect knowledge, the lightning which he generated destroyed him. He was struck by the heavenly fire, his body glowed with flame, and he fell dead in his laboratory amidst his instruments. Tullus Hostilius is the first known martyr in the field of electrical research. There is no real difference, then, between the premises of science and magic, only the savants of today dislike to recognize their kinship with the necromancers of antiquity.

Democritus, "the laughing philosopher," is seldom associated with metaphysics and magic, yet how shall we deny that he was schooled in the theurgic arts? His education was derived from the hierophants of Persia, Egypt, Ethiopa, and India, among whom he lived, and throughout his entire life he was devoted to the Pythagorean Mysteries. Modern science rejoices in the thought that this great atomist shared their contempt for supernatural phenomena. Their joy is short-lived, however, for Democritus did not reject miracles but, admitting their existence, maintained that they were natural rather than supernatural. To him, miracle-working was an aspect of science, and hence it was the duty of science to explain the miraculous and not to condemn it. Democritus defined a miracle as an effect, whose cause was unknown but which was necessarily equal to the effect which it produced. Having been initiated, he knew that transcendental magic depends upon and does not violate natural law as the uninformed claim. Democritus practiced divination, wrote prophecies, foretold events (presumably from the stars, astrology being the principal science of the Persians), and used charms and magical formulae for purposes of healing. Imagine the consternation in the world of letters when it is more universally known that Democritus, the father of experimental science, attributed numerous virtues to the left front foot of a chameleon and actually believed (see Pliny) that unguents could be prepared which would render the person using them invisible. Democritus had learned of atoms from Leucippus, and the knowledge passed from him to Epicurus. Then Lucretius took hold of it, and at last after many vicissitudes, John Dalton, "father of modern atomism," made his astonishing "discovery." Lucretius also declared that there were the seeds (semina) of things evil to life which fly about and cause disease and death, but Louis Pasteur and others are credited with discoveries in the field of infection which would have been impossible had not the ancient Greeks and Egyptians paved the royal road to learning.

In THE GREAT CHRONICLE OF BELGIUM, which was published in 1480, Albertus Magnus is referred to as "Magnus in magia, major in philosophia, maximus in theologia." This encomium is discounted practically in toto by Charles Singer, who writes: "Even the most learned of medieval writers—even Albertus Magnus himself—knew so piteously little compared to a modern scholar that it is possible, with sufficient application, to trace all the sources of his information." (See FROM MAGIC TO SCIENCE.) However, let us examine the "piteously little" knowledge possessed by the magician of Ratisbon to discover, if possible, in what measure he deserves the contumely of modern scholars. Albertus Magnus was a philosopher, a mystic, astrologer, alchemist, and transcendental magician—five branches of learning beyond the pale of present recognition. If it is, indeed, possible "to trace all the sources of his information," we would recommend that a logical point to begin would be the matter of his famous *android*. "It is related of Albertus, that he made an entire man of brass, putting together its limbs under various constellations, and occupying no less than thirty years in its formation. This man would answer all sorts of questions, and was even employed by its maker as a domestic. But what is more extraordinary, this machine is said to have become at length so garrulous, that Thomas Aquinas, being a pupil of Albertus, and finding himself perpetually disturbed in his abstrusest speculations by its uncontrollable loquacity, in a rage caught up a hammer and beat it to pieces." (See LIVES OF THE NECROMANCERS.) Such an automaton might provide a thrill even in this age of chronic ennui.

But Albertus was more than a creator of automata; he possessed other magical powers equally intriguing. The TRITHEMII CHRONICA describes how Albertus received and entertained William, Earl of Holland. The conjuror monk spread a magnificent repast in his monastery garden, but it was midwinter and the tables were laid in the snow. As the Earl and his courtiers seated themselves, Albertus waved his arm. "Suddenly the snow disappeared, and they felt not only the softness of spring, but even the parterre was filled with the most odoriferous flowers, the birds as in summer flew about or sung their most delightful notes, and the trees appeared in blossom." (See THE LIVES OF THE ALCHEMYSTICAL PHILOSOPHERS.) The banquet over, the vision disappeared as it had come, and the nobles were forced to hasten indoors because of the severity of the weather. It seems, then that this learned Dominican friar enjoyed a form of knowledge not available to the savants of this age. Of course, it will be denied that Albertus was favored with such gifts, but denial neither proves nor disproves anything. It might prove profitable, however, to be less contemptuous and examine this "piteously little" which Albertus knew; for there are still many secrets of Nature that retire abashed at the irreverent approach of the materialistic scientist.

Then there is Paracelsus, whom Dana styles "the Luther of physicians." Garrison also pays the great Aureolus several notable compliments.

"Paracelsus," he says, "was the precursor of chemical pharmacology and therapeutics, and the most original medical thinker of the sixteenth century. * * * Baas has compared reading Paracelsus to delving in a mine. We are in a strange world of mystic principles, macrocosms and microscosms, archæi and arcana, enlivened by gnomes, sylvans, spirits, and salamanders. Yet the author of all this high-flown verbiage, the actual Paracelsus, was a capable physician and surgeon." Garrison further notes that Paracelsus was the first to establish a correlation between cretinism and endemic goiter, was far ahead of his time in noting the geographic differences of disease, was almost the only asepsist between Mondevill and Lister, and introduced mineral baths. Should we not examine carefully the philosophical background of this man who, in the words of Ferguson, "revolutionized medicine" and who, according to Thomas Thompson, freed medical men from five centuries of bondage to wornout precedents?

Paracelsus confounded the professors of Basle by publicly burning the books of Galen and Avicenna as an introduction to his lecture course. "My accusers," he exclaims, "complain that I have not entered the temple of knowledge through the 'legitimate door.' But which one is the truly legitimate door? Galenus and Avicenna or Nature? I have entered through the door of Nature: her light, and not the lamp of an apothecary's shop, has illuminated my way." Paracelsus, the hermetist and the mystic, the original thinker who gained his knowledge not from long-coated pedagogues but from dervishes in Constantinople, witches, gypsies, and sorcerers; who invoked spirits, captured the rays of the celestial bodies in dew, of whom it is said that he cured the incurable, gave sight to the blind, cleansed the leper, and even raised the dead, and whose memory could turn aside a plague—this "magician" is the father of chemical medicine! We cannot do better than to summarize the achievements of Paracelsus in the words of Lessing: "Those who imagine that the medicine of Paracelsus is a system of superstitions which we have fortunately outgrown, will, if they once learn to know its principles, be surprised to find that it is based on a superior kind of knowledge which we have not yet attained, but into which we may hope to grow." (See PARACELSUS.)

No survey of the contributions of occultism to science would be complete without the achievements of Jan Baptista van Helmont, whom Dana dignifies with the appellation, "the Descartes of medicine." This noble Belgian mystic, disciple of the "divine" Paracelsus, was the founder of the Iatrochemical School, according to Garrison. "He was the first to recognize the physiologic importance of ferments and gases" (Garrison) and was the inventor of the term *gas* (Stillman). It has been said of van Helmont that no chemist has been cited more frequently or with greater respect. While still in his early thirties, he retired to an old castle near Brussels, where he remained "retired and almost unknown to his neighbors until his death in the sixty-seventh year of his age." The good name of van Helmont has suffered to some extent from the modern penchant for criticism depreciatory of earlier writers. He is accused of having pirated his opinions. The fact, however, appears to be that van Helmont's discoveries have been shamefully pirated by pretenders who came after him. The materialistic scientist is here confronted with an interesting dilemma. The man who first taught the chemistry of the human body and stated the true purpose of chemistry to be the preparation of medicines for the treatment of disease was an alchemist (*horrible dictu!*). In his treatise, DE VITAE ETERNA, van Helmont gives the following amazing testimony: "I have

—From Opera Medico-Chimica sive Paradoxa.

PARACELSUS, PRINCE OF PHYSICIANS
(1493-1541)

seen and I have touched the philosopher's stone more than once; the colour of it was like saffron in powder, but heavy and shining like pounded glass; I had once given me the fourth part of a grain, I call a grain that which takes 600 to make an ounce. I made projection with this fourth part of a grain, wrapped in paper, upon eight ounces of quicksilver, heated in a crucible." The result of the projection was eight ounces lacking eleven grains of the most pure gold, so that according to van Helmont one grain of the philosopher's stone could transmute 19,156 grains of quicksilver. It is interesting to note that van Helmont never professed to have ever actually prepared the philosopher's stone, but gained his knowledge of its appearance and power from alchemists whom he contacted during his years of research.

The place of Sir Francis Bacon (Lord Verulam) in the world of science is too thoroughly established to require defense. He has been called "the great Instaurator of all knowledge," accomplishing in himself the advancement of a whole generation and achieving in a few short years a restatement of the entire premise of learning.   There is evidence that Bacon "was strongly influenced and stimulated" by the writings of Paracelsus.   Far from being a materialist, he was profoundly impressed with the reality of spiritual values— a point well summarized by him in his treatise on atheism, wherein he writes: "A little philosophy inclineth man's mind to atheism; but depth in philosophy bringeth men's minds about to religion."   Bacon's confession of faith testifies that to this truly great thinker the purpose of knowledge was to discover a legitimate reason for hope; to demonstrate the integrity of faith, so that the intellect shall not attribute so much to secondary causes that it ignores First Cause.   Lord Bacon broke with scholasticism when he was sixteen years old, and from that time devoted his mind to the *Instauratio magno*, "the great restitution of learning."   He was self-taught, acknowledging no master among the pedants of his day.   To those laboring under the delusion that the memorization of other men's opinions is the beginning of education we submit a short extract from THE LIFE OF BACON by his faithful friend, William Rawley: "I have been induced to think that if there were a beam of knowledge derived from God, upon any man, in these modern times, it was upon him.   For though he was a great reader of books, yet he had not his knowledge from books but *from some grounds and notions from within himself*."   Our great author, then, is convicted of mysticism by his nearest friend.   And if more proof is needed that Bacon was at heart a Hermetist and a Rosicrucian, dedicated to a secret science, THE NEW ATLANTIS is more than sufficient.   Imagine the grand master of inductive reasoning, the man whose criteria of fact were observation and experimentation, delivering himself of the following scientific "heresy": "In the traditions of astrology the natures and dispositions of men are not without truth distinguished from the predominances of the planets; as that some are by Nature made and proportioned for contemplation, others for matters civil, others for war, others for advancement, others for arts, others for a changeable course of life."   (See THE ADVANCEMENT OF LEARNING.)

Roger Bacon, the Franciscan monk, preceded the illustrious Sir Francis by nearly four hundred years, but even the briefest consideration of science would be incomplete without some reference to the extraordinary measure of his genius.   Garrison thus surveys the field of his erudition: "Roger Bacon * * * was a comparative philologist, mathematician, astronomer, physicist, physical geographer, chemist and physician.   He reformed the calendar, did much for the theory of lenses and vision, anticipated spectacles, the telescope, gunpowder, diving bells, locomotives, and flying machines, and was a forerunner of inductive and experimental science."   And all this when Europe was in a period of intellectual obscurity!   He is actually believed to have "contrived a machine to rise in the air and convey a chariot more speedily than if drawn by horses."   He knew the art of putting statues in motion and drawing articulate sounds from a head of brass. Recent evidence has come to light that he actually assembled a microscope and was the first to investigate micro-organisms. Of course, Roger Bacon was an alchemist. He performed miracles, and of his medical writings which have survived the vandalism of time, the most important are concerned with astrology in its application to critical days and the use of planetary antipathies and sympathies in healing. Another scholastic heresiarch, shall we say?

Then there was Galen, "one of the very greatest and most creative biologists of all times" (see Charles Singer), who did not find spiritual mysteries antagonistic to physical learning. Nor can we overlook Ptolemy, chief of the cosmographers and geographers, and the founder of the principles of modern astrology. To continue this line of thought further would be to merit the accusation of tautology. The great Vesalius maintained that the study of the human soul was within the province of anatomy; and Robert Fludd, considered by De Quincey "to have been the immediate father of Freemasonry," and the chief of the philosophers by fire, was addicted to the earlier theories concerning the microcosm and the macrocosm. Copernicus and Galileo derived their theories from the metaphysical speculations of Pythagoras. Kepler and Tycho Brahe accepted the scientific integrity of astrology, as did also Flamsteed, the astronomer royal and founder of Greenwich Observatory. Halley, of comet fame, once criticised astrology in the presence of Sir Isaac Newton, the discoverer of the law of gravitation, who immediately rose to the defense of the ancient science by saying: "I have studied the subject, Mr. Halley; you have not."

From the foregoing, it would seem a reasonable conclusion that such major contributions to the body of scientific learning as chemistry, pharmacology, mathematics, astronomy, music, biology, physics, anatomy, bacteriology, atomism, electricity, and botany came from idealists and mystics, yes, even from magicians and astrologers. However, if transcendentalism is not admitted to be a distinct aid to the intellectual supremacy of these pioneers of learning, it cannot be shown, on the other hand, that it proved detrimental to them. It should mean something—or is it only a "coincidence"?—that the forerunners of science in nearly all its departments were the devotees of the theurgic and mystic arts. Hippocrates, the eldest of the sons of Asclepius, was the first physician. His *jusjurandum* (oath) is still "the most impressive document in medical ethics." In this work the duties of Asclepiads are defined for all occasions and all ages. Hippocrates was also the author of other *aphorismoi* equally "impressive," if not equally revered by the medical fraternity. The following is representative: "The man who is ignorant of the science of astrology, deserves the name of fool rather than that of physician."

—From Liber Divinorum Operum Simplicis Hominis.

HILDEGARD'S VISION OF THE GODHEAD, NATURE, AND MAN

CHAPTER III

THE MYSTERY OF THE THREE WORLDS

N accordance with the doctrines which had descended to them from their divine instructors, initiated priests of an older world regarded man as an epitome of the whole universal order and, therefore, a textbook of all mysteries, earthly and divine. Anatomy and physiology were cultivated as divine sciences and studied not for themselves alone but as aspects of sacred learning and keys to the heavenly arcanum. Benedictus Figulus writes that of the three books "from which I may learn very wisdom," the second "is the Small Book, which with all its leaves and pieces is taken from the larger work. This is man himself." In developing their concept of the relationship between the superior and the inferior orders of existence, the Cabalists denominated the ruler of the Macrocosm, *Macroprosophus*, "the Vast Countenance," and the ruler of the microcosm, *Microprosophus*, "the Lesser Countenance." According to at least one interpretation, "the Great Face" is God and "the Little Face," man— one the Supreme Agent, the other the miniature of that Agent; Deity enthroned in the divine sphere and man in the natural. "On man God stamped his seal and sign of his power, on him he has imprinted his own image and superscription, his arms and his portraiture. *Dixit Deus, faciamus hominum ad imaginem nostram, secundum similitudinem nostram.* * * * Hence he is called the microcosm, or little world, the recapitulation of all things, the ligament of angels and beasts, heavenly and earthly, spiritual and corporeal, the perfection of the whole work, the honour and miracle of nature." (Culpeper in THE FAMILY PHYSICIAN.)

Blinded by its own diversified achievements, the present generation is prone to underestimate the knowledge of anatomy and other sciences possessed by older civilizations. The ravages of time and the vandalism of man have obliterated most of the records of such ancient learning. Enough remains, however, to convince the open-minded that at some remote period there existed upon this planet a race of supermen who carved their wisdom into the face of mountains and marked the broad surface of earth with pyramids and other monuments. Professor James H. Breasted, of the University of Chicago, one of the greatest living Egyptologists, has recently translated a papyrus written seventeen centuries B.C. and presumably copied from an original still older by a thousand years. "For the first time recorded in human speech," he says, "our treatise contains the word 'brain,' which is unknown in any other language of this age, or any other treatise of the third millenium B.C. The earliest discussions of the brain have hitherto been found in Greek medical documents probably over two thousand years later than our Egyptian treatise." There is also evidence in the document that at least one old Egyptian understood the localization of brain control of muscles. (See the commentaries by Professor Breasted upon the Edwin Smith Surgical Papyrus.) With every passing day, it becomes more evident that the priest-physicians of the elder world acquired an amazing knowledge of certain occult or hidden processes continually going on in the human body, as yet unrecognized by the savants of our enlightened (?) age.

In his SECRET SOCIETIES OF ALL AGES, Charles Heckethorne describes the human figure set up in the sanctuaries of the learned not as an object for idolatrous worship but as a constant reminder of the harmonies and proportions of the world. Pythagoras declared that the Universal Creator had fashioned two bodies in His own image: The first was Cosmos, with its myriads of suns, moons, and planets; the second was man, in whose internal parts was reflected the entire universe, so that as Boehme has said, the human constitution bears the stamp or seal or signature of the whole mundane order. For this reason, the priests of the primitive tradition, in order to facilitate their study of the natural sciences, caused the statue of the Grand Man to be set up in the midst of the Holy Place to symbolize the divine power in all its intricate manifestations. This mysterious figure—the symbolic Adam or pattern of the species which stood above the primitive altars—was like certain similar figures found in some old books and occasionally met with in the Orient even today, that is, it was in the nature of a manikin and, like the emblematic hands found in the ruins of Roman cities, was covered with hieroglyphics either carved upon its surface or painted thereon with non-fading pigments. The statue may even have opened, revealing the relative position of the organs, bones, muscles, nerves, and other parts. Possibly the interior revealed the orbits of the planets, etc. One cannot but recall the Hermetic figure of Isis, her body covered with curious hieroglyphics and her belt studded with stars; or the Diana of Ephesus, bearing upon her parts the undeciphered words, *Aski-kataski-haix-tetrax-damnameneus-aision*, which, according to Hesychius, were engraved upon her belt or zone (see ŒDIPUS ÆGYPTIACUS. by Athanasius Kircher); or, again, the Sophia of the Gnostic vision, upon whose figure shone out in regular arrangement the letters of the Greek alphabet.

Gradually through ages of research the initiates of the various Mystery Schools contributed a mass of details to the fundamental principles set forth by the first philosophers, and by the time Egypt had reached the crowning glory of her civilization the manikin of the microcosm was a mass of intricate hieroglyphics and symbolic figures, each with a secret meaning reserved for the elect. The measurements of the symbolic man were a basic standard by which it was possible to measure by estimation and proportion every part of Cosmos. In its most perfect form, the manikin was a glorious composite emblem, witness to a knowledge possessed by the sages and hierophants of Isis, Osiris, and Serapis, and which by the Egyptians was communicated to the Greeks and other nations. The Grand Man seen by Nebuchadnezzar in his dream, with its golden head and feet of clay, as well as the mysterious figure which walked amidst the candlesticks of REVELATION refer unquestionably to this Universal Adam, this heroic epitome of all things. In an oracle delivered to the King of Cyprus, Serapis describes himself as the Universal Man in these words:

"A god I am such as I show to thee,
The Starry Heavens are my head, my trunk the sea,
Earth forms my feet, mine ears the air supplies,
The Sun's far-darting, brilliant rays, mine eyes."

Those initiated into the Mysteries became themselves, in turn, embodiments of the sacred truths. So we learn that those accepted into the Mithraic Rites were invested with loose tunics or capes on which, according to Maurice, in his INDIAN ANTIQUITIES, were depicted the celestial constellations, each with its zone or belt containing a representation of the figures of the zodiac. Like the starry hat which the gods bestowed upon Atys, these cloaks strewn with stars and constellations signified the new and heavenly body which the gods conferred upon the wise. The corporeal nature was transmuted by the Mysteries into a celestial nature, and men who had previously enveloped themselves in the dark raiment of form, having been "raised" into the presence of the immortals, put on a new and luminous garb resplendent with the heavenly lights. This is the same cloak to which Apuleius refers when he says that men devoted to the service of Divinity speak of it as the "Olympic garment."

In some old temple before an ancient altar long since crumbled away, but which then supported the radiant "philosophic manikin"—the very embodiment of wisdom—Hermes may have stood when he addressed the following words to his son, Tatian: "If thou wouldst contemplate the Creator even in perishable things, in things which are on the earth, or in the deep, reflect, O my son, on the formation of man in his mother's womb; contemplate the skill of the Workman; learn to know Him according to the divine beauty of the work. Who formed the orb of the eye? Who pierced the openings of the nostrils and of the ears? Who made the mouth to open? Who traced out the channels of the veins? Who made the bones hard? Who covered the flesh with skin? Who separated the fingers and the toes? Who made the feet broad? Who hollowed out the pores? Who spread out the spleen? Who formed the heart like a pyramid? Who made the sides wide? Who formed the caverns of the lungs? Who made the honorable parts of the body conspicuous and concealed the others? * * * Who made all these things? Who is the mother, who is the father, if it be not the only and invisible God who has created all things by His will?"

Then came the age of idolatry. The Mysteries decayed from within. The profane sat in the seats of wisdom. Wars destroyed the old orders. The light was swallowed up in darkness. The life departed and only the empty forms remained. None could be found to translate those symbols and emblems which constituted the secret language of the initiates. The identity of the manikin which stood over the altar was lost. It was only remembered that the figure was a sacred thing and had been revered by earlier ages as a glorious symbol of universal power. The "textbook of the philosophers" came to be looked upon as a god, even as the very god in whose image man had been made. The secret knowledge of the purpose for which the manikin had been constructed having been lost beyond recovery, the degenerate priestcrafts worshipped the actual wood and stone until finally the common lack of understanding brought down the temples in ruins and the statues crumbled away with the civilizations that had forgotten their meanings.

If we would be truly wise, we must be correctly informed as to the will of the Creative Agent as this will is manifested through the infinite diversity of creation. "The investigation of the use of the parts of the body," wrote the great Galen, "lays the foundation of a truly scientific theology which is much greater and more precious than all medicine." It was from the Hermetic premise set forth by the immortal Trismegistus upon the Smaragdine Tablet— "the inferior agrees with the superior and the superior with the inferior"—that the initiates of the old Mysteries established the science of correspondences. (See Swedenborg.) "Gnothi Seauthon" (Know thyself) was inscribed over the portals of the Secret House that those called to sacred matters might by pondering upon these words be fully informed as to the beginning of wisdom. Moving upon the Paracelsian premise that "visible forms are merely external expressions of invisible principles," it is possible through meditation upon the harmony of bodily form and function to discover those laws of life by which the symphony of being is maintained. Pythagoras places the instrument of wisdom in the hands of every man when he is made to say in THE NEW PEARL OF GREAT PRICE that "man is the measure of all things."

How can man in the smallness of his consciousness express a more glorious conception of the creative plan than through such a vision as Eliphas Levi gives us in his HISTORY OF MAGIC? "That synthesis of the word," writes the great Cabalist, "formulated by the human figure, ascended slowly and emerged from the water, like the sun in its rising. When the eyes appeared, light was made; when the mouth was manifested, there was the creation of spirits and the word passed into expression. The entire head was revealed, and this completed the first day of creation. The shoulders, the arms, the breast arose, and thereupon work began. With one hand the Divine Image put back the sea, while with the other it raised up continents and mountains. The Image grew and grew; the generative organs appeared, and all beings began to increase and multiply. The form stood at length erect, having one foot upon the earth and one upon the waters. Beholding itself at full length in the ocean of creation, it breathed on its own reflection and called its likeness into life. It said: Let us make man—and thus man was made. There is nothing so beautiful in the masterpiece of any poet as this vision of creation accomplished by the prototype of humanity. Hereby is man but the shadow of a shadow, and yet he is the image of divine power. He can also stretch forth his hands from East to West; to him is the earth given as a dominion. Such is Adam Kadmon, the primordial Adam of the Kaballists. Such is the sense in which he is depicted as a giant; and this is why Swedenborg, haunted in his dreams by reminiscences of the Kabalah, says that entire creation is only a titanic man and that we are made in the image of the universe."

In THE DIVINE PYMANDER it is written that Nature, having been embraced by the Man (the Protogonas, who contained within himself the concord of the

—From Myer's Qabbalah.

A FIGURE OF THE MICROCOSM SHOWING THE SEATS
OF THE TRINITY OF MAN

seven fiery and spiritual Governors), brought forth seven men in correspondence with the nature of the sidereal seven, and these seven men were male-female and moved in the air. They apparently correspond with the Kumaras, the virgin youths of the Vedas. They were the progenitors of the races and their origin was "the mystery kept hid until this day." (See THE THRICE GREATEST HERMES.) At this point we wish to establish certain arbitrary definitions for the words *androgyne* and *hermaphrodite*. Though generally regarded as synonymous, we would like to establish a fine point of difference between the terms. The word *androgyne* will be used to represent the equilibrium of the sexual potentialities in the soul, a state natural to the divine man. On the other hand, the word *hermaphrodite* is to be limited strictly to the phenomenon of incomplete sexual determination in the physical body.

The first man of the Judaistic system was created male-female, in the image of the Logoi, or the Elohim. He was the Celestial Androgyne, in whose likeness the second man (i.e., the terrestrial Adam) was formed. The lesser Adam in his terrestrial state was also androgynous, for he was an "air" or "sky" man—that is, he had not as yet become involved in material evolution. Only after Eve was taken out of him did he lose his divine completeness— that is, the one became two and the creative agent was distinguished as both agent and patient, or male and female. In THE ZOHAR it is stated that "Adam was created with two faces," and in another place, "And the Lord, blessed be He, parted him, and made two." Most ancient nations have legendary accounts of androgynous beings who existed at a remote time and were the progenitors of present humanity. These beings were metaphysical, however, possessed extraordinary powers, and were in all respects *superior* to mankind. Were these semi-divine creatures but mythological monsters of the imagination, or did they actually exist in the first ages only to vanish away like the mysterious Kings of Edom?

If life, the moulder of all form, is innately androgynous, we shall not be surprised to discover that the first physical bodies with which life invested itself bear evidence of this completeness. "All the invertebrate ancestors of man," writes Ernst Haeckel, "from the Gastraeda up to the Chordonia, must have been hermaphrodite. So, probably were the earliest skulled animals. One extremely weighty piece of evidence of this is afforded by the remarkable fact, that even in Vertebrates, in Man as well as other Vertebrates, the original rudiment of the sexual organs is hermaphrodite." (See THE EVOLUTION OF MAN.) Were the older writers, then, wiser and of greater vision than those who, coming after, ridiculed their words? Is the story of Adam and Eve a faithful narrative of evolutionary progress, setting forth what Haeckel would have called "the separation of the sexes," which took place in the "secondary" or "farther course of tribal history"? How many scientific mysteries are concealed under the religious and philosophic writings of classical and non-classical antiquity? What of the unnumbered specters of various forms, centaurs and double shapes which confronted Æneas at the gates of hell? What of the "one-eyed" men, the "winged" men, and the "hundred-armed" Briareus? Are the accounts of the "giants" and the "scorpion" men and the men with the "bodies of serpents" devoid of reason, or did they faithfully picture under figures and allegories facts in the genesis of form no more amazing than those now generally admitted by men of letters?

There is substance for thought in the fables of the ancients. Witness the "dragon" mines of the Chinese, where the teeth of prehistoric monsters are still excavated for medicinal purposes. The dragons which figure in the legends of Cathay most certainly existed, only science knows them under other names. They were the huge animals of another world and, were their bones not irrefutable testimony, would have been denied by this age as the chimeras of

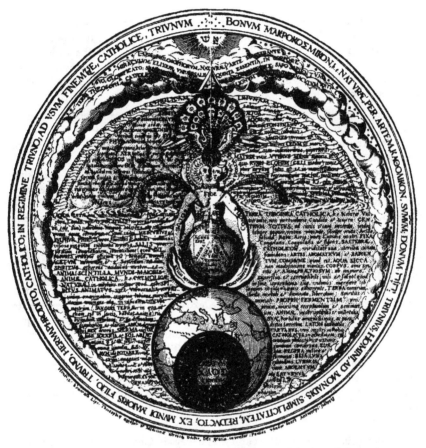

—From Amphitheatrum Sapientae Aeternae.

THE PHILOSOPHICAL ANDROGYNE ACCORDING TO
HEINRICH KHUNRATH

From the union of the sun and moon arises the bird Azoth, with its peacock tail. The bird symbolizes both the Philosopher's Stone and the soul.

a fevered dream. Plato declared that male and female are but the halves of a primitive androgyne which once existed as a separate type but was after-wards divided into kinds and thus lost its identity in its progeny. Of this undivided type he writes: "The Androgynes, for so they were called, had not only the male and female faces, but also possessed the sexual distinctions of both. Of these creatures, likewise, nothing now exists but the *name*, which survives as a *stigma*, and which is considered *infamous*." When Plato says that nothing remains of the androgynes but the name, he clearly indicates that this primitive creation is not to be confused with the hermaphrodites and inter-mediate types which most certainly existed in his day. Plato then goes on to explain the origin of the three kinds of beings, saying "that the males were formed by the *Sun;* the females by the *Earth;* and the mixed race of Andro-gynes by the *Moon:*—which partakes both of the *Sun* and the *Earth."* (See THE ROSICRUCIANS, by Hargrave Jennings.)

Here Plato is concealing a mystery as he did in his account of Atlantis. The sun which formed the males is the symbol of spirit and also of the gods or divinities who move through the agency of the solar power. The earth which formed the females is the symbol of matter and of mankind, the negative cre-ation, the matrix, etc. The moon which formed the androgynes, as "partaking of both," represents the soul, or mind, the spiritual androgyne, the middle race, the "heroes" or demigods, who partake of both qualities, and again of the initiates, the self-born, of whom the androgynous phœnix is the esoteric symbol. The intellect as the link between superiors and inferiors is in equil-ibrium and, being balanced, unites the virtues of both extremities. "The truth is," writes Coleridge, "a great mind must be androgynous." The soul is the first androgynous being to precipitate body out of itself without recourse to any other creature. As soul equilibrates itself in the body which it has pre-cipitated, the mystery of the Melchizedek will be revealed. According to THE SECRET DOCTRINE, humanity will, in the course of countless ages, again become male-female, achieving through evolution the potential equilibrium which has been within it since the beginning. The sympathetic nervous system (the soul ganglia) will gradually increase in significance and unite into a true spinal cord, so that man will have two complete parallel spinal systems. When this point has been reached, man will be negatively androgynous or philosoph-ically hermaphroditic—that is, he will be both sexes in one, each pole, however, manifesting through its own organism or bodily system.

Writing in the thirteenth century, Amaury de Chartres, held among what Hargrave Jennings terms "other fanciful notions" that at the end of the world both sexes would be reunited in the same person. This is in agreement with the ancient philosophical teachings that as man's human evolution approaches its end the cerebrospinal and sympathetic nervous systems will gradually draw together and ultimately "merge" into one. Soul will then be unified in body, resulting in what may be termed the ultimate type—the true androgyne, the man who is fashioned like his Father in heaven. In harmony with this doctrine, the ancient alchemists symbolized spiritual achievement by a two-headed bi-sexual figure. The androgynous Ishwara, is pictured by Inman in his ANCIENT FAITHS as having the right half of his body male and the left half female, and as the first man is the archetype of the human race in both its primitive and ultimate states. The Mystery gods, such as Serapis and Diony-sius, are usually shown heavily robed to conceal the fact that while they have the bearded faces of men, their bodies combine male and female attributes.

The Templars were accused of worshipping the androgynous Baphomet, and the bearded Venus was an object of veneration among the initiated Greeks and Latins.

Under the heading, "Hints on the Future," Madam Blavatsky writes: "As time passes on there will be more and more ether in the air. When ether fills the air, then will be born children without fathers. In Virginia there is an apple tree of a special kind. It does not blossom but bears fruit from a kind of berry without any seeds. This will gradually extend to animals and then to men. Women will bear children without impregnation, and in the Seventh Round there will appear men who can reproduce themselves. In the Seventh Race of the Fourth Round, men will change their skins every year and will have new toe and finger nails. People will become more psychic, then spiritual. Last of all in the Seventh Round, Buddhas will be born without sin." (See Vol. III, THE SECRET DOCTRINE.) The spiritual nature is neither male nor female, but both in perfect balance—the Ego is an androgynous entity. Hence, its perfect manifestation must be through an androgynous self-generating body, but ages must pass before the human race can sufficiently master the secrets of universal polarity for every man to become a complete entity in himself. Understanding is only possible when the positive and negative potentialities are in equilibrium; neither the male nor the female can be perfect of itself. Such is the mystery of the Priest-King Melchizedek, Prince of Salem, who was his own father and his own mother, and in whose footsteps all initiates of the Mysteries must follow if they would be priests forever after the Order of Melchizedek.

Interpreting the Orphic tradition, the Pythagorean initiates divided the universe into three parts, termed the *Supreme*, the *superior*, and the *inferior* worlds. From John Reuchlin's EXPLICATION OF THE PYTHAGORIC DOCTRINE, we learn that the Supreme world (which contains all the others and which consists of a single divine essence) is called that of Deity, and, being without beginning or end, is the eternal abode of existence, substance, essence, and Nature. The superior world (which "shineth" with incorporeal natures) is called that of the supermundane powers, the divine examplars and the "seals of the world." In it dwell also those divinities which, though of divine origin, are somewhat removed from First Cause and partake to a degree of natural substance. Here, too, reside those "heroes" who, though sons of the earth, have achieved to the state of demigod-hood by reason of transcendent virtues or accomplishments. The inferior world (which is the least of the three and is contained within both the others) is called that of the angels, gods, and dæmons. Here abide "bodies and magnitudes with their appropriate Intelligences, the Movers of the spheres, the Overseers and guardians of things generate and corruptible, and such as are assigned to take care of bodies." (See DE MYSTERIIS PYTHAGORICIS.) In general, the inferior world corresponded with the physical universe, or mundane sphere, the home of mortal spirits or, possibly more correctly, the temporary domicile of spirits in the state of mortality. In addition to such beings, who are the "mankind" of the philosophers the inferior universe included the three lower kingdoms of Nature: the mineral, plant, and animal; also the subterreous elemental deities and tutelary spirits. It was this concept of the universal order that moved Aristotle to the comment: "The Pythagoreans affirm that the whole and all things are terminated by three."

From these doctrines of the enlightened pagans the Fathers of the primitive Christian Church derived their opinions concerning the departments of cosmos. The creation they declared subsists in three departments, of which

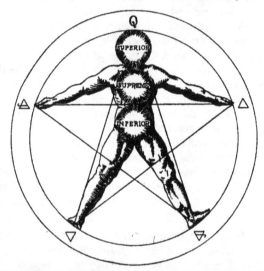

*THE PYTHAGOREAN PENTALPHA WITH THE PARTS OF THE WORLD
ASSIGNED TO THE THREE MAJOR BODILY CAVITIES*

the first is heaven, the second earth, and the third hell. The three crowns of the papal tiara signify the sovereignty of the Apostolic Church over the spiritual, temporal, and purgatorial spheres—the tripartite universe of the Orphic cosmologists. To the early Christian, the spiritual sphere was the abode of the Godhead in its triple aspect. The temporal sphere was originally the abode of the "hierarchies" and "saints" (the latter the "heroes" of the Greeks—the mortal immortals and the immortal mortals). Later the temporal sphere was identified with the world of mankind in general. The purgatorial sphere was originally the "sublunary estate," the abode of mortals (the Tartarus of the classical philosophers), but later the Church defined it as the posthumous state or condition of the soul after the death of the body, a condition in which sins were expiated, etc. Those informed upon such subjects realized heaven, earth, and hell to be qualities or conditions of being by which the One Life expressed itself through phases or aspects. Of these the three primary phases are Consciousness, Intelligence, and Force—the "Three Witnesses," the Trinity in Unity, and "the One in essence and Three in aspect" of the Hermetic Emerald. The three faces of the Deity are, therefore, the three worlds Plutarch so beautifully sets forth in his explanation of the Forty-seventh Problem of Euclid. By Consciousness the heavens were established; by Force the earth was lifted up from the deep and set upon its eternal foundations; and by Intelligence (the Homeric chain) heaven and earth were bound together—the Ark, the Anchor, and the Cable-Tow.

Applied to man generally, the three worlds correspond with the three major divisions of his composite nature—spirit, soul (or mind), and body. In his physical constitution, they have their analogy in the three major cavities of the body—the spirit to the thoracic, the soul (or mind) to the cranial, and the body to the abdominal. These are the three main chambers of the Pyramid and also the symbolic rooms in which are given the Entered Apprentice, Fellowcraft, and Master Mason's degrees in modern Freemasonry. Each of these three bodily cavities is, in turn, regarded as divisible into three parts, and all these together constitute nine, and finally enclosed within the greater cavity of the auric egg, produce the perfect human decad, or ten. Of these bodily cavities and their significance, Eliphas Levi hints in his TRANSCENDENTAL MAGIC: "Whatsoever is in the great world is reproduced in the small. Hence, we have three centers [analogous to the cavities of the classical writers] of fluidic attraction and projection—the brain, the heart, or epigastric region, and the genital organ." The Trinity in man, therefore, was believed to reside in the three great cavities of the body: Brahma in the heart, Vishnu in the brain, and Shiva (whose appropriate symbol is the *lingam*) in the generative system. Each of these deities has a threefold manifestation—the creative, preservative, and disintegrative aspects. These phases, in turn, were enthroned in lesser cavities contained within the greater ones. A good example of the secondary divisions of these major cavities will be found in the remarks concerning the doctrines of the Arabians in the section on the ventricles of the brain. (See page 140.)

In the correspondences between man and the three worlds, the heart came to be regarded as analogous to the heavens, the brain to the earth, and the generative system to hades, or the underworld. We learn from the Greeks that the awful caverns of Tartarus were under the very roots of Olympus and that the purgatorial chambers of initiation in the ancient temples were always subterranean, representing by their place and arrangement the windings of the intestinal tract. "Man is the mirror of the universe," wrote van Helmont, "and his *triple* nature stands in relationship to all things." The importance of recognizing the analogies upon which the philosophy of the microcosm was built up may not be at first apparent. As the mind penetrates farther into the mystery, it will become evident, however, that the whole universe is suspended like a foetus from its triform cause, termed in the Mysteries being, life, and intelligence. By *being* is intimated that which is the unmoved support of all existence; by *life* that which is the self-moving origin of all activity; and by *intellect* that which is moved. As Proclus might have said, good is that which abides, wisdom is that which moves, and beauty is that which is moved, manifesting the impulses of the first orders. "Like a foetus, he [man] is suspended, by all his three spirits, in the matrix of the Macrocosmos." (H. P. Blavatsky in ISIS UNVEILED.)

According to Pindar, the Pythagorean, the universe was an ensouled animal, and Plutarch adds that the sun is its heart, the moon its liver, etc.

—From Collectio Operum.

*A FIGURE FROM THE ROSICRUCIAN WRITINGS OF ROBERT FLUDD,
PORTRAYING THE ELEMENTAL WORLD IN ITS PRIMARY
STATE—THE CHAOS OF THE ELEMENTS*

Hence, we find man referred to as the "little animal" by Galen, the "little world" or the "little heaven" by Philo, the "little diacosm" by Porphyry, and the "lesser world" by Solon. (See ORPHEUS, by G. R. S. Mead.) After dividing the body into its noble and ignoble parts according to Laurentius, Burton follows the ancient order by recognizing three regions or the threefold division of the whole body: the head containing the animal organs; the chest "in which the Heart as King keeps his court"; and the abdomen, "in which the Liver resides as a *Legat a latere.*" Burton then invites his reader to enter into the contemplation of the mysteries of the body as though he had been brought into the presence of "some sacred Temple, or Majestical Palace, to behold not the matter only, but the singular Art, Workmanship, and counsel of this, our great Creator." Proclus correlates man to the world by saying that, like the universe, he has mind and reason, a divine body and a perishable body. Paracelsus adds the following testimony: "Whoever desires to be a practical philosopher ought to be able to indicate heaven and hell in the micro-cosm, and to find everything in man that exists in heaven and upon the earth."

In his analysis of the anatomy of the microcosm, Robert Fludd summarizes the opinions of earlier authorities by means of the curious figures reproduced herewith. In studying these diagrams, *one point particularly should be borne in mind.* The head as the highest part of the physical frame was used to represent the *empyrean,* or the highest part of the universe. The heart, however, is the noblest organ of the body and is, therefore, the true "head" in man and the actual source of all inspiration and truth. The cranium is but the outer bodily symbol of the heart. Thus, the highest part of the physical structure becomes analogous to the most spiritual organ, which is, there-fore, actually the "highest" part of man. In the universe, Deity is presumed to dwell in the furthermost and uppermost parts, but the philosophers understand His true abode to be in the heart of man, than which there is no higher place. The entire problem is not one of literalism, but of soul qualities abiding in higher dimen-sional vistas.

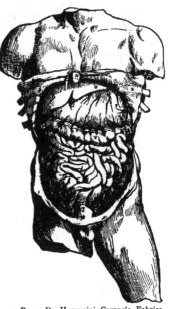

—From De Humanini Corporis Fabrica.

VESALIUS' DRAWING OF THE ABDOMINAL CAVITY AND ITS CONTENTS

By comparing this figure with that of Fludd's on the opposite page, it will be evident that the elemental world of the Rosicrucian was depicted in the general form of the intestinal tract.

In Fludd's first figure the human body is divided into three compartments by par-allel arcs. The upper division is called *Coelum Empyreum* and is assigned to the head. The central division is called *Coelum Æthereum* and is assigned to the thoracic cavity. The lower division is called *Coelum Elementarium* and is as-signed to the abdominal cavity. The heavenly world of the head is separated from the airy, or ethereal, world of the chest by the double line running through the shoulders. Fludd's interpretation of the three departments of the head will be found at the beginning of the section on the ventricles of the brain. The central, or thoracic, cavity is separated into a superior and an inferior half of the orbit of the sun (called *Sphaera Vitae,* "the sphere of life"), which is shown as moving on a plane with the human heart. This division of the chest is in harmony with Plato's disserta-tion on this subject in THE TIMÆUS, where he says: "And fearing to pollute the divine element, they gave the mortal soul a separate habitation in the breast,

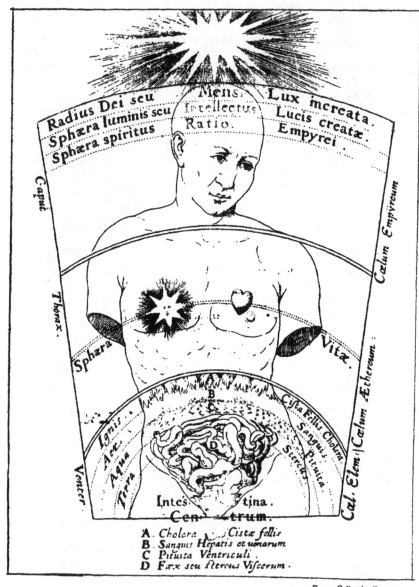

FLUDD'S KEY TO UNIVERSAL ANATOMY

The Cabalistic Adam as the first man and archetype of humanity.

parted off from the head by a narrow isthmus. And as in a house the women's apartments are divided from the men's, the cavity of the thorax was divided into two parts, a higher and a lower. The higher of the two, which is the seat of courage and anger, lies nearer to the head, between the midriff and the neck, and assists reason in restraining the desires. The heart is the house of guard in which all veins meet and through them reason sends her commands to the extremity of her kingdom. * * * The part of the soul which desires meat and drink was placed between the midriff and navel, where they made a sort of manger; and here they bound it down, like a wild animal, away from the council-chamber, leaving the better principle undisturbed to advise quietly for the good of the whole."

Although not depicted herein, the three superior planets (Saturn, Jupiter, and Mars) and the three inferior planets (Venus, Mercury, and the moon) should be regarded as moving in this region of the ethereal, or thoracic, heaven. By their position upon the body they would signify the vital organs distributed within the thorax and clustered about the sovereign sun (the heart). The orbit of the sun corresponds in general with the location of the diaphragm, Plato's "midriff," a muscle frequently used in mediæval symbolism to represent the low mountain or hill upon which stood the holy temple—the heart. Below the ethereal heaven and separated again by a double line are the spheres of the elements—the sublunary world, the land of darkness and death, marked A, B, C, and D in the diagram. In the occult anatomy of man this area is the true Inferno, the home of the beast of Babylon, the throne of Mammon, the temple of Beelzebub, and all the other infernal furies. At the base of the human spine burns the so-called infernal fire, and here, in the practice of black magic, the Witches' Sabbath is celebrated. In the Coelum Elementarium as depicted by Fludd, fire (A), the first of the elements, is associated with the bile of the liver and the contents of the gall bladder; air (B), the second of the elements, with the blood of the liver and blood vessels; water (C), the third of the elements, with the rheum or phlegm of the abdominal cavity; and earth (D), the fourth of the elements, with the waste or refuse of the "ignoble" abdominal viscera. The three general compartments of the diagram correspond excellently with the superior triad established by the physicians of the Dark Ages, who regarded man as a septenary composed of a triad and a quaternary. The three great cavities—cranial, thoracic, and abdominal—become the thrones of the three divine agencies, and the arms and legs the symbols of the elementary quaternary. In this system was perpetuated the doctrines of the Egyptians, who maintained that man consisted primarily of a triangle and a square.

In Fludd's second figure we have a full length human being surrounded by concentric circles, with the upper part, which constitutes the torso, further broken up by the arcs and circles of the harmonic intervals with which Fludd was deeply concerned. The largest of the circles surrounding the human form

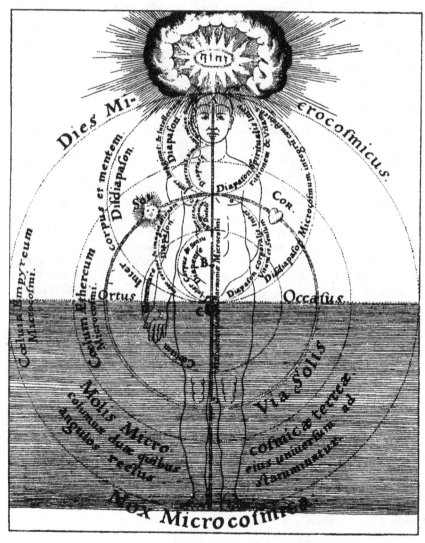

—From Collectio Operum.

THE HARMONIC INTERVALS OF THE HUMAN BODY

and including all others within it is called the *empyrean* heaven of the micro-cosm and represents the auric egg of man. It is divided by a horizontal line into an upper and a lower part—the day and night of the microcosm. The words *Ortus* and *Occasus* in large letters upon the horizon line signify the rising and the setting of the microcosmic sun. A cord is stretched from the feet of the man upward until its upper end is mingled with the rays of the divine glory above. In its ascent the cord passes through six spheres or planes —three in the dark half and three in the light half of the drawing. From the figure, it is evident that Fludd is attempting to portray not only the corre-spondence existing between man and the world, but also the harmonic structure of each, showing how, from the concordances set up in Nature, the proportions of all bodies are derived. According to one interpretation the human form represents the Greater Adam—the Heavenly Man—whose body extends over the entire interval between darkness and light, and in a more limited sense the physical body of mortal man, the latter setting forth in its parts and members a miniature of the whole world. That part of the figure above the median, or horizon, line actually represents the invisible constitution of man, for all the truly vital members of man exist only in the superphysical sphere.

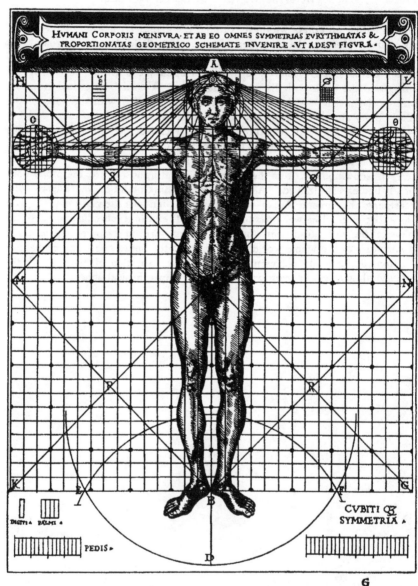

HVMANI CORPORIS MENSVRA· ET AB EO OMNES SVMMETRIAS EVRYTHMIATAS &
PROPORTIONATAS GEOMETRICO SCHEMATE INVENIRE ·VT ADEST FIGVRA·

DIGITI 4 PALMI 4

PEDIS ·

CVBITI
SYMMETRIA ·

G

THE MACROCOSM IN ITS CREATIVE ASPECT AS FABRICATOR
OF THE INFERIOR WORLD

CHAPTER IV

THE MACROCOSM AND THE MICROCOSM

O understand the doctrine of the Macrocosm and the microcosm, it is necessary to restore to these words their original
attributes. Both words primarily signify wholeness and correspond to the Leibnitzian theory of monads and the atomism of
Leucippus and Democritus. The Macrocosm is a vast monad,
the microcosm a relatively smaller monad similar in design but
less in quantity and contained within the larger organism. The terms *Macrocosm*
and *microcosm* do not necessarily imply the world and man, but rather signify
such correspondences as exist between two such constitutions. Man is a
microcosm when compared to the universe, but a macrocosm when compared
to some single organ within himself. According to the Pythagorean doctrine,
"wholes" are not actually composed of parts in the sense of fractions or fragments, but in reality of lesser "wholes," which are termed "parts" only when
compared to the greater unity which they conspire to make up. The heart is
primarily a body and only a part of the human body in a figurative sense.
Thus, by state it is an essential unity, but by place it assumes the accidental condition of an organ, which together with several others goes to make up the
greater wholeness of the body. Hence, every atom is a wholeness bearing
within it the stamp and signature of the whole world, every grain of sand an
image of the universe. When man is termed a microcosm, it is not to be
inferred that he is merely a "part" of the world but, rather, like all other
"parts" so-called, is in reality a miniature of the world. A somewhat more
adequate idea of this can be secured from a study of the symbolic tetrahedron
of the Pythagoreans. This pyramidal solid may be considered as constructed
from a prescribed number of smaller blocks, each of which is identical in shape
with the whole. Thus, a group of tetrahedrons built together results in a larger
form identical in shape with the units composing it, yet the term *tetrahedron*
is just as correctly applied to the smaller blocks as to the greater mass composed
of them. Again, if a cube be divided into eight smaller cubes of identical size,
each block will be as surely a cube as was the original. In this process, however, the large cube is a macrocosm and the smaller ones microcosms within it.
Macrocosms are, therefore, built up of aggregations of microcosms; and the
whole is similar to the parts and the parts to the whole, the difference lying in
magnitude rather than in quality.

This system of thought justified the ancients in correlating man to the
world, for to them all forms were concatenations of similars. "Every reptile
was a microcosm of man; man of the globe; the globe of the planetary system;
the planetary system of the universe; and the universe, of God; and thus, in
the image of God was man created—in the image of God, male and female,

created He him." (Godfrey Higgins, in ANACALYPSIS.) From the foregoing it becomes apparent why the earlier philosophers sought so enthusiastically to discover the inner workings of the human body and soul. They believed firmly that if once they could discover and classify the parts of man, they would possess the master-key to the whole mystery of life. "All is in all" was a motto of the Rosicrucians and, guided by this precept, they moved surely amid a mass of curious beliefs, dedicated to the proposition that wisdom always recognizes "wholeness," while ignorance is deceived by the appearance of "parts." Quoting from our ENCYCLOPEDIC OUTLINE OF SYMBOLISM, "Agrippa declares that, being a type of the lesser world, man contains in himself all numbers, measures, weights, motions, and elements. The secret doctrine of Freemasonry, like that of the Dionysiac Architects, is concerned primarily with the effort to measure or estimate philosophically the parts and proportions of the microcosm, so that by the knowledge derived therefrom the supreme ambition of their craft might be realized—the creation of a perfect man." The alchemists affirmed that all the metals were contained within each metal; the mystics that the whole universe was reflected within the human soul, and even Deity was mirrored in each atom. "O man, look at man! For man has in himself heavens and earth," exclaims the enraptured Hildegard. According to this concept, one tiny organism is not impressed with a certain aspect of divinity and a second organism with another aspect, but each is impressed with the whole universal order.

Similarly, each monad is actually a seed, for bearing the stamp of every aspect of existence upon and within itself, it is capable under certain conditions of releasing these potentialities. Hence, each tiny germ has the whole world locked within it, even as man is inwardly a potential divinity but outwardly only an animal. If the same signature be in all things, then it follows that one simple set of laws is applicable to the whole diversity of manifestation. Furthermore, any impulse conveyed to the Macrocosm (or Greater Part) is communicated ultimately to all the microcosms dependent from that Macrocosm. Any change in the whole is also reflected in all its aspects, which, for lack of a more accurate term, we call the "parts." "In the belief of the men of the Dark Ages," writes Charles Singer in FROM MAGIC TO SCIENCE, "there was a close relationship between the external and internal world, the Macrocosm and the microcosm. They discerned a parallel between the four ages of man and the four seasons, between the humors of the body and the solstices and equinoxes, between the four elements and the four cardinal points, and so on."

To visualize the relationship between the life of the Macrocosm and that of the microcosm, imagine a candle placed in the center of a room, the walls of which are composed of numerous small mirrors arranged to reflect the central light. The candle, for symbolic purposes, is the Spirit Flame of the Macrocosm and by reflecting its light each of the mirrors (the microcosmic monads) appear to possess the central light within itself. Thus, one light takes on the appearance of innumerable lights, even as the one man—the Protogonas—takes on the appearance of an innumerable mankind. Any change in the condition of the central flame causes a similar change to apparently take place in each of its reflections. So, if the central flame turns blue, all the reflections turn blue; if it flares up, all the reflections flare up; and if it dies out, all the reflections die with it. This is the basis of that widespread philosophy of sympathies between causes and their effects of which Isaac Myers writes in THE QABBALAH: "The doctrine of the sympathy between the spiritual man, his body, etc., and all other parts of the universe, as the affinity between the Macrocosm and the microcosm, was taught by the learned among the Hindus, Chinese, Egyptians, Chaldeans, Hebrews, Greeks, etc., and by Moses, Pythagoras, Plato, Aristotle, the Cabalists, Neo-Platonists, etc."

Flung through the wide vistas of space, suns, moons, and stars are but the separate bones of a great skeleton, the framework of the Universal Man. Our little lives are moved by the thrill of that infinite life which courses and throbs through the arteries and veins of space. We live isolated in the midst of an incomprehensible whole, on the one hand infinite greatness and on the other, infinite smallness; but on all sides, within and without, infinite wisdom. How profound were the words of Charron when in his work ON WISDOM, he exclaims: "The proper science and subject for man's contemplation is man himself." Pondering upon such mysteries as this, Moses Ibn Jacob ben Ezra was moved to declare that "the Microcosm greatly resembles by its compositions, derivation and creation, the Macrocosm." THE ZOHAR admonishes the wise not to look upon man as a creature of flesh, skin, bones, and veins, but as a living soul whose true constitution is spiritual rather than physical. Skin, flesh, bones, and veins are but a garment, a cloak worn during the period of physical existence and cast off at death. "Yet the different parts of the body conform to the secrets of the supreme wisdom," continues the ancient book. "The skin represents the firmament which extends everywhere and which covers everything, like a cloak. The flesh reminds us of the evil side of the universe (that is, as we have said before, the purely external and sensual element). The bones and the veins represent the celestial chariot, the forces which exist within the servants of God. However, all this is but a cloak; for the deep mystery of Celestial Man is within. * * * The mystery of terrestrial man is according to the mystery of the Celestial Adam. Yet, as we see in the all-covering firmament stars and planets which form different figures that contain hidden things and profound mysteries, so there are on the skin that covers our body certain figures and lines which are the planets and stars of our body. All these signs have a hidden meaning and attract the attention of the wise who can read the face of man."

According to St. Paul (*vide* I Cor. 15: 47 *et seq.*), there is a "mystery" which can be revealed only to the elect. He says there are two men, the first of the earth earthy, the second the Lord from heaven. In this statement the

Gnosticism of Paul is apparent. The man who is of the earth earthy is the human microcosm—that is, the shadow (soul) cast by spirit upon the surface of matter. The second man, who is the Lord from heaven, we will designate for lack of a better term, the human Macrocosm—the Oversoul, the ineffable summit above personality. This Macrocosm was called God. It was this divinity of man which, through the soul, impressed its shape upon the corporeal constitution. This Macrocosm was the God of the philosopher—*his* God, or that divinity which was himself. The wise sought union with this spirit and Plotinus, the illumined Neo-Platonist, makes mention of those rare occasions when he was lifted up into the presence of "his God." The God of every man is not in the heavens nor in the immeasurable vistas of space, for in those remote expanses dwells that vaster Spirit which is the God of the world—the Great Macrocosm. Man's God is his own divine part. It abides in the remoteness of his own auric bodies. To this spirit he addresses his prayers, in this spirit he invests his hope, towards this spirit he is led by his aspirations, and in union with this spirit he achieves immortality.

This spirit is his real self and his self is his Macrocosm—his vaster part. It is from this self that he had his beginning; it is in this self that he lives and moves and has his being during the period of his manifestation, and it is to this self that he returns again in the end. As all universal substances are vibrant with a divine force and radiant with a celestial fire, so the microcosm— i.e., the reflection—pulsates continually with the energy of the Macrocosm. Man searching for his God is matter seeking its own source. It is the shadow questing the substance of the shadow. The real man of St. Paul is *Anthropos,* the man who is in heaven or who is above the world, the radiant Protogonas, the heavenly likeness of all things which are below. This, then, is the mystery of the Macrocosm and the microcosm, the two Adams, and the plurality of divinities, which caused the ancients to assign to each man an *essential dæmon.*

The two plates from Cesariano's edition of Vitruvius reproduced herewith set forth the mystery of the Macrocosm and the microcosm. "No one can look at these two figures of Cesariano's," writes William Stirling in THE CANON, "without seeing that they are something more than mere anatomical patterns. In later editions they became so, but here we have clearly and distinctly a curious survival of the cosmic deity of Greece, copied and disfigured by the crude draughtsmen of the Middle Ages, but faithfully preserved, and recognizable to the last." The two figures are advanced as canons of proportion to be used in architecture, yet it is obvious that they would be of little practical value to a draughtsman engaged in the task of designing some public edifice. The figures are not intended to be taken literally, but their virtue lies in an obscure association with certain principles of Nature known to the initiated Dionysiacs. The first and greater figure is the world, the second or lesser figure is man. The ratios of proportion involved in the measurements pertain not to physical bodies alone, but, if interpreted Cabalistically, reveal the secret dimensions of God and Nature.

The body is laid out upon a background of nine hundred squares and the whole drawing is divided into twelve larger sections, of which four are square and eight triangular. It is significant that the background should be divided in the same manner as early horoscope blanks, which were square and divided by straight lines into twelve departments, which were the twelve members of the great Universal One. The body itself touches ten of these compartments and the two untouched are connected by an arc. In the zodiac of the ancient Mysteries, two signs were concealed from the profane, so that the divine man exoterically consisted of but ten members, a matter possibly suggested by the arrangement of Cesariano's man. As the horoscope blank was a symbolic figure of the heavens, the form upon it is very evidently a "heavenly" man, extending itself throughout the ethereal diffusion. The figures "of unknown origin" which appear in the earliest editions of Agrippa were evidently based upon the Vitruvius plates, and the fourth of these plates is quite similar in its divisions to Cesariano's Macrocosm. In the Agrippa figure the signs of the zodiac are added to the angles of the background, so that little doubt can remain as to what is intended.

Upon the forehead of Cesariano's figure is an upright triangle containing a small symbol resembling the sun, and from this radiate lines to the several parts of both arms. There are three circles, one surrounding the face and one enclosing each hand. The three circles represent the three Faces of the Zohar—the Crown, the father, and mother—Kether, Chocmah and Binah. Above the head is a large capital A, which indicates the starting point from which all the proportions and significant details should be estimated. The A may well have several meanings, for the man is Ain Soph, Adam or Anthropos, the starting point is Aries, and the whole scheme is reminiscent of the Gnostic Protogonas, whose body was marked and ornamented with letters and symbols. The Greek Alpha (A) was the symbol of the Macrocosm, and the Omega (O) of the microcosm. The rays from the head of the Grand Man are the hairs, and the lines from the face his beard, as mentioned in THE ZOHAR. That Leonardo da Vinci was acquainted with the figures of Vitruvius is apparent from a drawing which he left. In it he has united the Macrocosm and the microcosm—the soul and the body. His drawing is a symbolical squaring of the circle, a reminder that the answer to all riddles is man himself. (See figure on page 10.)

The Lesser Man from Cesariano's Vitruvius is described by William Stirling as "the mystery of the Microcosm," for it depicts the World Soul which, according to Plato, was crucified in space and sets its seal, or likeness, upon all inferior natures. "All the early Christians," he says, "who knew their Cabala declared that Plato had borrowed his ideas from Moses. Nor was Plato ignorant of that mystical symbol, the cross, which was a sacred emblem long before it emerged from obscurity in the first century. The allusion to the cross, in the famous passage in THE TIMÆUS, has often been commented upon, and there can be no doubt that it prefigures the mythos which afterwards appeared in the Christian gospel. It is quite plain that Plato, in describing the Demiurge, or Logos, compounded out of the zodiac, all the planets and the elements, is referring to the second and third persons of the Cabalistic triad, whose bodies comprise the material universe, created in the image of the Elohim, male and female. This Androgynous being the Creator 'divided lengthwise into two parts, which he joined to one another at the center like the letter X, and bound them into a circular form, connecting them with themselves and each other at the point opposite their original meeting point'." (See THE CANON.) Father Lundy refers to this as Plato's second God, "who impressed himself upon the universe in the form of the cross." Upon the authority of Porphyry, Proclus declares that a character similar to the letter X, surrounded by a circle, was with the Egyptians the symbol of the mundane soul.

In a writing called OCTAVIUS, a defense of the Christian religion, Minutius Felix addresses the Romans, declaring "your victorious trophies, not only represent a symbol of the cross, but a cross with a man on it." Godfrey Higgins considers this sufficient evidence that a crucified figure was among the standards carried by the Romans. The X-shaped cross, now called the St. Andrews cross, is reminiscent of the crucifixion of Ixion, who was suspended from the spokes of the world wheel. Semiramis was changed into a dove and in this form was crucified, and there are figures of Venus in the form of a dove crucified to a wheel with four spokes. Pindar refers to the bird, Iynx, bound to the wheel. Nimrod mentions the she-hawk of the wheel, which he interprets as the *anima mundi*, or divine soul of the world's rotation. The dove is called *Eros*, or love. By rearranging the letter $E R O S$ into $R O S E$, the rose, a secret symbol for Venus (or the world soul), is discovered. When this is crucified upon the cross—the cross referred to in THE CHEMICAL MARRIAGE of Christian Rosencreutz was a St. Andrews cross—the whole symbol becomes the figure of Plato's Logos, which, in turn, is unquestionably the Cabalistic Adam Kadmon and the Greek Protogonas.

Consider the figure of the Macrocosm and the microcosm by Saint Hildegard on page 36. The first and second persons of the Trinity are shown embracing the world, in the midst of which is a figure representing Christ extended throughout the elements and, like many such mediæval drawings, connected with lines to the various sidereal bodies. Such representations and the zodiacal man, or almanac figures, which have been derived therefrom, are all aspects of the world soul "crucified in space." Soul is the mediator between intellect and phenomenal existence. It is intimated that the limbs of the cross represent the Poles and the ecliptic. They are also the equinoxes and the solstices—the great sidereal cross upon which the sun itself is crucified. The

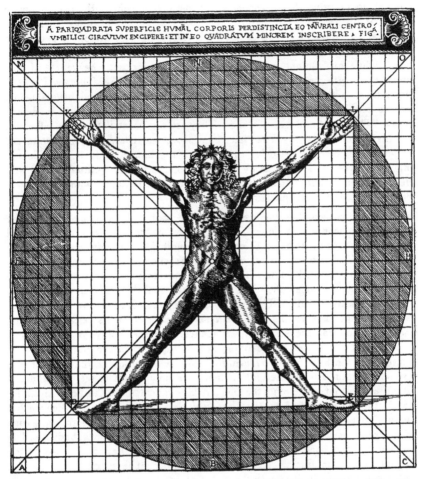

A PARIQVADRATA SVPERFICIE HVMANI CORPORIS PERDISTINCTA EO NATVRALI CENTRO VMBILICI CIRCVLVM EXCIPERE: ET IN EO QVADRATVM MINOREM INSCRIBERE, FIGª.

—From Cesariano's Edition of Vitruvius.

THE MICROCOSM IN ITS REDEMPTIVE ASPECT
Man is here portrayed as the World Soul—Dionysius, the cruciform Logos

annual crucifixion, death, and resurrection of the Solar (Soular) Man was set forth in the pageantry of the ancient initiatory dramas; for, as Clement of Alexandria said, they were the rituals of a "Brother slain by his Brethren."

Proclus, the Platonic successor, discoursed at length upon the analogies between the constitutions of man and the world. He established the sidereal aspects of the human body, recognizing not only the presence in man of the zodiacal but also the planetary agencies. "Thus it is that some assert that his [man's] noeric principle corresponds with the erratic sphere, the contemplative aspect of his reason with Saturn, the social aspect with Jupiter, while his irrational principle, the passional nature, corresponds with Mars, the expressive with Mercury, and the appetitive with the sun, and the vegetative with the moon, while his radiant vehicle [aura] corresponds with heaven, and this mortal body with the elemental (or sublunary) sphere." (See Thomas Taylor.) Here, then, is the origin of the many complicated astrological beliefs which rose to such high favor during the Middle Ages. Paracelsus was moved to say, "The world and man are one. They are one constellation, one influence, one breath, one harmony, one time, one metal, one fruit." By following the planetary analogies, it becomes evident that the human body is divisible not only into three parts in harmony with the aspects of the spiritual nature and the three worlds, but is again divisible into seven in harmony with the sidereal diffusion, i.e., the seven planetary harmonies.

Macrobius describes the descent of the soul and its assumption of the planetary vestments as follows: "The soul on its descent from the One and Indivisible source of its being in order to be united to its body, passes through the Milky Way into the Zodiac at their intersection in Cancer and Capricorn, called the 'gates of the Sun,' because the two solstices are placed in these signs. Through Cancer, the Gate of Man, the soul descends upon Earth, the which is spiritual death. Through Capricorn, the Gate of the Gods, it re-ascends up into heaven; its new birth taking place upon its release from the body. So soon as the soul has left Cancer and the Milky Way, it begins to lose its divine nature, and arriving at Leo enters upon the first phase of its future condition here below. During its downward progress, the soul, at first a sphere in form, is elongated into a cone, and now begins to feel the influence of matter, so that on joining the body it is intoxicated by the novel draught. This condition is typified by the Crater of Bacchus placed in the heaven between Cancer and Leo. The soul thus descending, as it passes through each sphere receives successive *coatings*, as it were, of a luminous body, and is furnished at the same time with the several faculties it has to exercise during its probation upon Earth. Accordingly in Saturn, it is supplied with reason and intelligence; in Jupiter, with the power of action; in Mars, with the irascible principle; in the Sun, with sensation and speculation; in Venus, with the appetites; in Mercury with the means of declaring and expressing thoughts; in the Moon, with the faculty of generating and augmenting the body."

Thus the planets became the symbols of a continually recurring septenary which stamps itself upon the face of Nature and is particularly noticeable in that microcosm which we call man. The persistent repetition of the seven cannot but appear significant to even the superficially-minded. It has been known through all ages as the most sacred of numbers and occurs more frequently in scriptural writings than any other number. The Cabalists have left much information concerning the application of the seven to universal mysteries and Madam Blavatsky bears witness to its frequency as a basic pattern in the human body. She writes: "Remember that physiology, imperfect as it is, shows septenary groups all over the exterior and interior body; the seven orifices, the seven 'organs' at the base of the brain, the seven plexuses (the pharyngeal, the laryngeal, cavernous, cardiac, epigastric [same as solar plexus], prostatic, and sacral plexus, etc.)." She might have added to her list of septenaries the seven sacred organs about the heart, the seven layers of the epidermis, the seven ductless glands of first importance, the seven methods by which the body is vitalized, the seven sacred breaths, the seven body systems (bones, nerves, arteries, muscles, etc.), the seven layers of the auric egg, the seven major divisions of the embryo, the seven senses (five awakened and two latent), and the seven-year periods into which human life is divided. All these are reminders that the seven primary Spirits, the first Monads, of which the planets are symbols rather than bodies, have become incarnated in the composite structure of man, and that the Elohim (Builders or Governors), are actually within his own nature, from their seven thrones molding him into an equilibrated septenary creature. Each of these powers corresponds to a color, a musical note, a planetary vibration, and a mystical dimension. Together these gods constitute natural consciousness and control jointly or by rotation the activities of the lesser world. "The same element which produced Mars, Venus, or Jupiter in the sky exists also in the body of man; because the latter is the son of the astral body of the Macrocosm in the same sense as the physical body of man is the son of the earth." (See Paracelsus.)

Writing in the first century A.D., Philo Judæus, a Hellenized Jew residing in Alexandria, in his work, ON THE CREATION OF THE WORLD, describes the harmony of the septenary in these words: "And since all the things on the earth depend upon the heavenly bodies according to a certain natural sympathy, it is in heaven too that the ratio of the number seven begins, and from this it descended to us also, coming down to visit the race of mortal men." Philo amplifies this statement with a detailed account of the natural and bodily septenaries. He says in substance that the soul is divided into seven parts: namely, the five senses, the vocal organ, and the generative power. The seven parts of the exterior body are the head, the chest, the abdomen, the two arms, and the two legs. The seven parts of the internal body (or the "entrails," as Philo calls them) are the stomach, the heart, the lungs, the spleen, the liver, and the two kidneys. [This latter division is based upon the speculative anatomy of his time.] The dominant part of an animal is the head which has seven "most necessary divisions," viz., the two eyes, the two ears, the two channels for the nostrils, and lastly the mouth, through which as Plato says, mortal things find their entrance and immortal things their exit. Into the mouth enters perishable food and drink, but from it proceed words—immortal laws of the immortal soul—by means of which rational life is regulated.

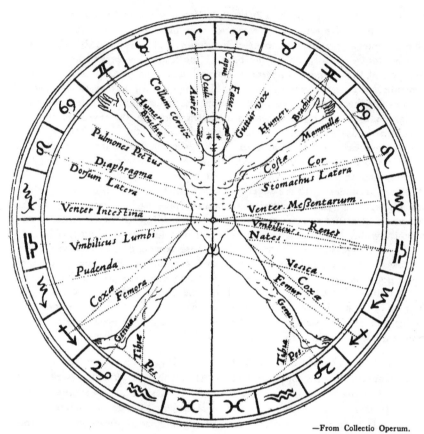

—From Collectio Operum.

THE SOUL AS IXION CRUCIFIED TO THE WHEEL OF A DOUBLE ZODIAC

Analyzing the sense perceptions, Philo declares sight to be the best, itself a sevenfold mystery, for the objects of its perception are seven: body, distance, shape, magnitude, color, motion, and tranquillity, for besides these there is nothing that can be seen. There are also seven modes or changes of the voice: the acute, the grave, the contracted, the aspirated, and three others which he calls the tone, the long sound, and the short sound. There are also seven motions possible to the body: motion upward, motion downward, to the right, to the left, forward, backward, and the rotary such as is manifest in those who dance. The excretions of the body are performed in the number seven: tears through the eyes, purification of the head through the nostrils, and saliva which is spit out through the mouth. Besides there are two direct channels for evacuation; the sixth is perspiration, and the seventh is the generative process. Philo concludes as follows: "Also children in the womb receive life at the end of seven months, so that a very extraordinary thing happens: for children who are born at the end of the seventh month live, while those who are born at the expiration of the eighth month are altogether incapable of surviving."

In the second part of the COLLECTIO OPERUM, which is devoted to the mysteries of Rosicrucian anatomy, Fludd publishes two figures which correspond in a general way with the Vitruvius plates in that they set forth the relationships of the Macrocosm and the microcosm. In the first figure a zodiacal man is shown stretched out in the great circle of the world surrounded by a double zodiac. Though the text accompanying this figure is extremely meagre and obscure, its significance is apparent. He is the Macrocosm and the microcosm in one—the Grand Man and the Lesser Man—one represented by the zodiac upon the left and the other by the zodiac upon the right. Fludd's Logos is an amplified and completed form of the zodiacal man. From each of the signs upon the sphere of the zodiacal wheel rays converge towards the various parts of the human figure. These indicate the following relationships between the zodiacal hierarchies and the bodily members and organs: Aries is assigned to the head, the eyes, the face, and the ears; Taurus to the neck and the larynx; Gemini to the shoulders, arms, and hands; Cancer to the lungs, chest, breasts, and ribs; Leo to the diaphragm, the back and sides, the heart, and the stomach. [By most astrologers the stomach is associated with Cancer.] Virgo is assigned to the abdominal cavity and its contents; Libra to the kidneys, the umbilicus, the loins, the navel, and the nates; Scorpio to the pudenda and the bladder; Sagittarius to the hips and thighs; Capricorn to the knees; Aquarius to the lower legs; and Pisces to the feet.

According to the astro-anatomists, the zodiacal signs controlled the body systems of man rather than special areas of the human form. To them, man is the composite product of twelve distinct systems, or "lesser men." Thus, Aries becomes the marrow man, Taurus the muscular man, Gemini the cerebrospinal man, Cancer the sympathetic nervous man, Leo the arterial man, Virgo the assimilative man, Libra the glandular man, Scorpio the venous man, Sagittarius the motor nerve man, Capricorn the bony man, Aquarius the respiratory man, and Pisces the lymphatic man. Like the disciples of old, these twelve men gather around the thirteenth power—the Light of the Soul—and are the agencies through which the soul is distributed and interpreted into terms of action. Fludd's second figure is the sidereal, or astral, man—the microcosm—as the embryo within the body of the Macrocosm. Here the planets instead of the signs focus their rays upon the body. Fludd gives the analogies between the bodily members and the planets thus: To Saturn he assigns dominion over the right ear, the teeth, the spleen, and the bladder; to Jupiter dominion over the lungs, ribs, pulse, semen, and the liver; to Mars dominion over the left ear, kidneys, and the pudenda; to the sun dominion over the right eye, the brain, and the heart; to Venus dominion over the throat, liver, breasts, womb, loins, and genitals; to Mercury dominion over the tongue, the hands, the finger, the

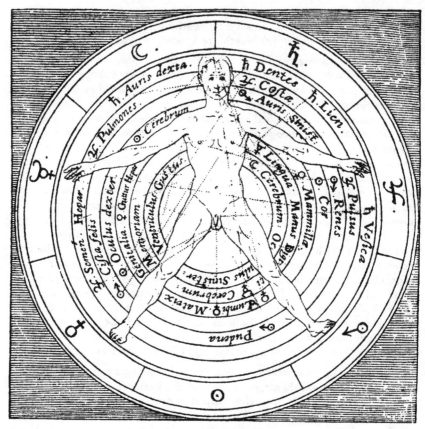

—From Collectio Operum.

THE ASTRAL MAN BOUND TO THE PLANETARY SPHERE AND RECEIVING
INTO HIMSELF THE SIDEREAL IMPULSES

brain, and memory; to the moon dominion over the brain, the left eye, the stomach, and taste.

While the many writers on astrology are without complete agreement as to the planetary rulerships over certain parts and organs of the body, they are in full accord as to the principle involved. Some have even gone so far as to recognize world within world, affirming each organ to be broken up into its zodiacal and planetary systems, each part of which is again susceptible to a similar division. Even cells are worlds in miniature. Each vibrant atom that conspires with countless others to build up the physical framework of Nature is a star in its own right, a macrocosm and a microcosm in itself, containing a heaven and an earth, together with all the elements which hang suspended betwixt these two. Thus it is that Oriental peoples came to write of the parts of the human body, bestowing upon each a distinguishing title and a hieroglyphical form suitable to its qualities. The Tantrikas, a sect of Oriental mystics, according to Madam Blavatsky, give proper names to nerves, cells, and arteries, identifying various parts of the body with deities, endowing functions and physiological processes with intelligence, etc. The vertebrae, fibers, ganglia, the cord, etc., of the spinal column; the heart, its four chambers, auricles and ventricles, valves and the rest; stomach, liver, lungs, and spleen, everything has its special deific name, is believed to act consciously and to act under the potent will of the Yogi, whose head and heart are the seats of Brahma, and the various parts of whose body are all the pleasure grounds of this or another deity. (See KOSMIC MIND.)

When the student of occult anatomy has thoroughly familiarized himself with these terms and their peculiar adaptation, a new world of analogies will open to him. He can then understand how there can be a heart in the world and a world in the heart; how man is in God and God in man; how the planets are in the vital organs and the vital organs in the planets; how each is in all and all is in each; how the world grows up in God and God grows up in the world; how atoms make stars and stars make atoms; how there are macrocosms and microcosms; how man, blinded by the single sun of heaven, supports a hundred million suns within himself. Before one can study the mysteries of the world, he must free his mind from the limitations of beliefs based upon caution and precedent. He must frame a new alphabet, devising its letters from his own learning; he must form these letters into new words that men have never dared to speak before, and with these words shape new writings, revealing secrets hidden from the ages. When he can accomplish this, he can fully comprehend how God fashioned the first man in His own likeness and how this first man, in turn, fashioned Nature in the likeness of himself.

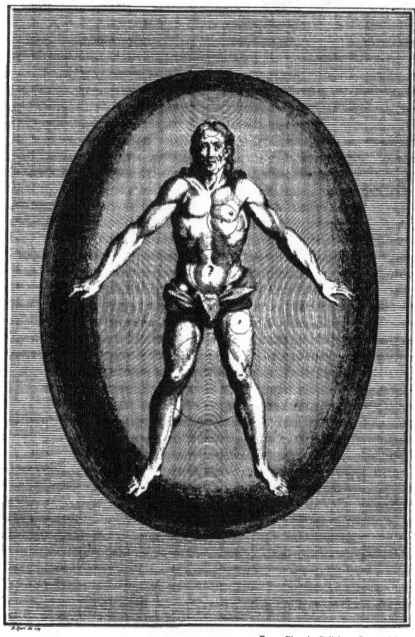

—From Picart's Religious Ceremonials.

BRAHMA IN HIS EGG
The fourteen creative potencies are shown as circles upon the parts of his body

CHAPTER V

THE SYMBOLISM OF THE WORLD EGG

THE old philosophers, initiated into the "Mysteries of the World Mother," beheld a universe perpetuated through a process of divine generation and suspended from an ungenerated but ever generating principle. The Supreme Wisdom which had raised all things from the Abyss and maintains them from its own sufficiency was greatly revered by the sages of antiquity. They not only deified this cause itself as the foundation of all good, but also regarded as worthy of veneration the qualities and attributes (the conditioned states) which emanated therefrom. As the means by which the "perpetual animal" (i.e., the world) perpetuated itself, generation was esteemed by some as the "summit" and by others as the foundation of corporeal existence. Generation is the essential point around which, in eccentric orbits, circle accident and incident. That which Divinity dictates man must needs accept not only as the most necessary but also as the greatest good. The nineteenth and twentieth centuries have attempted to substitute machines for men on the earth below and mechanisms for Divinity in the heavens above. As one writer has said, "To the moderns creation is mechanism, to the ancients, it was generation."

The egg was both the theoretical and also the practical symbol of generation. Both the world and the gods who govern it were recognized as "egg-born" in early theogonies. Primitive thinkers also anticipated the conclusions of modern science when they declared man himself to be an oviparous creature, for it is now accepted without question that the egg is one of the two essentials of reproduction in all vertebrates. Aristotle based his conclusions as to the origin and development of bodies upon the examination of chicken eggs, and from his discovery that the heart was the first organ to be distinguishable therein declared this to be the seat of the soul, in defiance of the opinions of his own master, Plato. Three fundamental aspects or expressions of the generating principle were recognized by the philosophers. The first generation is the world, itself a god and the support of inferior divinities. The second generation is man as a temporal being, the most noble of all creatures and the epitome of the world. The third generation is the soul— the "new" man, the regenerated and perfected creature, the Melchizedek, the Hermetic Adam. The whole mystery of origin and destiny is concealed in the symbolism of that radiant gold egg suspended from the dome of the Temple of the Dioscuri in Laconia. It was declared that such as understood this mystery had risen above all temporal limitations. To paraphrase the closing words of the Golden Verses of the Pythagoreans, such a man, then stripped of flesh, up to free ether soars, a deathless god divine, mortal no more.

In the theological system of the Orphics from which Plato derived his inspiration, Chronos (Time) is the first of the gods. He is the son of Ouranos (Heaven) and corresponds with the Pythagorean concept of number, for he defines the limits of magnitude, multitude, and duration. All things exist within Time and Time, in turn, reposes in the "infinite bosom of duration." The first progeny of Time are Ether and Chaos—that is, Beginning and End, or the corresponding qualitative opposites. Thus the first triad of intelligible gods was established. In this symbolism, the Great Egg represents the simple Unity, the First and Unaging One—philosophically, the only reality.

Before the beginning of the worlds, the gods and the Great Egg existed together; but when the hour of creation struck, the gods broke through the shell of the egg and came forth in all their splendor. The breaking of the heavenly egg symbolized the shattering of unity and the loss of identity. The parts of the broken shell became departments of existence and the homogeneity which preceded manifestation gave place to the diversity of the generating universe. Number became numbers, in the Pythagorean formula. From the egg came forth Phanes, the shining one, the sun, or, as the Neo-Platonists called him, "the intellect of the world." Phanes is described as "an incorruptible god, bearing wings on his shoulders; but in his inward parts naturally possessing the heads of bulls, upon which heads a mighty dragon appears, invested with all various forms of wild beasts." (See Thomas Taylor's INTRODUCTION TO PROCLUS.) The god is more exactly defined as having four heads —the first that of a lion, the second that of a bull, the third that of a dragon, and in the midst of these a fourth, his own divine and radiant countenance. Here, then, is the Cherubim of Ezekiel.

The interpretation of this fable is not difficult. Phanes is the intellectual body of the world born from and reflecting the qualities of the Empyrean or encircling heavens—the Egg. The heads are the four corners of creation, the fixed cross of the zodiac, the four elements and, symbolically, the kingdom of Nature. Phanes is winged to signify that, etherlike, he is diffused and, unlike gross matter, is not dominated by inertia. The mighty dragon twisted about Phanes and itself "invested with all various form of wild beasts," is the zodiacal serpent, which in the language of the Mysteries encircles the body of the world. In a Hindu drawing of the World Egg reproduced by Isaac Myer, the egg is shown encircled by the great serpent of Cosmic Time, Ananta, that crushes all things in its coils, and about the meridian of the egg is the band of the zodiac, the starry belt of the god. It is important also to note that in Myer's figure the egg is pierced by five openings which this learned Cabbalist believes represent the senses, thus identifying the egg as a symbol of the microcosm, or man. Among the Mithraic sculpturings are figures of the Protogonas standing or seated in an egg. This figure serves two purposes, indicating not only the origin of the sun but also of man. Upon the authority of Bryant, the Persians relate that when Ormuzd formed mankind he enclosed them or concealed them in an egg. The Syrians also speak of their ancestors, whom they later confuse with gods, as the progeny of eggs.

In the rites of the Samothracians there was a nocturnal ceremony consisting of the consecration of an egg. During this ritual those who had been accepted into the order were instructed in the secret significance of the myth of Castor and Pollux. Varro says: "In the initiation into the Mysteries at Samothrace, heaven and earth are regarded as the first two divinities." These twin gods (Castor and Pollux) were born from the same egg, and when they had issued forth used the halves of the shell for caps. Ibykos, an initiated poet, wrote thus of the twin gods: "Like aged and equal headed and one body, both born in a silver egg." (See ZEUS by Arthur Bernard Cook.) In an early Persian zodiac, the sign of Gemini (Castor and Pollux) is formed of a figure with one body and two heads. Castor and Pollux are the Hermetic androgyne—the two-headed Mercury of the alchemists. They are, therefore, the soul born from the silver egg—the Mysteries. This symbolism was very carefully preserved and appears in the mediæval renaissance of Hermeticism.

Eusebius, on the authority of Porphyry, wrote that the Egyptians ackowledged one intellectual author or creator of the world; that they worshipped him in a statue of human form and dark blue complexion (the heavens), holding in his hand a girdle (the zodiac) and a scepter (the Pole), wearing upon his head a royal plume (universal Law), and thrusting forth an egg (the world) out of his mouth (i.e., through the power of the Creative Word). The Egyptians hymned their Creator as the god who fashioned the egg and formed himself into the twin gods that were born therefrom. The god Ptah is represented in the papyri as a potter shaping the Cosmic Egg on his wheel. "The chief seat of the god [Seb, the Creator] appears to have been at Heliopolis, where he and his female counterpart, Nut, produced the great Egg where out sprang the sun-God under the form of the phœnix." (See THE GODS OF THE EGYPTIANS by E. A. Wallis-Budge.)

As Phanes bursts from the Orphic Egg, so the god Ra (the sun) emerges from the dark Egg of Seb. In the Hermetic arcanum, the phœnix is again double-headed, symbolic of the Great Work, and it rises victoriously from the Hermetic Egg which bore the strange appellation, *Rebis*. The accompanying diagram from the alchemical writings of the illustrious adept, Basilius Valentinus, sets forth the whole mystery. The symbol is made to say: "I am the Egg of Nature, known to the Sages only, who, pious and modest, engender from me the Microcosm. * * * By the Philosophers I am called by the name of Mercury." From Albert Pike's interpretation of this figure in the SEPHAR H'DEBARIM, we abridge the following: The human figure has one body with two heads—a man on the right and a woman on the left. The man's hand holds the compasses and the woman's the square. These symbols have a Hermetic origin. The compasses evidently indicate the generative potency or creative energy of the Deity, and the square the productive capacity. The figure is Brahma-Maya, Osiris-Isis. On the side of the male head is the sun, always the symbol of generative power; on the left of the female head, the moon, always the symbol of productive capacity. In the middle over the two heads is the sign of Mercury—Hermes Trismegistus, or Thoth, "the Master of the Lodge" (the universe). On the winged globe under the fire-breathing dragon are an equilateral triangle and a square, one numbered 4 and the other 3, and together composing 7, a most significant number. Castor and Pollux are here shown standing upon the back of the dragon, which crouches upon the World Egg. Ra as the sun-god of the Egyptians assumes the form of the phœnix

—From Materia Prima.

THE EGG OF NATURE AND OF THE PHILOSOPHERS,
ACCORDING TO F. BASILUS VALENTINUS

in his aspect as the light of the soul. When the sun is said to incarnate in the sphere of wisdom, it takes upon itself the body of the phœnix, which, in turn, stands for the initiate—Melchizedek, or the perfected man.

The sacred writings of the Hindus are rich in allusions to the World Egg. In the KHANDOGYA UPANISHAD it is written that in the beginning was the Akasha, which is described as existing in a non-existent state. This Brahmanical paradox was understood by the wise as signifying unconditioned life, called *Aditi* (Cosmic Space). The Upanishad then describes how the non-existent became existent. Existence increased; it gradually assumed the form of an egg. The egg "lay," or rested, for one year of Brahma—a Great Age. At the expiration of this vast infinity, the egg broke open. Of the two hemispheres of the egg, the upper was of gold and the lower of silver. The silver hemisphere became the world (the mundane creation). The golden hemisphere became the sky (the celestial expanse). In some accounts, the golden yolk

of the egg became the sun; in others, it was viewed as the earth surrounded
by the albuminous portion (the terrestrial waters). Within the egg also were
the mountains, the valleys, and the elemental strata, each symbolized by an
appropriate part of the membrane. So it is written, "the small veins are the
rivers, the fluid of the sea." The sage describes the World Egg thus: "In
that egg, O Brahman, were the continents, the seas and mountains, the planets
and divisions of the universe, the gods, demons, and mankind."

According to the RIG-VEDA, Aditi (the Akasha) had eight sons, but the
eigthth—Martanda—who is called the "egg-born," she cast away, or rejected,
having brought him forth "to be born and to die." The same thought is
contained in the KALEVALA, the epic of Finland, which introduces a beautiful
duck that, nesting in the Ocean of Eternity, laid six golden eggs and the
seventh an egg of iron. The numbers are changed, but the principle involved
is identical. In the rites of Samothrace there were seven gods called Cabiri,
and an eighth, a mystery god named Esmun. That the "egg-born" in the
Vedic allegory represents the sun is evident from the statement that he was
brought forth to be born and to die, which is indicative of the diurnal and
nocturnal aspects of the solar orb. The RIG-VEDA also describes the birth of
the golden child, Hiranyagarbha, a word which, according to Max Müller,
means literally the golden embryo, the golden germ or child, or born from a
golden womb or egg. In the old books it is also written that the waters of
space (the Great Deep, the universal amniotic fluid) produced from itself an
embryo; or, more correctly, Brahm assumed the form of Kalahansa, "the swan
of eternity," and at the beginning of each Great Age lays the golden egg of
the cycle. (See THE SECRET DOCTRINE.)

From the old records we gather the following: Narayana, an epithet of
Vishnu, contemplating the creation of the universe, first generated the *waters
of causation.* Then, moving upon the face of the waters, he dropped the seed
of the world into the deep. Within the egg was born Purusha, the Heavenly
Man, resplendent as the sun—the Greek Phanes. Within the egg also are all
the *lokas,* or worlds, by which is meant all the aspects of existence which can
be sensed by the perceptions of created things; and also within the egg is the
physical world "composed of seven islands." The egg was described as being
originally without consciousness, but the Creator, having entered into the
consciousness of time, destiny, and law, the egg became alive and Purusha—
the Protogonas—issued forth with a thousand heads, a thousand eyes, and a
thousand arms. The fourteen worlds came forth with him and are called the
limbs of the Grand Man. Purusha is named "the egg golden," the father of
the Pitris and all beings.

The Persian Mysteries also enlarged upon the doctrine of the World Egg.
There are early figures representing Ormuzd and Ahriman under the forms of
the good and evil serpents contesting for the possession of the World Egg.
Plutarch, in his dissertation ON PROVIDENCE AND DESTINY, supports his opinions

by advancing the mystic egg of Zoroaster and Mithras. By this he intimated the zodiac, the celestial hierarchies of which were the administrators of fate and the custodians of divine law. According to Albert Pike, the 48 gods described as enclosed within the ample circumference of the Universal Egg were the constellations set within the concavity of the world sphere. The seven eggs referred to in the KALEVALA are explained by the early Gnostic and Hermetic fragments, which declared the planetary gods to have been fashioned in the form of eggs, a term used to signify spheres but suggesting not only the shape but also the inherent fertility of the globes. Ormuzd is described in THE MYSTERIES OF ISIS AND OSIRIS as forming 24 gods and putting them into an egg. Here the egg becomes the symbol of the day, the gods being the hours. This symbolism was preserved in the Arthurian cycle, wherein are described the 24 knights seated about the Round Table; and, again, the elders of the Apocalypse. The Persian mysticism surrounds the world with a shell pierced with 360 openings. This is the annual egg, of which Virgil writes that the sacred bull breaks the egg of the year with its horns.

Among the Pahlavi texts translated in the sacred books of the East is a part in which the "Spirit of Wisdom" describes the world in these words: "The sky and earth and water, and whatever else is within them are egg-like, just as it were like the egg of a bird. The sky is arranged above the earth, like an egg, by the handiwork of the Creator, Ahura-Mazda; and the semblance of the earth in the midst of the sky, is just like as it were the yolk within the egg; and the water within the earth and sky is such as the water within the egg." (See THE OPINIONS OF THE SPIRIT OF WISDOM.) This quotation is startlingly similar to one appearing among the writings of Paracelsus and indicates that this great occultist was unquestionably acquainted through the Arabs with the metaphysical mysteries of the East. "The yolk of an egg," wrote the Swiss Hermes, "rests in the albumen without sinking to the bottom of the shell. The yolk represents the Earth, and the white represents the invisible surroundings of the Earth, and the invisible part acts upon the visible one, but only the philosopher perceives the way in which the action takes place." When Paracelsus declares the invisible to act upon the visible, he infers the albuminous part of the egg to represent the invisible superphysical planes of Nature, from which, unknown to the average person, flows the life by which the mortal fabric is sustained.

It is unfortunately not possible in this remote time to follow the advice of Macrobius, who recommended that those who would understand the hidden wisdom should "consult the initiates of the Mystery of Bacchus, who honor with special veneration the sacred egg." We learn from other authorities, however, that the philosophers used this figure to represent the Ark, for it is pictured floating upon the water and "exposed to the fury of Typhon, or the Deluge." As the egg, according to Bryant, contained the elements of life, it was thought no improper emblem of the Ark in which were preserved the rudiments of the future world. By the bursting of the egg was denoted the opening of the Ark and release into manifestation of the powers it contained.

Among the Druids, the *ovum anguinum*, or serpent's egg, was highly sacred; in fact, it was termed *insigne Druidis*, "the distinguishing mark of a Druid." According to Pliny, the test of the genuineness of the Druidic egg was that it would float upon the surface of water, supporting not only itself but the heavy golden setting which contained it. The Druidic egg was called "the involved ball, which casts its rays to a distance, the splendid product of the adder, shot forth by serpents." Edward Davies writes of the Mysteries of Britain: "The Druids themselves were called *adders* by the Welsh bards. The Druids, therefore, *were* the serpents which assembled at a certain time in the summer to prepare these emblems of *creirwy* [the eggs], and to conceal within them certain discrimination tokens, which probably were kept as a profound secret from the persons who received them. Pliny saw one of these eggs, but he had not the curiosity to examine it any further than its cartilaginous integument; otherwise, he would probably have discovered that it contained either a *lunette of glass*, or a small ring of the same material." (See THE MYTHOLOGY OF THE BRITISH DRUIDS.)

The same author then expresses himself of the opinion that the Druidical eggs were almost certainly artificial and of various colors, some blue, some white, some green, and others regularly variegated with stripes of these colors. Some had the appearance of glass, others again were simply composed of earth and glazed over. The color of the eggs give a certain clue to their significance, for these colors were identical with those worn by the members of the several grades of the Druid order. The eggs could only be prepared at certain times of the moon, and in the ovolatry of most ancient nations the moon occupied a prominent place. The Greeks believed the moon to be inhabited by a race of beings who issued from great eggs. There is a legend that the beautiful Helen, for whom was fought the Trojan war, was born out of an egg that fell from the moon. Serpent eggs were believed by the Druids to be impregnated directly by the solar ray, and the preparation of these mysterious eggs represented the process by which the body of the Druid was caused to generate within itself the serpent of wisdom. There can be no question but that the Druidic adder was identical with the Kundalini of the Tantric cults. In the CHALDEAN ORACLES, the mundane god is described as possessing "a winding form." (See Cory's ANCIENT FRAGMENTS.) The birth of the serpent from the egg was then the releasing of the spinal fire—"the winding god"—and the Druids themselves were called snakes because they were masters of the serpent power.

The egg which, according to Plutarch, was an image of the universe which engenders everything and contains everything in its bosom, is described by Albert Pike as follows: "Thus the symbolic Egg, that issued from the mouth of the invisible Egyptian God KNEPH; known to the Grecian Mysteries as the

Orphic Egg; from which issued the God CHUMONG of the Coresians, and the Egyptian OSIRIS, and PHANES, God and Principle of Light; from which, broken by the Sacred Bull of the Japanese, the world emerged; and which the Greeks placed at the feet of BACCHUS TAURI-CORNUS; the Magian Egg or Ormuzd, from which came the Amshaspands and Devs; was divided into two halves, and equally apportioned between the Good and Evil Constellations and Angels." We have already noted that in the doctrines of the Cabala the word *cranium*, or *skull*, was used to signify the monads, or unities, which circumscribe all the manifestations of existence. "When the skull-like, wide-yawning egg did break" is a statement attributed to Orpheus which links the Greek and Jewish systems.

The egg, then, is identical with the great cranium of THE ZOHAR, the spherical envelope surrounding the world. The serpent entwined about the Orphic egg stands for the active agent of creation and the egg itself for the patient. The serpent is the sperm and the egg the ovum. "When the egg and serpent are represented,' writes G. R. S. Mead, "they stand for 'Chaos' and 'Ether,' matter and spirit; but when united they represent the hermaphrodite or male-female first principle of the universe, spirit-matter." (See THE THRICE GREATEST HERMES.) The egg was warmed from within and, according to Aristophanes, love was hatched from the egg. Here love represents a spiritual quality, a transmuted or perfected nature issuing from the philosophic egg (the soul).

The philosophic egg of the Hermetists is derived from these ancient sources and, restated in the alchemical terminology of the Middle ages, was incorporated into the mystical symbolism of the Rosicrucians. In describing the origin of the Fraternity of the Rose Cross, John Heydon declared the order to be maintained by a group of mysterious adepts who perpetuate themselves from age to age by returning periodically into a philosophic womb, where they rest for a prescribed time and then come forth once more renewed in life and years. Heydon speaks of the Brother C. R. C. as 'in a proper womb quickening." This womb was a glass casket or container, an alchemical vessel in which the Brothers were buried. It was properly called the philosophic egg. At regular intervals the philosopher, breaking the shell of his egg, took up again the concerns of life, later to retire once more into his shell of glass. From the Greek accounts we learn that the Cosmic Egg was also called in the language of the Mysteries, "the brilliant *chiton*" or "the cloud." The Macroscosmic Egg is the universe with its hypothetical boundaries, and the Microcosmic Egg is the human aura, the brilliant cloud in which man lives and moves and has his being.

The average scientist is not equipped to investigate the mysteries of man's spiritual constitution. Plutarch, for example, in describing the vision of Thespesius, notes that the spirit guiding this worthy through the underworld discoursed thus upon the colorations of the soul: "Observe the colours of the souls of every shade and sort: that greasy, brown-grey is the pigment of sordidness and selfishness; that blood-red, inflamed shade is a sign of a savage and venomous nature; wherever blue-grey is, from such a nature incontinence in pleasure is not easily eradicated; innate malignity, mingled with envy, causes that livid discoloration, in the same way as cuttle-fish eject their sepia." Philo, in commenting on "Jacob's dream of the white, and spotted, and ring-straked, and speckled kine," declared that these markings referred to the qualities of souls. (See THRICE-GREATEST HERMES.) Here are the auras examined by the clairvoyant eyes of ancient seers and called by mediœval mystics "insensible perspirations." In 1920, Walter J. Kilner, B.A., M.B., (Cantab.), M.R.C.P., etc., late electrician to St. Thomas's Hospital, London, published his sensational work, THE HUMAN ATMOSPHERE. After carefully emphasizing the fact that he was neither a clairvoyant nor an occulist, he demonstrates that with the aid of glass screens (or rather cells filled with an alcoholic solution of dicyanin) the average person can both see and analyze the human aura. The nimbi around the heads of saints are not figments of the imagination but actually exist and, to quote Dr. Kilner: "There is no more charlatanism in the detection of the human aura by the means employed than in distinguishing microbes by the aid of the microscope."

After a certain period of physical functioning, the potentialities constituting the objective life of man retire again into the auric body. When the soul deserts the physical fabric and retires into its own substances, the body is referred to as dead and returns to the elements from which it came. Between lives, therefore, the philosopher was said to be sleeping in his egg—that is, existing in the invisible worlds or, more correctly, in his own invisible bodies. Periodically he precipitates "the golden germ," builds a new external form, and abides in it temporarily. He is then said to have emerged from his egg. The breaking of the egg had also another and very recondite significance, for it represented the attainment of Nirvana, or absolute unity with the formless Cause of existence. The breaking of the egg was the shattering of personality and the release of the spiritual nature into that Universal Being from which it originally emanated. The auric egg of man is so complex in its structure that all the description which applies to the universal system is equally applicable to the human auric envelope. Within man's aura are the zones and belts; the stars, the planets, and the elements; the gods, the angels, and the demons. Man is a universe and at his present state of development his physical personality is a golden embryo suspended within the brilliant shell of his auric sheaths. As the Rosicrucian would say, he is in a proper womb quickening, preparing himself to come gloriously forth with all the radiance and beauty of the Orphic Phanes.

THE TITLE PAGE OF AN INCUNABULA BIBLE IN WHICH THE WORLD IS SHOWN IN THE FORM OF THE EXTRA-EMBRYONIC FŒTAL MEMBRANES WITH THEIR CONTENTS

CHAPTER VI

INTRODUCTION TO OCCULT EMBRYOLOGY

HE propagation of the human species depends upon the union of the two reproductive elements, the spermatozoon and the ovum, referred to in Oriental mysticism as the "ray" and the "germ." The human spermatozoon, or seminal filament, is about 1-500th of an inch in length and consists of three distinct sections, which are called the head, the middle piece, and the tail piece. The spermatozoon resembles a microscopic pollywog and is capable of rapid motion due to what Hertwig calls "a peculiar serpentine [!] motion in virtue of its contractile properties." The ovum, or human egg, is considerably larger than the sperm cell; in fact, it is the largest cell in the human body, having a diameter of about 1-100th of an inch. Suspended in the protoplasm of the ovum are "dropules and granules" and the whole cell is protected by a delicate vitelline membrane. The ovum is a passive cell in contradistinction to the active qualities of the spermatozoon. An examination of these reproductive elements cannot but impress the philosophically-minded with the exquisite resourcefulness of Nature which finds such an ingenious method for launching life into objective existence.

Realizing that the vital facts involved in the processes of maturation and fertilization of the ovum are utterly beyond the analysis of ontogenists, it is not surprising that many curious opinions have been advanced to explain the chemistry of physical origin. If there is one point at which metaphysics impinges itself upon physics—or the metaphysical upon the physical—it is that point at which the spermatozoon, having pierced the wall of the ovum, vanishes into the substances of that cell. Two early theories were advanced. The Spermists assumed the potential man to be contained within the head of the spermatozoon, the ovum contributing, so to speak, the nutritive environment for its development. The Ovists, on the other hand, affirmed the ovum to contain the whole of the future embryo, and that the sperm merely released this potential activity, quickening, as it were, the ovum. Both these theories have given way to Epigenesis, and it is the present opinion that both the sperm and the ovum, through their minglings, supply the substances of the future man.

Dr. William E. Kellicott gives the following summary of embryology, its purposes and accomplishments: "The province of Embryology is not merely thus to describe the upbuilding and unfolding of the structure and form of the new organism * * * it is, further, to describe the more fundamental *processes* involved in this development, and still further, to summarize these descriptions of both kinds in the formation of simple general statements or laws." So far, so good. The Professor of biology continues: "This physiological aspect of Embryology is concerned more with *how* development occurs, *how,* and through the operation of what factors or mechanisms, one condition leads to another." [Here the Doctor gets on dangerous ground and qualifies himself accordingly!] "In a way this is also the *why* of development—not 'why' in the philosophical sense of course, but the the sense of 'how does it happen that' these things occur in development." (See A TEXT-BOOK OF GENERAL EMBRYOLOGY.) Ontogenists were not the originators of the intriguing formula that in matters scientific *why* should be interpreted as *how*. *Why* is the most dangerous word in the field of learning. It is almost certain to invoke a sickening realization of ignorance and a torrent of *hows*. Great minds have wrestled with *why* all through the night even as Jacob wrestled with the angel.

On the authority of Father Sinistrari, of Ameno, Pererieus, speaking for the physicians of his day, declared that the whole strength and efficiency of the human sperm resides in certain "spirits" which it contains. These spirits were believed to have been derived from the vital parts of the parent organism. The "marrow," the heart, the brain, and so forth, through the blood were the origin of the active qualities of the spermatozoon. Thus, man is said to "beget from his own substances." Though this theory, in company with many others, has been relegated to the limbo, it may not prove unprofitable to examine it more closely, especially since Sir Michael Foster, an eminent authority in physiology, admitted that knowledge in this direction "is almost a blank." That certain forces or agencies too elusive to be seen or analyzed, even with the aid of the most powerful microscope, are present within the germinal cell cannot be denied; and if there be applied the pragmatic yardstick —that the meaning and nature of things are to be discovered from consideration of their consequences—the paramount importance of these indistinguishable elements is apparent. "It is humiliating to the pride of man," wrote Pliny, "to consider the pitiable origin of this most arrogant of all the animals." Pitiable as may seem these little drops of life oozing from the very substance of the Infinite, their depths are no less a mystery than the heavens. Fearful and wonderful are these seeds which carry within their nearly transparent substances the rudiments of a new world and, strange as it may seem, dominate that new world to the very end. Yes, even beyond the end, for the cell is the basis of racial continuance, and all that has gone before is locked within it to foreshadow that which is yet to come. Physical man is the product of the cleavages taking place within this single cell, whose impress is stamped upon every vital part of him. Though the complexities of the organism and its functions conceal this fact from the profane, man never escapes from the domination of that invisible agent which abides somewhere within the germinal cell from which he sprang.

It was the belief of the ancient philosophers—and science is essentially a branch of philosophy—that bodies, in and of themselves, are relatively inanimate; nor again are they origins of life, but rather vehicles or carriers of divine or vital principles.   These principles may not always be discernible through the structure of their physical mediums, but their presence is evidenced (1) by the activities which they bestow upon bodies and (2) by the potentialities which they release through such physical chemistry as the fertilization of the ovum.   In harmony with this opinion, Paracelsus held the physical sperm to be the carrier of superphysical essence which he calls the *aura seminalis,* or the aura of the seed.   This *aura seminalis,* in turn, has its origin in the *liquor vitae,* or ethereal life fluid.   In DE GENERATIO HOMINIS, Paracelsus describes the *liquor vitae* as a highly refined super nerve fluid, in which is contained "nature, quality, character, and essence."   The great Aureolus affirmed the physical body, which he termed the microcosm, to be contained potentially in a vitaplasmic field, wherein all its aspects and attributes existed in a fluidic state.   This potential creature, composed entirely of an ethereal life fluid, Paracelsus termed the invisible or hidden man—the unrecognized source of bodily function and action, and the origin of the apparently spontaneous changes which take place in the outward constitution. The *liquor vitae* is thus man in a state of solution in nerve essence.   The *aura seminalis* is an emanation from the *liquor vitae;* that is, it is exuded from it or tinctured by it.   As the *liquor vitae* is man in a psycho-fluidic state, so each drop of this fluid contains the image and likeness of the *whole* man.   The *liquor vitae* bestows this whole image upon its emanation, the *aura seminalis,* which by virtue thereof carries the quality aspects of a complete man within its substances.

The sexual cell of the male is but the physical medium for the activity of the *aura seminalis,* which radiates from it and is the superphysical cause of its virility.   Therefore, Paracelsus says that the fructifying principle does not exist in the sperm or seed but in the

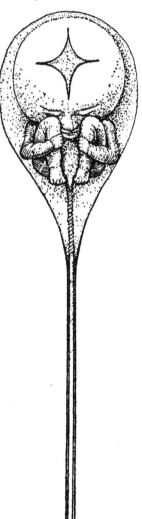

—From Hartsoeker.

AN EARLY DRAWING OF THE HUMAN SPERM

The embryo is shown as a complete organism curled up in the head of the spermatozoon.

spirit. To classify the rationale of this procedure, first there is the *tincture*, (in Paracelsian terminology) the cause; then the *liquor vitae*, the spiritual impulse; then the *aura seminalis*, the astral agent; and lastly, the sperm, the physical carrier. Here, then, are the four worlds of THE ZOHAR—Atziluth, Briah, Yetzirah, and Assiah—and also the four Adams or men again recurring in the four castes authorized by the Brahmanic Vedas. An examination of Cabalistic literature shows the first world to be associated with the abstract names or qualities of Divinity, the second with the zodiacal hierarchies, the third with the planetary regencies, and the fourth and last with the physical

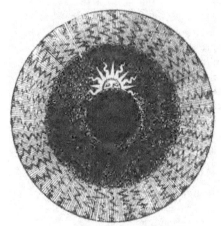

—From Collectio Operum.

FLUDD'S DIAGRAM OF THE ORIGIN
AND RISING OF THE SUN

In this figure, designed in 1617, present-day knowledge concerning the structure and appearance of the cell is anticipated to a remarkable degree.

elements and the infernal state, which are always associated in metaphysical tradition with our corporeal existence. "We may judge what kind of life is allotted to us by Nature," wrote Seneca, "since it is ordained, as an omen, that we should come weeping into the world."

All the organs of the human system in Paracelsian ontogeny, together with all their powers and attributes, contribute alike to the formation of the true seed—that is, the spiritual sperm. "They are, therefore,' he affirms, "germinally contained in the seminal fluid that is necessary for the reproduction of the human organism. The spiritual seed is, so to say, the essence of the human body, containing all the organs of the latter in an ideal form." This thought is restated by a more modern writer when he says that "the one cell represents the whole individual," and has the characteristics of the individual with the organs and parts of organs imprinted in it. Peering through a microscope at the tiny spermatozoon lashing its way through the seminal fluid, it seems incredible that one small organism should possess such significance. Yet there is not a single atom vibrating in space but which bears similar evidence of divine order and purpose.

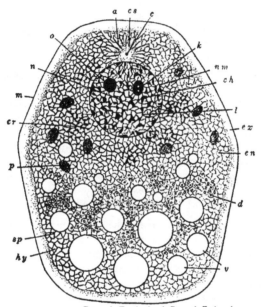

—From A Textbook of General Embryology.

DIAGRAM OF A TYPICAL CELL (after Kellicott)

By comparing this diagram with the Rosicrucian figure on the opposite page, it will be seen that the centrosome (c), above the nucleus (n), is startlingly similar to Fludd's symbol of the sun rising above the chaos of the primitive earth; yet in Fludd's time the present theories of cell development were presumably unknown and the centrosome undiscovered.

From a consideration of the qualities of the spermatozoon, let us now turn to an analysis of the ovum, which also evidences in a superlative degree the wisdom of the Universal Architect. Paracelsus was a philosophical Spermist: that is, he maintained that the pattern for the coming creature was resident in the sperm. In fact, he considered the male body primarily spermlike or intrinsically sperminal. On the other hand, the female body not only produced the ovum but was essentially egglike in qualities, which Paracelsus explains as follows: "The whole of man's body is potentially contained in the seed and the whole of the body of the mother is, so to say, the soil in which the future man is made to ripen." Most of the original cosmogonists assumed water to be the parent of all generated things, explaining that the water was rendered productive through impregnation by the solar ray. These theories probably gave rise to such terms as *Father God* and *Mother Nature*. The father was the bestower of life and the quickener of animate things, while the mother was the incubator of these germs, supplying nutriment and protection to them during their fœtal period.

The shadow of the world lay sleeping in the depths of the Great Ocean, and the gods, moving upon the face of the deep, called the shadow forth from its abyss, or, as recounted in THE VISHNU PURANA, the Lord of the World, in the form of a great boar, dove into the Ocean of Matter and reappeared elevating the rescued world upon its tusks. The ovum contains within it the Water of Eternity, and it is upon or in this that the god who is worshipped in the form of a serpent—the spermatozoon—"moves." "As the Spirit of God in the beginning of creation," writes Paracelsus, "moved upon the surface of the waters (the soul), likewise the human spirit, being diffused through the whole of man's organism, moves upon the fluid, out of which the human form developed." From the union of Ether and Chaos—the germ and the egg—the world comes into being, and by recourse to the cosmogony myths, which for the most part are founded upon embryology, we can secure a very adequate account of the development of the "world animal."

From an occult standpoint, then, the spermatozoon is the carrier of the archetype. It is a little *ark* in which the seeds of life are carried upon the surface of the waters that at the appointed time they may replenish the earth. A triad of forces—spiritual, psychical, and material—are contained within the head of the sperm. This triad originated from the three great centers of man referred to exoterically as the heart, the head, and the navel. The sperm also contains the Logoi, or generating gods—the Builders—those who are to establish their foundations in the deep and upbuild their thrones in the midst of the waters. With them come also hierarchies of celestial powers—the star spirits—pioneer gods going forth to build new worlds. In the ovum is the plastic stuff which is to be molded by the heavenly powers. In the ovum lies the sleeping world, awaiting the dawn of manvantaric day. In it lurk the Chhaya forms of time and place. Suddenly above the dark horizon of the ovum appears the blazing spermatic sun. Its ray shoots into the deep. The mother ocean thrills. The sperm follows the ray and vanishes in the mother. The germ achieves immortality by ceasing of itself and continuing in its progeny. The mother ovum is fertile. She produces the lesser sun—the Demiurge, or the Builder. The law is established. The Builder calls forth the world form. The One becomes two; unity is swallowed up in diversity. Fission begins; by cleavage the One releases the many. The gods are released. They group around the Poles. The zones are established. Each of the gods releases from himself a host of lesser spirits. The germ layers come into being. The gods gather about the North Pole. The shape is bent inward upon itself. The mineral becomes a plant, the plant an animal, and the animal a man. The Builders take up their places in the organs and the parts, and the Father Cell beholds the work from His hidden place, and He sees that it is good.

From a state analogous to that of the mineral, the body of the future man recapitulates its descent by passing rapidly through the several kingdoms with each of which it is temporarily correlated, at least in appearance. "At the end of three or four weeks," writes H. P. Blavatsky, "the ovum has assumed a plant-like appearance, one extremity having become spheroidal and the other tapering, like a carrot. Upon dissection it is found to be composed, like an onion, of very delicate laminæ or coats, enclosing a liquid. The laminæ approach each other at the lower end, and the embryo hangs from the root of the umbilicus almost like a fruit from the bough. The stone has now become changed, by metempsychosis, into a plant. Then the embryonic creature begins to shoot out, from the inside outward, its limbs, and develops its features. The eyes are visible as two black dots; the ears, nose, and mouth form depressions, like the points of a pineapple, before they begin to project. The embryo develops into an animal-like fœtus—the shape of a tadpole—and like an amphibious reptile lives in water, and develops from it. Its monad has not yet become either human or immortal, for the Kabalists tell us that that only comes at the 'fourth hour.' One by one the fœtus assumes the characteristics of the human being, the first flutter of the immortal breath passes through his being; he moves: nature opens the way for him; ushers him into the world; and the divine essence settles in the infant frame, which it will inhabit until the moment of physical death, when man becomes a spirit." (See ISIS UNVEILED.)

By scientific means it is possible to examine and classify the phenomenal changes taking place during fertilization, cleavage, etc. The spiritual processes, however, which precipitate the physical phenomena are more difficult of perception and analysis. We predict that in time science will "discover" them, possibly through instruments capable of producing a mechanical clairvoyance, as the Kilner screens. Until that day comes, we must depend upon the testimony of "exceptional" types who possess within themselves the faculty of superphysical vision. The causal activities which precipitate the physical man are luminous qualities which have a color, form, and sound existence in what the ancients called "æther." This æther is the metaphysical counterpart of the hypothetical medium of science. A play of vibratory activity precedes every modification of physical matter, being the necessary but as yet unrecognized cause of such change. Impregnation is primarily a spiritual process. By "spiritual" we mean superphysical but not supernatural.

The new entity first incarnates through a neutral area caused by the blending of the magnetic fields, or auras, of the parents. During normal copulation this neutral zone is established as a low pressure area in the akashic field. Through this focal point the new life is ushered into physical being.

If abnormalities exist in either parent, these are registered in the aura and may prevent the establishment of this harmonic interval, and under such conditions impregnation cannot result. "At connubial intercourse on earth," declares THE ZOHAR, "the Holy One, blessed be he, sends a human form which bears the impress of the divine stamp. This form is present at intercourse, and if we were permitted to see it we should perceive over our heads an image resembling the human face; and it is in this image that we are formed. As long as this image is not sent by God and does not descend and hover over our heads, there can be no conception. * * * This image receives us when we enter the world, it develops us when we grow, and accompanies us when we depart this life."

This image is that of the Heavenly Man—that is, the ego and its super-physical vestments—man clothed in his "Adamic" flesh (his astral body). As the aura of the incarnating entity impresses itself upon the area formed by the impingement of the parental auras, a symbolic triad becomes apparent, which may best be described by the 47th proposition of Euclid. The "Great Face" referred to in THE ZOHAR represents again the. Upper Face of the Sephirothic Tree. It is Macroprosophus in its human aspect—the "heavenly father." The rapprochement of the three auras results in a more or less complete sympathy between the factors involved in the mystery of generation, i.e., father, mother, and child. During the prenatal period the ego works upon its new body in three ways: (1) By spinning threads between itself and the evolving germ it is enabled to diffuse its qualities throughout the embryonic body; (2) it insinuates itself into the new body by tincturing the auras of the parents; (It is erroneous to assume that the father contributes nothing but the sperm.) (3) it envelopes the embryo as an "atmosphere," pouring its forces upon the little form as the stars focus their rays upon the earth. The consciousness of the incoming ego does not immediately enter the embryo, but takes up its abode there gradually as the increasing complexity of development demands the presence of an intellectual force. The PISTIS SOPHIA describes in these words how the builders, or workmen, which have been emanated from the higher principles of the incoming man descend into the fertilized ovum: "And forth-with the three hundred and sixty-five workmen of the Rulers enter into her [the mother], to take up their abode in her. The workmen of the two parts [the sperm and the ovum] are all there together."

The auric entity overshadowing the embryo is inseparable from that of the mother; that is, it accompanies her, partly diffusing itself through her magnetic bodies. This frequently results in a peculiar vital intoxication, causing the mother to be indifferent to disturbing conditions and greatly removing the probability of emotional excess. The body of the embryo is actually built from the aura of the incarnating entity. The body of the mother is only the medium through which these forces work. In a manuscript copy of Hildegard's SCIVAS, the circumstances attendant upon the descent of the soul into the body at birth are admirably set forth. The mother is lying in the foreground at the bottom of an egg-shaped nimbus, in which ten figures are shown bringing fruits, foods, etc. These are the Hindu Prajapatis, or builders. Above the aura of the mother is the trisected spiritual body of the incoming soul. This is filled with eyes, symbols of spiritual power and enlightenment, and is connected by a tube which descends and enters the head of the fœtus. Hildegard describes the ego as descending through this tube as a shapeless but luminous mystery, which tinctures the new form with life and gradually develops into a glorious spiritual organ. "And I saw the likeness of a woman," wrote the seeress, "having a complete human form within her womb. And then, by a secret disposition of the Most High Craftsman, a fiery sphere having none of the lineaments of a human body possessed the heart of the form, and reached the brain and transfused itself through all the members."

The process of "quickening" is described by an old medical author as "that instantaneous, yet undescribable motion of the vital principle, which, the instant the fœtus has acquired a sufficient degree of animal heat, and is completely formed in all its parts, rushes like an electric shock, or flash of lightning, conducted by the sanguiferous and nervous fluids, from the heart and brain of the mother, to the heart and brain of the child. At this moment the circulation begins; the infant fabric is completely set in motion; and the child becomes a living *soul*." (See A KEY TO PHYSICS.) But there is more to the mystery than this, for in the words of John Heydon (who speaks upon the authority of Epicharmus, Cebes, Psellus, and Proclus), "it is not the mother's soul that efforms the embryo." The *anima mundi*, or "soul of the world," is diffused through the embryo at all times, so that from the beginning it is alive in the sense that all natural bodies are alive. Science seemingly recognizes no point of demarkation between life and entity, but occultism, following Plato and the old masters, maintains that at a certain time the soul takes up its abode, especially in the blood. The theological concept that the soul descends directly from God has more of truth in it than the scientific belief that life is chemical in its origin. The term *God* is broadly used to signify the universe in its causal aspect, and the ego most certainly verges from cause towards effect. Having perfected a body for its residence, the soul is drawn thereinto by the same fateful destiny which led Narcissus to plunge after his reflection in the pool. Having once been united with its corporeal fabric, the soul after drinking of the waters of Lethe loses all memory of its original state and must remain beset by doubts until philosophy or death shall release it.

The material on Paracelsian ontogeny in the first part of this chapter is not in conflict with the Cabalistic and Gnostic doctrines just described. The apparent contradiction is due to the angle of approach. Paracelsus described the chemistry by which the physical body itself came into being, whereas THE ZOHAR and PISTIS SOPHIA are concerned with the entity which is ensouling that body. The principles of the animal constitution are, indeed, derived from the *liquor vitae*, but these principles do not become the organs and departments of man until they are ensouled by the incarnating entity. The archetypal organs and members derived from the parents are focal points for the incoming life. By setting these primary vortices in motion with its own peculiar rate of vibration, the new entity gradually imposes itself—that is, its will and purpose—upon the form resulting from the union of the sperm and the ovum. Paracelsus tells the story of the physical processes relating only to the establishment of the bodily nuclei, whereas the Jewish and Egyptian mystics set forth the phenomena of the descent of conscious life into the newly-prepared vehicle. By comparing the two accounts in this way, it will be evident that they amount to a complete record of human generation.

Herein is also contained a clue to such mysteries as heredity and prenatal influence. Heredity is traceable to two factors. In the first place, since morality, culture, genius, etc., are reducible to rates of vibration pervading the mother's aura, they also exert a powerful influence upon the external life. Thus, while neutral zones are established at the time of copulation, there are qualitative differences in these zones caused by the intellectuality, morality, and spirituality of the parents. Incarnating egos seeking rebirth are drawn to these neutral zones by the law of attraction—that is, through sympathy or antipathy. If the psychical vortices set up by the parents are inconsistent with the purposes of the incoming life, conception will not take place. "If a child," writes Dr. Franz Hartmann, "as is often the case, manifests the same tastes, talents, and inclinations as those of his father or as other members of the same family, it does by no means necessarily follow that these tastes, etc., have been inherited by him from his parents, and the contrary often takes place. A similarity of tastes, etc., between the child and his parents would rather go to show that the monad, having developed its tendencies in a previous incarnation, was attracted to a particular family on account of an already existing similarity of its own tastes with those of its future parents." In the second place, it is possible during the sensitive embryonic period for either parent—but more especially the mother—to modify the bodily chemistry of the child through what Paracelsus calls will and imagination. According to Paracelsus, "the imagination of the mother exerts a great constructive influence upon the development of the fœtus, and upon this fact is based the similarity existing between children and parents." He further asserts that the imagination of the father activates the creative power which is necessary to the generation of a human being, and the imagination of the mother furnishes the materials for the formation and development of this being. The rational principle of the child, however, is separate and distinct from that of the parents, having its own eternal subsistence.

The creative aspect of human thought is now recognized in so far as it impels physical action. Going beyond this, occultism maintains, however, that thoughts have a life of their own and are capable of molding matter from a subjective plane. Therefore, the old maxim: "Thoughts are things." When Professor Haupt, in FUNDAMENTALS OF BIOLOGY, passes on to modern youth the prevailing opinion among scientific men that there is no nerve connection between the mother and the embryo and, "consequently, there is no way in which the mental state of the mother—her thoughts, desires, or fears—can influence the unborn offspring," he is affirming as a fact an opinion not justified by its own premise. The absence of physical nerve connection—if this can be proved beyond all doubt—is no more conclusive proof of the impossibility of sympathetic contact than is the absence of wires *prima facie* evidence that the radio receiver has no possible connection with the broadcasting station. Ether is a highway for subtle vibratory impulses, and Professor Haupt is, indeed, to be congratulated if he has exhausted possibilities to the point of negative certainties. It is scarcely necessary to bring evidence to support the phenomenon of prenatal influence, as the theory has not yet been intelligently assailed. To those, however, who would examine the matter of monstrosities and malformations more carefully, we would recommend a careful perusal of the writings of the great Jan Baptist van Helmont, who sets forth much historical data and well classified original research.

If science, too, must have its superstitions and pass theories off as facts, why should it not promulgate the opinions which contribute definitely to human well-being? The race is imperilled by narrowness. Only by the deepening and broadening of the intellect can man escape the unhappy fate of all narrowness. What has modern science to offer comparable in splendor with the universal vision of the Cabalist? Let us depart from the *sub verme* sphere of the materialist to a concept of life worthy of man and to some measure, at least, consistent with cosmic magnitudes. The ancients discovered in embryology an answer to the riddle of the world. Let us apply knowledge to its reasonable end, uniting all the diversified discoveries of mankind to one sacred duty— the perfection of humanity. Behold the vision! "As the fœtus develops from the *liquor amnii* in the womb, so the earths germinate from the universal ether, or astral fluid, in the womb of the universe. These cosmic children, like their pigmy inhabitants, are first nuclei; then ovules; then gradually mature; and becoming mothers in their turn, develop mineral, vegetable, animal, and human forms. From center to circumference, from the imperceptible vesicle to the uttermost conceivable bounds of the cosmos, these glorious thinkers, the Kabalists, trace cycle merging into cycle, containing and contained in an endless series. The embryo envoling in its prenatal sphere, the individual in his family, the family in the state, the state in mankind, the earth in our system, that system in its central universe, the universe in the cosmos, and the cosmos in the First Cause:—the Boundless and Endless." (See ISIS UNVEILED.)

—From Kabbala Denudata.

TITLE PAGE OF THE GREATEST OF CABALISTIC BOOKS

Profoundly versed in the mysteries of Nature and of man, the Cabalists veiled their discoveries behind crude and apparently meaningless figures, thus preserving themselves from persecution. The radiant sun towards which the female figure looks has vast symbolic import for those with eyes to see.

CHAPTER VII

THE STORY OF THE CELL

N discussing the process of fertilization in the human ovum, it is necessary to bear in mind the very incomplete state of the research done in this field. During the past fifty years, a host of very able men have attempted to classify the phenomena, but there is an unfortunate lack of agreement in their findings. This discrepancy is unquestionably due to the elusiveness of the factors under consideration. There is a vanishing point at which the patient disappears into the agent—or, at least, cannot be distinguished therefrom with present equipment, optical and instrumental. When the minute bodies responsible for our physical existence refuse stain, they vanish, at least from the observational standpoint. At this point speculation dominates the situation and irreconcilable theories spring up. The state of affairs is briefly summed up by Professor Leslie Brainerd Arey, of Northwestern University, in a recent publication: "There are no observations on the fertilization of the human ova." (See DEVELOPMENTAL ANATOMY.) Other available authorities concur. The Professor then adds that the "general course" for man is undoubtedly like that of the Tarsius or of the mouse. It serves our purpose admirably to confine the present writings to this "general course" and let others to whom this subject is their special province find their way through the labyrinth of confused opinions. From the mass of data accumulated through observation of the fertilizing process in slugs, maw-worms, squash-bugs, fruit-flies, frogs, sea-urchins, lemurs, etc., speculation concerning the process of human fertilization is, for the most part, derived. As surely as these creatures differ in their final estate, so they vary—though less perceptibly—in their origin. Hence, the state of information on the subject is far too imperfect to warrant dogmatic conclusions respecting particulars.

All authorities agree that in the process of fertilization the male cell (the spermatozoon) approaches the female cell (the ovum) and, having reached the outer surface of the ovum, bores its way through the cell membrane, impelled by the motion of its tail. The instant the spermatozoon has forced its way into the female cell, the ovum—which is apparently supersensitive throughout its structure—prevents multiple fertilization by transforming its surface into a membrane called the vitelline membrane. Having actually entered into the protoplasmic field of the ovum, the sperm undergoes immediate modification. The tail disappears, but the head pushes its way on towards the center of the ovum, increasing in size by absorbing into itself substances from the cytoplasm—that is, the protoplasmic ground substances of the ovum— and becoming what is called the male pronucleus. From the neck, or body, of the spermatozoon, which also disappears, is presumably derived another smaller body called the male centrosome, which appears as a small spherical mass much less in size than the sperm nucleus and surrounded by radii, or starlike rays. As it approaches the female pronucleus—that is, the nucleus in the female cell—the male pronucleus rotates approximately 180°, so that the little centrosome which appeared in the place of the neck piece of the spermatozoon now moves in front of the male pronucleus towards the female pronucleus. In the meantime, the female pronucleus in the ovum has cast off from itself three small cells called polar bodies.

As far as known, these polar cells have no part in the development of the embryo other than to reduce the number of the chromosomes, which will be described later. Hertwig was of the opinion that the polar bodies were abortive eggs, which perish because the egg mother-cell in the process of fertilization appropriates to its own use the entire mass of egg yolk. The female pronucleus is apparently acompanied by what is called the female centrosome, but the fate of this is extremely obscure. As yet, there is hardly organized speculation on the subject. The two pronuclei—the smaller from the sperm, the larger from the ovum—are drawn towards each other by an occult attraction. As the sperm pronucleus approaches the ovum pronucleus, the little radiant male centrosome is the first to reach the female pronucleus. When the centrosome gets in contact with the egg nucleus, it becomes double and takes up its position at what may be termed the pole of the female pronucleus. The sperm pronucleus, moving up behind the centrosome, impinges itself upon the larger egg nucleus. At first the two remain only in close contact, but later the lines of demarkation fade out and the substances of the two pronuclei mingle to form a common nuclear vesicle. The nucleus formed by the two pronuclei is now termed the cleavage nucleus. The cleavage nucleus now lies in the center of the cytoplasmic field, and the two centrosomes with their radii, or asters, lie close to the two poles of the cleavage nucleus and may be termed the polar centrosomes. Boveri, a distinguished investigator, came to the following conclusion which, according to Edmund B. Wilson, Professor of Zoology at Columbia University, have been supported by numerous later observers. "The ripe egg possesses all of the organs and qualities necessary for division excepting the centrosome, by which division is initiated. The spermatozoon, on the other hand, is provided with a centrosome, but lacks the substance in which this organ of division may exert its activity. Through the union of the two cells in fertilization, all of the essential organs necessary for division are brought together; the egg now contains a centrosome which by its own division leads the way in the embryonic development." (See THE CELL IN DEVELOPMENT AND INHERITANCE.)

Mitosis, or the segmentation of cells, follows naturally upon fertilization. The cleavage nucleus contains a substance called chromatin, which in the resting state of the nucleus takes the form of small masses of substance scattered throughout the structure of the cleavage nucleus. When the cell is preparing for division, the chromatin gradually changes its appearance and organizes itself into a fine convoluted thread, which is known as the skein, or spireme. This becomes thicker and finally breaks up into a number of little rods, some straight, some curved into irregular shapes. These rods are called

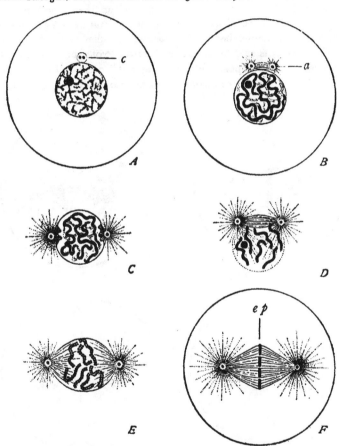

—From The Cell in Development and Inheritance.

DIAGRAMS SHOWING THE FORMATION OF THE MITOTIC SPINDLE

A. *A resting cell. The large central nucleus contains chromatin and a black spot which represents the nucleus. The small letter c indicates the position of the centrosome, which has become double.*

B. *The centrosomes (a) are dividing and moving towards the poles of the nucleus, and the chromatin is gradually forming into the spireme.*

C. *and* D. *Two variations in the development of the spindle.*

E. *The continuation of C. The wall of the nucleus is disappearing.*

F. *The mitotic spindle is now complete. The spireme has broken into chromosomes which have arranged themselves in the form of a hollow disk called the equatorial plate (e p).*

the chromosomes. "Every species of plant or animal," says Professor Wilson, "has a fixed and characteristic number of chromosomes, which regularly recur in the division of all cells; and in all forms arising by sexual reproduction, the number is even." Van Beneden affirmed that when the two pronuclei meet and mingle in the formation of the cleavage nucleus, the chromatin from each of the two pronuclei retained its original identity. Authorities at various times have differed as to the number of chromosomes peculiar to the human species. "In man the number is said to be sixteen," writes Professor Wilson. "In man thirty-two chromosomes appear in a dividing cell," declares Professor Charles Edward Walker. "There are forty-eight chromosomes in the eggs and sperms

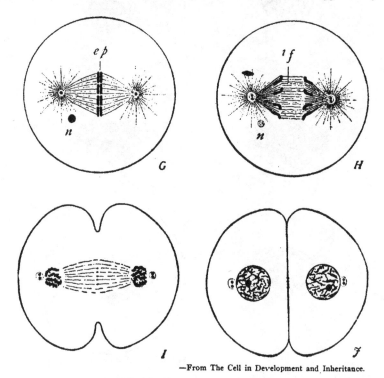

—From The Cell in Development and Inheritance.

DIAGRAMS SHOWING SEGMENTATION OF THE CELL

G. *Longitudinal splitting of the chromosomes on the equatorial plate. The small letter* n *indicates the cast-off nucleus.*

H. *Chromosomes diverging towards the poles of the spindle,* i f *indicates the interzonal fibers and* n *the nucleolus fading out.*

I. *The daughter nuclei in process of formation.*

J. *Division complete. The chromosomes of the daughter nuclei have returned to the state of chromatin, a nucleolus has reappeared, the centrosomes have doubled, and the daughter nuclei have assumed all the aspects of the parent nucleus.*

of man," announce Messrs. H. M. Evans and Olove Swezy. The last figure is now regarded as most nearly correct and was arrived at after the most painstaking research under exceptional conditions.

As the chromosomes are breaking up into separate pieces, the nuclear membrane which surrounds the cleavage nucleus gradually disappears and the chromosomes are said to lie naked in the cell. They should be visualized as a number of little twisted rods lying between the radiant bodies of the two polar centrosomes already described. Simultaneous with the changes in the nucleus itself, a curious form called the amphiaster gradually appears. The latter is the spindle and it seems to radiate from the centrosomes themselves and encloses within it the little chromosome rods. The centrosomes themselves also double "in anticipation" of the division of the chromosomes. As the spindle forms, "the chromosomes group themselves in a plane passing through the equator of the spindle, and thus form what is known as the equatorial plate." (Professor Wilson.) Each of the chromosomes now splits longitudinally, becoming as it were double. Gradually, they separate, diverging towards the poles of the spindle—that is, the centrosomes. After they have separated they are called daughter chromosomes, and as they separate thin fibrous threads connect them across the ever-increasing interval. As they diverge towards the centrosomes, the daughter chromosomes bunch gradually together. Mitosis is complete by the entire body of the cell dividing in a plane which passes through the equator of the spindle, "each of the daughter cells receiving a group of chromosomes, half of the spindle, and one of the asters with its centrosome." Having thus become two complete daughter organisms, the new cells establish their nuclei and pass into a resting state in preparation for further division. The centrosome in each of the daughter cells has already divided preparatory to moving towards the poles of the daughter nucleus for further segmentation. Some authorities give the time required for mitosis from the rest period of the mother nucleus to the rest period of the daughter nuclei as approximately two hours. The magnificent task of building up a body by this process is apparent when we realize that "According to Donaldson there are 12,000 million cells in the cortex of the cerebral hemispheres of the human brain. These are all formed by the process of mitosis and all before birth, so that nearly 12,000 million mitoses have occurred in the prenatal period in forming the cells of this region alone." (See PIERSOL'S NORMAL HISTOLOGY.) Each of this inconceivable number of cells produced in this fashion is working out a common destiny with a diligence and integrity staggering to the human intellect.

In this epitome of one of the most complicated subjects in the field of human learning certain points clearly impinge upon the metaphysical. Science has placed definite limitations upon itself by choosing to consider primary causes and reasons as beyond its province. A mass of data has been accumulated and each year sees more added. It is amazing, however, how much man can discover and at the same time how little he can know. Science has built empires. It has contributed infinitely to man's well-being and to almost an equal degree has placed in his hands the instruments of his own destruction. Yet learning falters upon the doorstep of wisdom. Science can explain nearly everything except the scientist himself. Man thinks but knows not wherewith he thinks. He aspires yet he knows not wherewith he aspires. He lives yet he knows not wherewith he lives. He is here upon the earth yet he knows not where he came from, how he got here, why Nature should precipitate him into such a state, or where he is going at the expiration of his mortal span. How unfortunate, then, is the lot of this poor animal, whose learning can but reveal to him how much there is he does not know!

The first step in an occult analysis of the human cell is the establishment of the septenary; that is, to discover therein the seven principles of life—the "seeds" from which grow the sevenfold nature of man. A clue to this is given in THE SECRET DOCTRINE: "When the seed of the animal man is cast into the soil of the animal woman, that seed cannot germinate unless it has been fructified by the five virtues (the fluid in, or the emanation from the principles) of the sevenfold Heavenly man." This passage is derived from a very rare work entitled ANTHROPOS, and in her commentary upon it, Madam Blavatsky completes the septenary by declaring that man's seventh principle "is but one of the beams of the Universal Sun." In occultism, the septenary always consists of a triad and a quaternary, of which the former is nearly always obscure and the latter more or less evident. What, then, are the major parts of the cell? First, and most evident, is the protoplasmic field—the cytoplasm. Second, there is the nucleus. Third, there is the centrosome, and fourth, the archoplasm surrounding the centrosome. In addition to these, there is also a fifth extremely obscure body located in the nucleus, namely, the nucleolus. The latter is a mystery sphere which performs some unknown task and then is cast off and disappears. This does not mean necessarily that the nucleolus ceases to exist, but rather that it passes into an unobservable condition. The nucleolus is the fifth element in the cell and, like the sphere of the heavenly fire of Plato, partakes too much of the abstract, or divine, to be susceptible of human analysis. The following analogies are advanced at this time subject to revision upon more critical consideration. The occultist recognizes the planets as symbols of *qualities,* and in this case they will be used to represent five qualifications or modifications of the Life Force, or Soul, termed by the Orientals *Jiva.* The cytoplasm we will assign to the sun, the nucleus to Saturn, the centrosome to the moon, the archoplasm to Mars, and the nucleolus to Venus. This leaves Jupiter and Mercury unassigned, and we will regard them as lying undifferentiated within the field of the nucleolus. The cytoplasm, the nucleus, the centrosome, and the archoplasm will constitute our quaternary. We shall regard them as the "builders," corresponding to the four fixed signs of the zodiac. The nucleolus with its as yet undifferentiated contents will be the triad, and in this way we shall arrive at a working hypothetical septenary, which must then be analyzed as to the consistency of such an arbitrary arrangement.

We will examine first the nucleus with its contents, always remembering, of course, that in the process of fertilization two complete cells mingle their septenaries—the active septenary, so-called, derived from the sperm, and the passive septenary from the ovum. Thus, the seven which are above (or within) unite with the seven which are below (or without), thereby permitting the gods (the active processes) to come into manifestation by union with their *shaktis* (or negative aspects). From this point on, it should be carefully noted that the qualities attributed to the parts of the cell are intended solely to set forth certain analogies or correspondences between spiritual and physical phenomena. The processes in the cell are taking place in a physical world with physical substances, yet these substances are actors in a sense—that is, they play a world drama on their own little stage. We have said that the nucleus corresponds with Saturn; that is, *Kama-Manas*, or the animal mind, and that it carries within itself the nucleolus—Venus, or true *Manas*—within which again are Jupiter (Atma) and Mercury (Buddhi). Thus, the nucleolus constitutes the causal triad, of which only Manas, the third and lowest aspect, is visible. The whole nucleus, then, is a Kama-Manasic field, which is called chromatin and from which the chromosomes originate. In nearly all the ancient systems of mythology, the original God is dethroned by those who come after him; that is, his progeny. This occurs with the nucleolus, which is cast off and vanishes, but which from some invisible throne continues to dominate cellular development. The nucleus carries the universe in suspension within it. By the "universe" we now mean man in his ideal state—a pattern or archetype, the parts of which will be released into expression as the rapidly multiplying cells are rendered available for such purpose.

The centrosome is the initiator of action and is also believed to be a mass of "active motor plasm." It is under the control of the moon, which is the equivalent of the etheric double, and is surrounded by "astral rays," that is, the specialization of the archoplasm. This radiant body is under Mars, or Kama (desire, action), by which the world is called into wakefulness. The cytoplasm, or protoplasm, is ruled by the sun, for it represents Prana, the solar nutriment by which growth will be nourished. The order is as follows: (1) Atma, the ray of the Universal Sun, corresponding to the auric egg of man; (2) Buddhi, the inter-nucleolar bodies, the Buddhic sheath in the aura of man; (3) Manas, the nucleolus itself, the builder, the higher mental body in man; (4) Kama-Manas, the nucleus, the first of the impermanent vehicles, the lower mental body in man; (5) Kama, the archoplasm or radii, the astral body in the cell, the seat of emotion and desire, the emotional body in man; (6) Prana, living matter, protoplasm, the source of form, the vital fluid in the human body; (7) the Linga Sharira, the centrosome, the lunar ancestor, the etheric double of man. These are the agents, and together they fashioned an eighth—the physical man—which is sustained and suspended from them.

In the writings of the Rosicrucians and Cabalists, the order is somewhat different, but the principle involved is the same. The seven gods or powers through whose conspiracy man is produced were concealed by them under the symbolism of metals and the planets assigned to the metals. As the Philosopher's Stone was produced by the mingling of the spiritual counterparts of the metals within specially prepared vessels, so the embryo—the golden child—is called into being by divine chemistry (alchemy). From a study of early

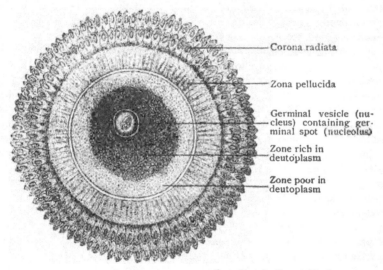

Corona radiata

Zona pellucida

Germinal vesicle (nucleus) containing germinal spot (nucleolus)

Zone rich in deutoplasm

Zone poor in deutoplasm

—From Piersol's Normal Histology.

A FULLY DEVELOPED UNFERTILIZED OVUM

religious and philosophic writings, it is not difficult to gather that the ancients were accurately informed at least concerning some of the processes involved in the generation of the species. Although they concealed their knowledge under various symbols, thus protecting themselves against the persecutions of an unenlightened age, the Rosicrucians and Hermetists set forth their opinions for the edification of the elect.

Let us compare the ovum reproduced in PIERSOL'S NORMAL HISTOLOGY (1929) with a figure of the world published by Robert Fludd in 1617, considerably prior to the advent of modern ontological viewpoints. Fludd is generally remembered for the number of people who have attempted to refute him. He has been "convicted" of nearly every error of reasoning of which the human mind is capable. Yet, with it all, he is now credited with the construction of the first barometer, which should earn for him some small measure

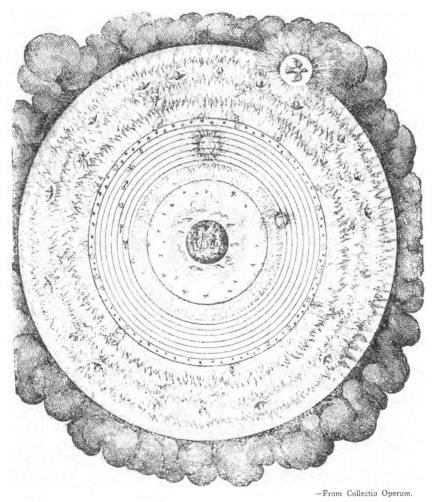

—From Collectio Operum.

FLUDD'S FIGURE OF THE WORLD CELL

of renown. First note the amazing similarity in the general appearance of the two figures. The *Corona radiata*, or radiating crown of elongated cells which surrounds Piersol's illustration, finds a perfect analogy in the radiating corona of flames which surrounds Fludd's "Macrocosm." The *Zona pellucida* of the ovum is Fludd's circle of fixed stars, the jeweled or radiant belt or zone in which are seated the celestial hierarchies. Retiring towards the center of the ovum, we find first a zone poor in deutoplasm and then another zone rich in deutoplasm. These correspond with the orbits of the planets, which are divided into an outer (or superior) and an inner (or inferior) half by the orbit of the sun. Near the center of the ovum lies the germinal vesicle, or nucleus, which is also clearly shown in Fludd's diagram; and in the very center of this the germinal spots, or nucleoli, apparently personified by Fludd in the form of Adam and Eve. In Fludd's engraving, the sperm in the form of a bird is shown entering the ovum. Note the birds, fishes, and other creatures within the nucleus. They remind one of the chromatin and the chromosomes. Robert Fludd was a mystic, his learning—like that of Lord Bacon—coming not from books but from some place within himself. Deep consideration of Fludd's diagram is apt to prove more enlightening than the speculations of some later authorities, whose stock phrase seems to be that about this-and-that "much uncertainty exists."

We now pass from the first aspect of our problem, that of cell segmentation, to those morphogenetic processes by which the embryo with its rudiments of organs and systems is formed from the vitelline spheres, or cleavage cells. We are confronted with a problem which as yet lies beyond "the farthest outposts of cell research." The modern temper is to shift responsibility. Heredity presents itself and is eagerly fixed upon. The agent responsible for the mechanism of embryonic development is regarded as an inheritance from the generations gone before. The ancient and honorable riddle as to whether the hen or the egg came first is thus solved more or *less* satisfactorily. *Vox scientiae est vox Dei!* It will be a sorry day for biologists when they run out of "foregoing generations" to account for the origin of life and are confronted with the necessity of admitting the existence of a metaphysical or spiritual reality behind the "shadows" which they have classified so industriously. "I see it, therefore it is" thunders science. "It is, but I can see only certain of its consequences" retorts philosophy. The "is"-ness has not been contested, which is about all that may be said without danger of contradiction. We, therefore, pass on to the mechanics of embryonic development, mindful of the words of Professor Wilson that "an explanation of development is at present beyond our reach." In his disillusionment over the paucity of facts, Omar, the tent-maker, was by no means unique.

We have already traced the steps of cell cleavage by which the mother-cell divides into two daughter cells. We should then visualize this division continuing until a mass of cells has been produced. The details of cleavage differ with the various species. The egg of the *Amphioxus lanceolatus*, a primitive chordate whose name is greatly out of proportion to its size and importance, is a general favorite in the study of early embryonic stages. The cleavage results in what is called a *morula*, a spherical mass made up of smaller spherical cells. These are of two kinds. Those of the animal pole, which are called animal cells, are smaller and increase more rapidly than those at the vegative pole, which are nutritive cells. The morula is a solid mass, but gradually the cells move toward the circumference, leaving a central cavity called the cleavage cavity. "The embryo is now said to be in the *blastula* stage, a blastula being merely a hollow sphere consisting of a single layer of cells surrounding a cavity." (Prof. Arthur W. Haupt.) The next step is *gastrulation*, which may be described as the process by which the lower, or vegative, part of the blastula —that is the part made up of vegative cells—first flattens and then invaginates, gradually filling the concavity of the upper, or animal, part. When the cells of the upper and the lower part have met, the blastodermic sphere is changed into a sac-like or cup-shaped structure consisting of an outer layer of animal cells and an inner layer of vegative cells. Between these two primary layers of cells, the outer of which is now called the *ectoderm* and the inner the *endoderm*, there next appears a middle layer called the mesoderm. From these three

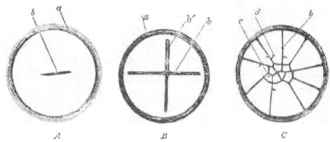

FURROWING OF GERMINAL DISK IN PROCESS OF UNEQUAL CLEAVAGE

A shows the first furrow, B the second, by which the figure of the cross is formed, and C the multiple cleavage

layers of cells—the outer, or ectoderm; the central, or mesoderm; and the inner, or endoderm—arise the sets of specialized tissues. We may now turn from the *Amphioxus* with its comparatively simple process to a consideration of the more complicated phenomena taking place in the higher mammals and also presumably in man.

In man—that is, judging from bats, guinea pigs, mice, etc.—cell segmentation is decidedly unequal, the animal cells at the upper pole of the ovum increasing far more rapidly than the vegative cells at the lower pole. Furthermore, the segmentation is not general throughout the structure of the ovum, but begins in the area of the animal pole, producing what may be termed a polar cap of cells. This germinal polar disk "is not sharply separated from the remainder of the ovum," but the two graduate insensibly into each other. The relative lack of yolk substance in the human ovum results in comparatively little segmentation among the vegative cells and no morula is formed. The process of segmentation, then, is for the most part limited to the upper pole, wherein a furrow first appears, which is crossed by another at right angles. A cruciform figure results. Is this Plato's Logos impressing itself upon the new world in the form of a cross? This aspect of the subject does not seem to have been previously considered.

Other furrows appear bisecting the first two until a considerable mass of animal cells has come into existence. These constitute the "polar continent," the sacred island of the Eastern Mysteries. This is the imperishable land which endures from the beginning to the end. The phenomenon of mitosis, or segmentation, is not limited to the surface of the ovum alone, but the germinal area deepens into the body of the ovum. It is on the under side of this cap of animal cells—that is, on the side towards the body of the egg—that the vegative cells from the lower hemisphere make their appearance and align themselves in the form of a thin layer. These two layers, the outer of animal cells and the inner of vegative cells, are the ectoderm and endoderm respectively, as in the *Amphioxus,* and as in the case of that primitive chordate, the third layer, or mesoderm, arises between the ectoderm and the endoderm. Thus, the human embryo has achieved the same end that was accomplished in the *Amphioxus:* namely, the specialization of three sets of tissue from which both the body of the embryo itself and its foetal membranes will be developed. From the ectoderm (outer layer) are derived the epidermis, hair, nails, sweat glands, the parts of the nervous system both central and peripheral, the enamel of the teeth, the most important parts of the special sensory organs, the pituitary body, pineal gland, etc. From the mesoderm (central layer) are derived the whole of the vascular system, the skeleton, muscles, lymphatics, the connective tissues, sexual organs, etc. From the endoderm (inner or secretory layer) are derived the epithelial linings of the digestive and respiratory tracts(with certain exceptions), the thyroid, parathyroid, thymus body, etc.

Thus we see that the process of development in the human embryo presumably differs from that of the *Amphioxus* and other lower forms in that instead of invagination and the forming of two cell layers, the cleavage starts in a sort of cap or disk and development begins by the folding, or furrowing, of the margin. As the layer of animal cells increases, it extends downward in all directions from the animal pole, spreading in the form of a thin layer between the vitelline membrane and the yolk. This extension of the animal cells continues until the entire yolk is covered. The development of a primitive membrane may be traced generally for man through observation of the phenomena in the hen's egg. The amnion will serve as an example. A fold appears in the germ layer on each side of the embryo. These folds consist of an outer layer of ectoderm and an inner layer of mesoderm. The folds increase and, arching up over the embryo, finally meet and fuse to form the walls of the amnion. By this process the embryo is caused to retire from the upper surface of the egg and is isolated in the amniotic cavity, which is now filled with a fluid called the amniotic fluid and in which the little body seems to float protected from injury and shock. The embryo is further isolated from direct contact with the yolk by a constriction of membranes until only a stem remains. The extra-embryonic foetal membranes—that is, the chorion, the amnion, the yolk sac, and the allantois—rise from the three primitive *dermi.* A double septenary is thus set up. The embryo itself consisting of seven parts and its extra-embryonic membrane being similarly divided, the occult maxim becomes applicable: "There are seven within and seven without."

In her ESOTERIC INSTRUCTIONS, Madam Blavatsky establishes certain correspondences between the contents of the sidereal and human uteri. She refers to the seven contents of the chorion thus: "Now, each of these seven continents severally corresponds with, and is formed after, an antitype, one on each of the seven planes of being, with each in their turn correspond the seven states of Matter and all other forces, sensational and functional, in Nature." Her direct analogies are as follows: (1) The terrestrial embryo which contains the future man with all his potentialities is the mathematical point, the cosmic seed, the monad of Leibnitz which contains the whole universe as the acorn contains the oak. (2) The amniotic fluid which exudes from the embryo is the akasa which proceeds from the ten divinities of the sun. (3) The amnion, the membrane containing the amniotic fluid, is the ether of space, which in its external aspect is the plastic crust supposed to envelope the sun. (4) The umbilical vesicle which serves, according to science, to nourish the embryo originally, is the sidereal contents of ether, the substantial parts thereof. (5) The allantois, a protrusion from the embryo, which spreads itself between the amnion and the chorion, is the life currents in the ether, having their origin in the sun, through which the vital principle passes to nourish everything on the earth. (6) The allantois is divided into two layers. They are the double radiation, psychical and physical, called in occultism the upper, or divine astral light, and the lower, or material astral light. (7) The chorion, the outer layer of the membranes which go to form man, is the outer crust of every sidereal body, corresponding to the shell of the mundane egg; or, in the terrestrial plane, corresponding to air which, like the skin of man, is built in seven layers.

Physical birth, so-called, does not actually free man from an embryonic state, for throughout physical life his body remains an embryo suspended in the magnetic field of his aura. The extra-embryonic membranes which he discards with the rupturing of the umbilical cord are to a certain degree the physical counterparts of superphysical bodies called auras, which continue to nourish and protect him and within which he lives and moves and has his being. It has already been noted that the embryo corresponds to Atma when viewed as the monad with which the seven bodily systems develop. It is, therefore, Neo-Platonically, the apex of body—the unity from which diversity arises. The embryo thus corresponds to the auric egg, which is to the whole of man— spiritual, psychical, and physical—what the embryo is to his physical part alone: namely, its source and all-inclusive aspect. The amniotic fluid finds analogy in the second department of the aura, which is called the Buddhic sheath, and the amnion with the third department of the aura, or the Manasic field. The umbilicus represents the fourth department of the aura, the Kama-Rupic sheath; the fifth, or allantois, with Prana; the sixth, or the interspace, with the Linga Sharira; and the seventh, or chorion, with the physical body, or rather the substances from which the physical body is made. There are possible alternative renderings of the last three, owing to the confusion existing between such terms as the astral body, the emotional body, the vital body, and the etheric double.

The analogies between the embryo and its extra-membranes and the sidereal creation are derived from the accounts in the various PURANAS. For example, in THE VISHNU PURANA, creation is described as taking place within the womb of Meru. The section is translated thus by Wilson: "This vast egg, O sage, compounded of the elements, and resting on the waters, was the excellent natural abode of Vishnu in the form of Brahma; and there Vishnu, the lord of the universe, whose essence is inscrutable, assumed a perceptible form; and even he himself abided in it, in the character of Brahma. Its womb, vast as the mountain Meru, was composed of the mountains; and the mighty oceans were the waters that filled its cavity." We must break the quotation at this point to insert a note by Fitzedward Hall, who edited Wilson's translation. He declares that many of the manuscripts prefer to translate the sentence beginning "Its womb" thus: "Meru was its amnion, and the *other* mountains *were* its chorion." Continuing with Wilson's text: "In that egg, O Brahman, were the continents and seas and mountains, the planets and divisions of the universe, the gods, the demons, and mankind. And this egg was externally invested by seven natural envelopes; or by water, air, fire, ether, and Ahamkara, the origin of the elements, each tenfold the extent of that which it invested; next came the principle of Intelligence; and, finally, the whole was surrounded by the indiscrete Principle; resembling, thus, the cocoa-nut, filled interiorly with pulp, and exteriorly covered by husk and rind."

When the esoteric comentators declare the embryo, or "golden child," to be a symbol of the sun bearing the ten gods within itself, they affirm no more than is set forth in the curious title page of that rarest of all *published* Cabalistic writings, the KABBALA DENUDATA by C. Knorr Von Rosenroth. At the top of the figure reproduced herewith is a blazing Cabalistic-Pythagorean sun containing the ten circles of the Sephirothic Tree arranged in three larger spheres. This diagram in itself reveals a secret which has not been elucidated in the text. The ten little circles are the ten Prajapatis—the Lords of Being, the Builders. An embryonic analogy may be drawn. The three first and highest contained within the upper sphere have their physical correspondence in the dermi, or primitive tissues—ectoderm, mesoderm, and endoderm. They are the hidden foundation, the primary divisions of the one physical substance, the hidden face of THE ZOHAR. The six little circles in the central sphere are the active forces—the Macrocosmic Hexagon. They are born out of the first three. They spring from the fathers. They mold the substances and build the septenary world from the three primitive states (the dermi). The tenth and last of the circles, placed alone in the lowest sphere, is the fruitage of their workings. It is the external and revealed world—man—called in the Cabala the Kingdom, "that which is established."

These are the numbers, the sacred numerals, the potencies locked within the sun, universal and embryonic. Once fertilization begins the process of releasing power, it is the task of the Builders to order the mass of tissue and shape it into the likeness of the world. The spiritual world is upheld upon the points of Shiva's trident (the Hebrew letter *Shin*). The psychical world is elevated upon the seven planetary foundations, and the physical world is hung by cords from all the higher spheres. Realizing the antiquity of the Hindu PURANAS, the Cabalistic ZOHAR, and other writings in which these analogies appear, it is evident that the ancients possessed a knowledge of embryonic processes entirely inconsistent with the state of scientific development we have ascribed to them. Even if we abide with the most conservative authorities who allow the antiquity of THE PURANAS to be but a thousand years, we find in its vision of creative processes an extraordinary enlightenment and an ideal far more beautiful, satisfying, and complete than that of most modern authorities.

In the old Mysteries it was taught that space itself was surrounded by great mountains and cliffs—the Ring Pass Not, the eyebrows of Ymir, the sidereal chorion. The universe was created in the midst of the waters, not such water as we know but the divine universal water, the ethers of space, and is symbolized as floating in a great sea of this substance. Thales held a similar opinion. After the island (the embryo) was established, the gods descended to it by coming down a ladder (the umbilical cord). The rivers described in Genesis (the blood vessels of the umbilical cord) flow into the new land. In some distant day science will come to realize that allegories are statements of hidden truths and will then achieve a greater understanding of the nature of man through a contemplation of sacred writings and recognition of the similitudes existing between universal cosmogony and the beginnings of human life.

VISHNU SLEEPING UPON THE COILS OF THE SERPENT OF COSMIC TIME

CHAPTER VIII

THE INCARNATIONS OF VISHNU

HE word *Vishnu* is from the root, *vish,* "to pervade." The god Vishnu, in his most abstract form, signifies the Divine Spirit either of the universe or of man. Itself unconditioned, this Spirit passes through a sequential order of conditioned aspects which are termed the divine avataras, or incarnations. This motion of the god from form to form—or, more correctly, from condition to condition—is called a stride or step of Vishnu and is the true explanation of the transitions constantly taking place in Nature. The "god who takes any form at will" has chosen to take all forms, to ensoul them, to grow up through them, and to glorify himself in their perfection. Vishnu thus becomes the root of all sentient and insentient life. In the MAHABHARATA, he declares himself the maker and the unmaker of the universe, besides which there is no other. From him creations are suspended "as hangs a row of pearls upon its string." He is the vital air moving in all that moves, the wisdom of the wise, and the intellect of the informed. "He who pervades" is not contained within the world, however, any more than the spirit of man is within his body, but rather the god contains the world within himself, even as the physical body of man is suspended fœtus-like within the cavity of the auric egg. The VEDAS are rich in references to Vishnu and his numerous attributes. Chief among these accounts are the ten great incarnations. The god, coming forth "when virtue fails upon the earth," delivers his creation from the machinations of evil and preserves it against premature destruction.

Since Pythagoras was initiated into the Brahmanic Mysteries, it is quite probable that his numerical philosophy was founded upon the same esoteric truths which underlie the story of Vishnu's incarnation. The ten dots which constitute the Pythagorean *tetractys* were advanced by the initiates of the Italic School as the perfect key to the Universal Arcanum, setting forth the mystery of Number flowing into objective existence through the numerals. The Cabalists were certainly acquainted with the doctrines of the Masters of Eastern Wisdom. The ten Sephiroth, or jewels—like the avataras of Vishnu— were the aspects of one eternal life principle. These aspects, reflected into the substances of the several worlds, became planes, spheres, states, and eventually the Ten Commandments, or Laws. There are definite and most intriguing correspondences between the forms assumed by Vishnu during his incarnations and the development of the embryo and fœtus during the nine months of the prenatal epoch. Every modification and specialization of bodily form and function testifies to changes taking place within the soul, or superphysical structure behind form. Bodies only seem to grow of themselves, this appearance of development being part of the illusion which deceives the unenlightened.

What we call growth is really life expanding and extending itself through form. Vishnu, the force of the Spirit, is ever building nobler mansions. These are really temples to himself, and in all parts of creation forms are rising up, each a shrine, an altar or a monument to the one all-pervading life.

In the steps through which the embryo passes in its development we may behold as in panorama a recapitulation of man's condition throughout all the remote ages of the past. Man has no conscious memory of these steps by which he became himself or, rather, life became man through him. But locked deep within the memory of each evolving cell is the story of all that has gone before. Each time the human being comes into physical incarnation a body must be built. Each body is a universe and is organized according to universal laws. It follows that those who have a key to the embryological mystery may perceive shadowed forth therein the pervading god building his world. He overshadows the form which is to come, impresses himself as ten conditions upon it, moves through these conditions, focussing his energies, in turn, upon them and gradually shaping the rude mass into the organized instrument of his purpose. Vishnu is thus to be considered both the fabricator and the fabric of the world structure. He is the deity in whom men live and move and have their being. He is the objective power which manifests the eternal subjective condition of Brahma, the first person of the Creative Triad. He stands between the superior heavens which are of the nature of Brahma and the inferior world which is of the nature of Shiva. Therefore, he is the sun which, according to the Mysteries, occupies the focal (foetal) point between abstraction and con-cretion. As lord of the sun, he is the patron of all creatures and forms, the bestower of life and the giver of abundance. He is often represented with blue skin, the blue representing the heavens, which are his abode, and also the invisible subtle ethers. In Indian art, Vishnu is often depicted sleeping through the Night of Cosmic Darkness upon the coils of a great serpent. In one sense of the word, Vishnu—like the Greek Chronos—destroys the power of his father and usurps his authority as lord of the world. When Vishnu fabricates the universe, he absorbs into it the great Brahma, for in the last analysis he forms the universe out of the nature of Brahma, the Universal One, of whose constitution he is also a part.

The ten incarnations of Vishnu are, therefore, widely accepted in Asia as representing those creative efforts by which the gods (the divine forces of life) attempted to establish themselves in the various substances of the world. This Eastern doctrine is not inharmonious with the evolutionary theories that have come into favor in the Western world. In moving from generals to par-ticulars, it is well to pause a moment to consider the correspondences between the incarnations of Vishnu and the origin of life upon this planet. "In this diagram of avatars," writes Madam Blavatsky, "we see traced the gradual evolution and transformation of all species out of the ante-Silurian mud of Darwin and the *ilus* of Sanchoniathon and Berosus. Beginning with the Azoic

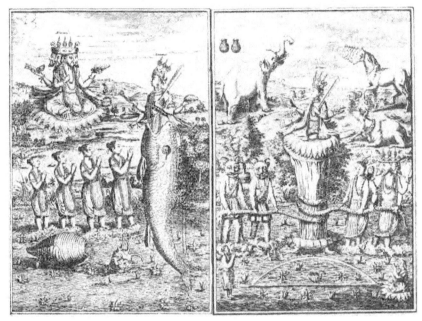

—From Picart's Religious Ceremonials.

FIRST AND SECOND INCARNATIONS OF VISHNU

time, corresponding to the *ilus* in which Brahma implants the creative germ, we pass through the Palæozoic and Mesozoic times, covered by the first and second incarnations as the fish and tortoise; and the Cenozoic, which is embraced by the incarnations in the animal and semi-human forms of the boar and man-lion; and we come to the fifth and crowning geological period, designated as the 'era of mind, or age of man,' whose symbol in the Hindu mythology is the dwarf—the first attempt of nature at the creature of men. * * * From a fish the progress of this dual transformation carries on the physical form through the shape of a tortoise, a boar, and a man-lion; and then, appearing in the dwarf of humanity, it shows Parasu Rama physically, a perfect, spiritually, an undeveloped entity, until it carries mankind personified by one god-like man, to the apex of physical and spiritual perfection—a god on earth." (See ISIS UNVEILED.)

From this point, the analogies between the origin of life upon the planet and the development of the embryo in the womb are apparent. We have already seen how the beginnings of the universe are recapitulated in the fertilization and cleavage of the cell. Ages so vast that the human mind cannot invoke even a shadow of their duration in the intellect are summarized in the activities following immediately upon the union of the sperm and the ovum.

As the shadow of the embryo itself appears, the more intimate development of man up from the first slime of matter is pictured forth. At this point, then, it is that the analogies between the incarnations of Vishnu and the months of the prenatal epoch begin. The first avatara of Vishnu is termed the *Matsya,* or fish incarnation. According to the legends, there was a very early time in the history of the world when so great a corruption blighted mankind that the gods determined to destroy the human race with a great flood. The prince who ruled at that time was a very pious man, and he and the seven Rishis, or wise men, their wives, and pairs of all the animals, and other forms of life entered an ark. The lord Vishnu then took upon himself the body of a fish and fastened the ark to his own body by means of a cable fashioned out of a serpent. When the flood subsided, Vishnu slew an evil monster who had stolen the VEDAS, or sacred books of the law. The books being returned, a new human race was formed, who treasured the sacred writings and obeyed them implicitly.

In the sacred writings of the Hindus the story of the first avatara requires 14,000 verses for its recital. This incarnation corresponds with the first month of the prenatal epoch. During this period, which is under the control of Saturn, the rudiments of the coming organism are laid down. During the first week fertilization is progressing apace, but there is very little enlargement of the ovum. During the second week, it increases rapidly in size, and about the fourteenth day the first indications of the embryo appear. By the end of the third week, the nervous system and the brain are discernible, and the extremities have appeared as short buds. The close of the first month finds the heart separated into a right and a left part, considerable extension of the caudal extremity, which is considerably more prominent than the lower limbs, and even the appearance of the spinal ganglia. There are many points of similarity between the embryo and a fish at this time. There is no more interesting department of human learning than that which may be termed the science of rudimentary organs. These are nearly all remnants of structures at one time vital to survival but which are now in the words of Haeckel, "useless to its organism, valueless for life-purposes, worthless for its function." By these so-called purpose-less parts we are related definitely with the past. The endocrine system is extremely rich in rudimentary organs, for several of the more important glands have been readapted from some primitive but now obsolete function. Man is linked with the fish not only by the gill clefts but by that small crescent-shaped fold of skin in the inner corner of the eye called the nictitating membrane, which is the remnant of a third inner eyelid, highly developed in our first cousins, the sharks, but serving no known purpose in man.

The second avatara of Vishnu is termed the *Kurma,* or the tortoise incarnation. This incarnation is also connected indirectly with the flood, for in it Vishnu took upon himself the body of a turtle, supporting with his shell the sacred mountain, *Mandara.* Using the great serpent for a rope and the sacred

—From Picart's Religious Ceremonials.

THIRD AND FOURTH INCARNATIONS OF VISHNU

mountain for an axis, the gods and demons churned the great ocean in order
to regain the sacred *amrita,* or beverage of the gods. By this churning process
fourteen sacred articles were discovered. These are shown in the picture as
grouped about the central mountain and in the hands of the deities. The
second month of the prenatal epoch is under the control of Jupiter. During
this period there is rapid expansion throughout the embryo, which according
to the Hindu myth is passing through an amphibious state symbolized by the
turtle. During the fifth week, the first traces of hands and feet appear. This
is a most significant point, for it is among the Amphibians that the cartilaginous
rays which form the fins of fishes develop into the five-toed form of foot from
which man inherited his present hands and feet. In the sixth week, the bones
assume a cartilaginous condition. In the seventh, the muscles appear, and by
the end of the eighth, the sympathetic nerve is discernible. During this whole
period, the organs have been establishing themselves and developing gradually
from the simple to the complex. By the end of the second month it is possible
to distinguish between the embryo of man and that of other mammals, but not
as yet between man and the simians. The distinguishing features are the
comparatively greater size and complexity of the brain development and the
decreasing importance of the tail, or caudal appendage.

The third avatara of Vishnu is termed the *Varaha*, or boar incarnation. In this incarnation Vishnu is generally depicted upholding the earth with his tusks, the earth being deposited in the concavity of a lunar crescent. According to the allegory, there was once a *Daitya*, or Titan, who desired to become the ruler of the earth. He ultimately became so powerful that he stole the planet and carried it with him into the depths of the ocean. Vishnu, assuming the form of a boar, dived into the abyss and fought with this monster for one thousand years. Ultimately slaying the evil one, Vishnu restored the earth to its proper position by raising it upon his tusks. The third month of the prenatal epoch is under the control of Mars. This is the fiery *Lohitanga* of the Hindus, and it is not surprising that during this time the sexual organs should be differentiated. The boar is the symbol of the ungulate, or hoofed, mammals, most of which are herbivorous, and signifies in the period of embryonic development not only man's recapitulation of the animal state but also summarizes the mystery of the division of the sexes, which in human evolution took place in the third, or Lemurian, root race of the present earth. A curious survival in man to bear witness of his "boar" incarnation is the muscle of the external ear. There was evidently a time when man possessed the power of "pricking up," or erecting, his ears to catch sounds more readily. As the ages passed, man intensified certain of his sense perceptions by sacrificing the acuteness and radius of others. It was in this way that he lost control of his ear muscles, and now they remain without any other function than that of proving human kinship with the animal world. It is not surprising that the gall bladder should appear during the reign of Mars, and the third month finds the organization of the body continuing, with the rudiments of the eyelids, the hair, and the nails forming, according to Beaunis and Bouchard.

The fourth avatara of Vishnu is termed the *Narasingha*, or man-lion incarnation. This is the story of a holy man who for ten thousand years prayed and meditated for the boons of universal monarchy and everlasting life. Having become very great through the one-pointedness of his purpose, he also grew equally selfish and arrogant. The gods led him into debate with his own son concerning the omnipresence of Deity. When his son told the proud monarch that God was everywhere, even in the pillars supporting the roof of the palace, the evil prince in anger and blasphemy struck the column with his sword. Splitting in half, the pillar revealed "fearful" Vishnu with the head of a lion, who after fighting with the egotistic prince for an hour, dragged him into the hollow pillar and destroyed him, thus delivering the world from his arrogance. The fourth month of the prenatal epoch is under the control of the sun, which in symbolism is nearly always associated with the lion. In the Ptolemaic order of the planets, the sun occupies the middle point, dividing the three remote (or superior) planets from the nearer (or inferior) planets. In the incarnations of Vishnu, the man-lion avatara reveals the transitional stage between the animal and human forms, embodying both within itself. In the fourth month

FIFTH AND SIXTH INCARNATIONS OF VISHNU

in the development of man "the embryo takes the human shape, the face gets human features, the embryo is now called foetus." (Again authorities differ.) Individualization is a keyword of the sun. From the fourth month on, according to Haeckel, there arise in the foetus distinguishing characteristics by which it is divided from all other vertebrates and its true destiny is revealed. In other words, from this point on man himself appears. By the end of the fourth month the cartilaginous arches of the spine have closed, the tonsils have made their appearance, and ossification is preparing the bony support of the future man. The man-lion is reminiscent of a race of creatures described by early historians as existing in a remote time and combining, like the symbolic centaur, the bodies and attributes of both man and beast. Such accounts refer to the descent of man as a spiritual equation into the animal body. The sphinx is such a *composita*—a man-lion and a monument to Harmackis, the sun-god.

The fifth avatara of Vishnu is termed the *Vamana*, or dwarf incarnation. In this case, a great monarch, becoming proud of the fact that he ruled over three worlds—that is, heaven, earth, and hell—neglected the performance of the proper ceremonials to the gods. In the form of a dwarf Vishnu appeared before the king, requesting a boon, that is, as much land as he could pace off with three steps. The king granted the request and ratified his promise by pouring water on the hands of the dwarf. Immediately the tiny figure increased in size until it filled the entire universe, and taking its three paces, owned the world, but out of kindly consideration for the virtues of the king it permitted him to retain the government of hell. The fifth month of the prenatal epoch is under the control of Venus, which in occult philosophy is curiously associated with the ape. Although the fifth incarnation is called that of a dwarf rather than a monkey, it represents the first imperfect effort in the formation of a human creature and, like Gabriel Max's conception of the missing link, has points of correspondence with the ape. At this stage, the parts of the body are being more closely knit together. The germs of the permanent teeth appear, there is hair on the head, the lymphatic glands are noted, and there is further development of the genital organs. The dwarf incarnation of Vishnu is further reminiscent of man's kinship with the ape. The vermiform appendix in man invokes a retrospective mood. It links us with our vegetarian ancestors of the boar incarnation and "is of considerable size and of great physiological importance" to herbivorous animals, and is an appendage which we share wtih the apes and rodents. It is also important to note that three to four months before its birth, the human fœtus is usually covered "by a thick coating of delicate woolly hairs." The three strides by which Vishnu measures the whole world represent the three aspects of human consciousness, by virtue of which man so greatly increased in power that heaven, earth, and hell came under the dominion of his enlightenment.

The sixth avatara of Vishnu is termed the *Parasu Rama* incarnation. This is the first of the series of true human incarnations of the god. Parasu Rama was the son of a very aged holy man to whom the god Indra had entrusted the sacred cow. One of the Rajahs, desiring to possess the cow, connived to bring about the death of the holy man, whose wife then committed suttee, or suicide, praying with her last words that the gods would avenge the murder of her husband. Vishnu, answering the call, assumed the personality of Parasu Rama and, after twenty terrific battles, slew the evil Rajah. The sixth month of the prenatal epoch is under the control of Mercury, and it is during this period that very rapid brain development is evident in the fœtus. The cerebral hemispheres increase and cover the cerebellum, in this way bringing about the withdrawal of the pineal gland, or third eye, to its deep position in the central part of the cranium. The fœtus moves, there is definite nerve stimuli, and the new organism is capable of breathing but not yet of surviving if subjected to the conditions of the external world. The vital agent, imperceptible to modern science, is taking hold of the new organism, even as Vishnu took upon himself the body of Parasu Rama.

The seventh avatara of Vishnu, termed the *Rama Chandra* incarnation, is the subject of the great Indian epic, THE RAMAYANA. Ravana, the evil king of Lanka (which is now Ceylon), stole Sita, the ideal of East Indian womanhood from her beloved husband, Rama. Assisted by Hunaman, the king of

—From Picart's Religious Ceremonials.

SEVENTH AND EIGHTH INCARNATIONS OF VISHNU

the apes, Rama Chandra won back Sita who, by submitting to the ordeal of fire, proved her fidelity to him.   The apes in a single night built a stone bridge connecting Lanka with the mainland.   Ravana, in order to torture Hunaman, the ape-king, set fire to his tail.   Running through the streets of Lanka with his blazing appendage, Hunaman set fire to the city, thus virtually destroying the power of Ravana, who eventually fell in battle before the prowess of the divine Rama.   The seventh month of the prenatal epoch is under the control of the moon, the last of the ancient planetary septenary, which closes the first cycle of the prenatal epoch.   The child may be born at the end of seven months and live by virtue of the qualities of the lunar ray.   The pattern of the body is now complete, the cerebral convolutions appear, and details are added to the general bodily structure.   The man-animal has been formed. Now the process continues to bring about the production of the man-god.   "As the seven months' old unborn baby," writes H. P. Blavatsky, "though quite ready, yet needs two months more in which to acquire strength and consolidate; so man, having perfected his evolution in seven rounds, remains two periods more in the womb of Mother-Nature before he is born, or rather reborn a Dhyani." (See THE SECRET DOCTRINE.)   Man is more than a bodily perfection, and while those parts of him which we can see have assumed the outward semblance of perfection, the soul is spinning the threads which are not only to bind the parts together but to connect them all with itself. For this reason, a child born in the seventh month is very often what is popularly termed "psychic," sensitive or high-strung. These terms may all indicate that because of the premature delivery the soul is not as tightly bound to the body as in the case of those who have completed the prenatal span.

The eighth avatara of Vishnu is termed the *Krishna* incarnation. The story of Krishna is so well known that it hardly requires any elaborate description. The illustration depicts the birth of Krishna and also the legend of his escape from death while an infant by being carried across the river in a basket. The water rose, threatening to destroy the bearer of the sacred child. To prevent this calamity, Krishna permitted one of his feet to hang over the edge of the basket, whereupon the water subsided. Numerous incidents in the life of Krishna parallel the experiences of Jesus. These include the slaughter of the innocents, the transfiguration, the crucifixion, the resurrection, and the ascension. Krishna is considered as a personification of the sun, and his consort, Radha, is the embodiment of the earth. With the eighth incarnation, a new planetary cycle begins. So the eighth month of the prenatal epoch is under the control of Saturn. To the ancients, Saturn was the symbol of crystallization and death. The major changes of the embryo during this month consist of the addition of points to the sacral vertebrae of the spine and the solidification of the bony structure which is under the particular dominion of this god. As lord of death, Saturn is presumed to prevent a child born in the eighth month from surviving. The number eight was called "the little holy number" by the Eleusinian initiates and by them was associated with the Kundalini and the spinal fire. The eighth month is related by analogy to the condition of the superman. During this period the potentialities of adeptship arise in the fœtus.

The ninth avatara of Vishnu is generally termed the *Buddha* incarnation, although a great number of Hindus disagree with this. Some Orientalists have gone so far as to declare that the Christ of Christendom represents the ninth avatara, or incarnation, of Vishnu. The life of Buddha is beautifully set forth in Sir Edwin Arnold's LIGHT OF ASIA. Buddha was an Indian prince who, inspired by the needs of humanity, renounced his kingdom and dedicated himself to the service of mankind. After many years of renunciation and prayer the two great laws of life—reincarnation and karma—were revealed to him. He lifted the Buddhist faith from comparative obscurity to the dignity of the world's greatest religion, and at his death, or translation, a great number of Indian nobles were present. It was found impossible to light the funeral pyre until the body burst into flames by the release of spiritual energy from a great emerald which adorned the body of the dead sage. The ninth and last month of the prenatal epoch is under the control of Jupiter, the great benefic, and it is under his kindly influence that the fœtus is prepared to emerge and assume its place in the objective world. The bones grow more firmly together and

—From The History of Hindoostan.

VISHNU IN THE FORM OF KRISHNA CHARMING ALL NATURE WITH THE MUSIC OF HIS FLUTE

—From Picart's Religious Ceremonials.

NINTH AND TENTH INCARNATIONS OF VISHNU

the body is preparing itself for the shock of life. The potentialities of the demigod are being distributed seedlike throughout the structure of the subjective man. In the early months of the prenatal epoch the incoming life works upon its vehicles from without, molding them as a sculptor might shape clay or wax. At the time of "quickening," however, the life gradually insinuates itself into the new body, taking hold of the parts and members one by one and shaping them from within. The contact points between the soul and its vehicle are in this way perfected and the vital principle adjusts itself to the limitations of the mortal fabric. As a man putting on a new glove opens and closes his fingers to accustom his hand to such a covering, so the spontaneous motions of the embryo are of such nature that the little body thrills, turns, and even strikes out with its newly-formed extremities. The active agent is taking up the threads of function and motion and, having accomplished this, is ready to launch itself upon the ocean of outrageous fortune. Completing these various preparations, the new man emerges from the dark cavern of his beginnings.

The tenth avatara of Vishnu is termed *Kalki*, or horse, incarnation and is the one which is yet to come. This incarnation is generally symbolized by a picture of a man leading a riderless white horse. The animal is sometimes shown with wings like the fabled Pegasus of the Greeks.   Among many nations the horse is an emblem of the animal world, or the lower sphere of being. In this sense it may infer that when Vishnu appears for the last time he will be mounted upon the world—that is, victorious over the substances of inferior Nature. The Brahmans believe that in his tenth avatara Vishnu will act as the true Savior of the world, redeeming the faithful from the sorrows and limitations of mortal existence. No man knows the day of his coming, but the Hindus are positive that when the great need arises he will be there to preserve and redeem those who have been faithful to his laws and tenets. The tenth avatara of Vishnu has no correspondence in the prenatal state of man, but rather corresponds to his whole life after birth. If a planet were assigned to this tenth period, it would have to be Mars, which reminds one that the lord of the world comes "not with peace but with a sword." The tenth sephira of the Cabalistic Tree is Malkuth, the Kingdom, inferred by the words in the Lord's Prayer: "Thy Kingdom Come." The attendant leads the white horse but the man who is seated thereon is invisible, for in the last incarnation man becomes a spiritual rather than a temporal reality. Vishnu, "he who pervades," comes forth for the last time not as a man but rather through man. He is the invisible god who rules in the chariot of the human heart. The world awaits the coming of its Redeemer—the perfect man. To the philosopher, this perfect man is rather the perfection in man. The immortality that lay asleep in the germ from which man sprang awakens and, in the course of countless ages, releases itself, tincturing all bodies and lifting all men into the perfection of its own state.

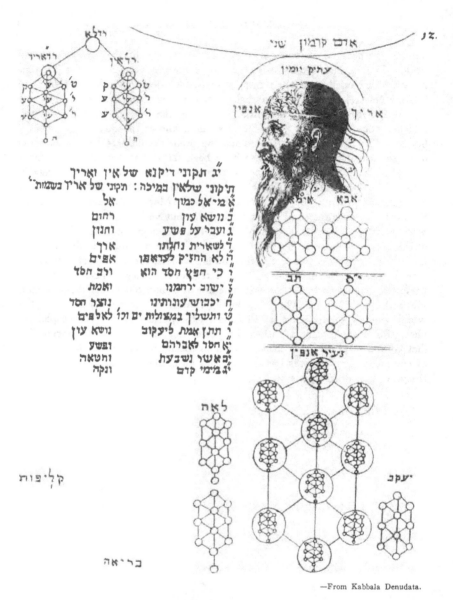

—From Kabbala Denudata.

THE GREAT HEAD OF THE ZOHAR

In the cranium of the Most Ancient One is distilled the heavenly moisture which, dropping downward, forms the worlds. The Trees of Creation have their beginning in the Great Head. This is the first Adam, the origin of all generations.

CHAPTER IX

THE BRAIN AND THE RELEASE OF THE SOUL

HE BRAIN is enclosed by the walls of the skull, which Plato describes as being an imitation of the peripheric constitution of the world. In the Gothic Mysteries, the skull of the hoarfrost giant, Ymir, forms the wall of the heavens. The cranium, then, is that microscopic heaven which Atlas (the upper vertebrae of the spinal column) bears upon his shoulders, according to the Orphic tradition. The spine, therefore, like the Tat pillar of the Egyptians, which is its symbol, supports the superior world upon its upper end. The skull consists of 22 bones, of which 8 make up the cranium and 14 the face. Realizing the proclivity of the Cabalists to discover analogies between universal mysteries and the human body, the number of these bones suggests the arrangement described in the SEPHER YETZIRAH, wherein is set forth how the Lord, "Blessed be he," arranged the 22 letters in the form of a wall, etc.

The skull is of particular interest to the occultist because of the ancient belief that somewhere in it is the door through which the spirit makes its egress at death. In THE HARMONY OF THE WORLDS, John Heydon advances what he terms to be a Rosicrucian theory. He explains that when the time for the departure of the soul has come, the *anima* collects herself either in the heart, from whence she can easily depart through the lungs and mouth, or else she gathers her spirits in the head "out of which there are more doors opened than I will stand to number." St. Hildegard represents the soul as departing from the mouth in the form of a naked human figure, in accordance with the early belief that the life principle escaped with the exhalation of the last breath. The secret tradition affirms the existence of ten apertures in the body, of which nine are apparent in the outward parts but the tenth is concealed and is the door of God.

The *Brahma-randhra* (usually translated "The Gate of Brahma") is said by the Hindus to be located at the back part of the head near the crown in about the position of the *parietal foramen*. Some writers have identified it with the occipito-parietal suture of Western anatomists, others with the *anterior fontanelle*. This is the "little door" in the wall of heaven through which St. John passed in his vision of the Apocalypse, and in the VISISHTADVAITA CATECHISM the soul is described as breaking through the crown of the head and departing into the region of the sun. "On Mount Saokant (Meru) there is a golden tube coming up from the root of the earth," says the UTTARA-GITA. From the commentary, Mount Saokant is very evidently the *Brahma-randhra*, the high place of the earth. When through discipline and regeneration, the Yogi can turn his face to this "mountain," he can attain to *Moksha*. Moses (cabalistically, the sun) ascended into the mountain and there the Law was revealed to him and he received the Ten Commandments, which are also the mysterious breaths and the superior Sephiroth referred to by Thomas Vickery, a mediæval anatomist, as the ten cells of the brain.

Calvary *(calvaria)*, "a bare skull," is from the Latin *calva*, the scalp without hair, or *calvus*, which means bald. The Hebrew word is *Gulgoleth* (Golgotha), which means both a skull and a burial place. Here is a definite link between the mysteries of the spirit and those of the body, and also a clue to the esoteric significance of the tonsure. The secret of the Gate of the Father was perpetuated among the early Christians by the ceremony of shaving off a circular portion of the hair on the crown of the head as a symbol of the ecclesiastical state. Thus we have the origin of the shaven corona of the Roman Catholic Church and the cranial sunbursts of the Pagan Mysteries.

Dr. Vasant G. Rele, in analyzing the word *Brahma-randhra*, reminds his readers that the word *randhra* may as well be translated "cavity" as "hole." He, therefore, visualizes the Brahma-randhra not as an opening but as a cavity surrounded "by a chakra or plexus of a thousand branches, known as *Sahas-rara*," which, in turn, he identifies with the cerebrum. Is the door, then, the great cavity of Brahma, the interior of the cranium itself, the seventh cavity of the brain which, according to H. P. Blavatsky, is the "synthesis" of all? It is evident that no literal hole is necessary in the head to allow the soul to depart, as this tenuous body would find physical substance no impediment to its progress. The rolling away of the stone must, therefore, be regarded as a spiritual rather than a material fact; and, as Golgotha in one of its meanings is a burial place, a clue is given to at least one interpretation of the Holy Sepulchre. The cross of Christ was raised upon the skull of Adam, declares the *Aurea Legenda*. The Brahma-randhra must be understood, therefore, as a quality or condition rather than a place. It is the attenuated medium through which the soul flows to the sun. The amazing resemblance between the top of the skull marked with the courses of the sutures and the outline of the Egyptian *scarabeus* may account for the use of this insect as a symbol of the resurrection of the human soul. If the skull is Golgotha, or burial place, then the Egyptian paintings, which depict the soul in the form of the man-headed hawk ascending from the tomb containing the mummy through a chimney-like vent, require no further explanation.

The Oriental divinities are often figured as wearing tight-fitting lotus-shaped caps, the petals spread out over the crown of the head like a sunburst from a plain central disk. The museum at Cairo contains several Egyptian mummy cases bearing these symbolic lotus blooms over the head area. One of the most extraordinary archeological fragments ever discovered on the American Continent is the massive head of dark green diorite in the Hall of the Monoliths in the National Museum at Mexico City. The figure is called *Tlahuizcalpantecuhtli* (Morning Star), "The Light of the Morning." The features have a definitely Oriental cast and the headdress consists of an inverted lotus-like cap, a perfectly symbolic representation of the *sahasrara*, or brain lotus, with the plain circular center—Brahma-randhra.   How curiously the name of the figure—Light of the Morning—agrees with the Yogi doctrine that this lotus of the soul opens and expands its petals when the sun rises above the horizon and sheds its rays upon the flower!   Explorations in the Mimbres Valley in New Mexico, during 1928 and 1929, resulted in the discovery of nearly four hundred primitive Indian bowls at least 1,400 years old.   The majority of these bowls were found inverted over the heads of mummies and

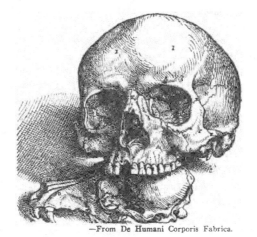

—From De Humani Corporis Fabrica.

THE HUMAN SKULL (After Vesalius)

in nearly every instance a small hole had been chipped out of the bottom of the bowl. Is it possible that these primitive Americans were acquainted with the Asiatic philosophy relating to the departure of life through the crown of the head and had these openings made so that the soul might make its exit?

The old Egyptian bas-reliefs and papyri often depict the soul of the deceased hovering as a man-headed hawk above the mortuary couch upon which lies the mummified body. Being the royal bird of the sun, the hawk indicates the luminous splendor of the soul and also intimates the kinship between the soul and the sun, as suggested in the Oriental writings. We are indebted to Andrew Jackson Davis, the seer of Poughkeepsie, for one of the best descriptions extant of the soul's departure from the body at physical death. He first describes how the various internal organs of the body appear to resist the withdrawal of the animating soul.   The muscles sought to regain the element of motion, the arteries the element of life, the nerves the element of sensation, and the brain the principle of intellect. These internal conflicts gave rise to the appearance of suffering, which, however, was not actual, for the whole process of death is according to natural and immutable law.   Next, according to the seer, the head became enveloped in a mellow, luminous atmosphere.   The cerebrum and cerebellum expanded their interior portions and discontinued their appropriate galvanic functions.   Next the brain became highly charged with vital electricity and vital magnetism, "that is to say, the brain, as a whole, suddenly declared itself to be tenfold more positive, over the lesser portions of the body, than it ever was during the period of health. This phenomenon invariably precedes physical dissolution."

The brain next began to attract the elements of electricity, magnetism, motion, life, and sensation into its various departments.   The head became intensely brilliant to the same proportion that the extremities of the body grew darker.   Gradually in the mellow, spiritual atmosphere which surrounded the head the indistinct outlines of another head appeared.   This was "eliminated and organized from out of, and above, the material head."   As this new spiritual head appeared, the brilliant atmosphere that had surrounded the brain of the old body contributed its light to the new organ and gradually faded out of the corporeal brain.   This process of progressive development continued until a complete body had been exuded, more radiant and beautiful than the physical organism but similar in general appearance.   "The spirit rose at right angles from the head or brain of the deserted body."   But at the final dissolution of the relationship between the two constitutions, Andrew Jackson Davis saw "playing energetically between the feet of the elevated spiritual body and the head of the prostrate physical body—a bright stream or current of vital electricity."   This current he termed an umbilical thread capable of being drawn out "into the finest possible medium of sympathetic connection" when the spirit leaves the body for clairvoyant research.   At death, the physical umbilical thread is broken, however, and a certain amount of the electrical element which moves through it flows back into the physical body, where diffusing itself, it prevents immediate decomposition.   In the case under analysis, the time required for the complete release was approximately two and one-half hours, but this is not advanced as a rule. (See THE GREAT HARMONIA.)

The word *spirit* generally invokes an erroneous conclusion.   Andrew Jackson Davis did not actually see the spirit departing from the body; he rather beheld a subtle body separating itself from a grosser one.   The spiritual *ens* is imperceptible in its own state, depending upon a chain of emanations for its recognition.   In the Paracelsian terminology, the soul is the sidereal body as distinguished from the physical form, which is called the elementary body.   The phenomenon of the etheric granules arranging themselves into a duplicate of the physical body is most significant from an occult standpoint. The units of physical substance from which the material body is built were originally oozed out of etheric granules and are, so to speak, the negative poles of these granules.   Man's etheric body corresponds, atom for atom, with his dense form.   Davis noted that the "spiritual" body has organs, and it is known to the sages that man's etheric body is in every respect as completely organized as the physical. It exists in a more attenuated sphere, however, breathing a subtler atmosphere and nourishing itself from its proper environment. When the physical form is discarded, the etheric body serves as a bridge between two distinct states of being—substantial and transubstantial. It is the wing which extends across the gulf in the old Mysteries. The brilliance of the ether particles prevented the seer from examining the still higher auras, whose delicate shadings bespoke the presence of the divine man.

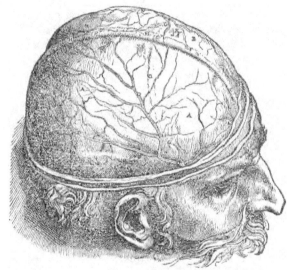

—From De Humani Corporis Fabrica.

THE OUTER SURFACE OF THE BRAIN AND ITS MEMBRANES (After Vesalius)

If we examine the writings of the older masters, we will discover the whole mystery of death set forth in the veiled language of the adepts. To Plotinus, life itself was but a "reasonable preparation" for death. From Hermes we learn the course of the soul after its departure from the body. The soul gradually disentangles itself from the discordances of the animal nature and returns to that divine or godlike condition, which is its natural aspect. Death was defined by the philosophers as "a change of place," or the passing of life from a previous to a subsequent state. However violent may seem the transition, the procedure is perfectly normal and in accord with the laws of life.

In THE GNOSTICS AND THEIR REMAINS is contained a summary of "the doctrines of the servants of Saturn" derived from Plutarch's treatise, ON THE FACE OF THE MOON. The substance of the account is as follows: In the generation of man, the earth supplies the body, the moon the animal soul, and the sun the *nous* (that is, the ego clothed in abstract mental substance.) This composite nature in its return to a simple state undergoes a double death. In the first, the goddess, Demeter, whose companion is the earthly, or supernal, Hermes (as the *psychopomp*, or lord of souls), forcibly separates the animal soul from the body. After a certain interval of penance in the middle sphere, in order to purify it from the pollutions of the flesh, this animal soul is caught up into the moon and passes through the earth's shadow during an eclipse. If the wicked attempt to enter the paradisiacal state before their purification is complete, they are frightened away by what is termed "the terrible Face." The good abide in the moon in the enjoyment of perfect tranquillity and, becoming genii, busy themselves with the regulation of human affairs upon the earth, rendering oracles and similar services to mankind. But should these beatified spirits misconduct themselves, they are put again into a human body and sent down to earth. After a certain time, however, in this middle paradise, the *nous* (the Self within) aspires to reascend to its fountain-head, the sun. When the proper time for this has arrived, the goddess, Proserpine, with her colleague, the celestial Hermes, separates *nous* "with gentleness and by slow degrees" from the animal soul. This is the second death. The liberated *nous* flies upward to the sun to mingle its essence with the universal life. The animal soul, however, remains in the sphere of the moon, continuing a dreamy sort of existence until gradually absorbed into the lunar substance, a process identical with that by which the earth gradually absorbs into itself the deserted physical body. Calm and philosophic souls—those in whom reason has acquired domination over the passions—are easily absorbed into the lunar field. Active, passionate, and erotic natures are very difficult to dissipate. They wander about in mid-space divested of the *nous*, becoming *Tityi* and *Typhones*.

The reader should not be deterred by the allegorical nature of the narrative from making a serious examination of its philosophical elements. The *nous*, or the intellectual Self, is revealed as sustaining the same relations to the animal soul that the latter bears to the physical body. Thus, the entire mystery of the death of the soul is explained, for "the soul that sinneth, it shall die," but "the spirit returns to God who gave it." The radiant form which Andrew Jackson Davis saw separating itself from the dying physical body was the Orphic "crater," or etheric vessel, containing the animal soul which, in turn, was permeated by the *nous*, as shown in St. Hildegard's figure of the microcosm (see page 36). Pythagoras discouraged communion with departed spirits because he maintained that, while a change of place, death was not necessarily a change of condition. Some of the Mysteries taught that man's elementary body was composed of five elements (as recognized by Plato) and the animal soul, or sidereal body, of seven elements. *Nous* was regarded either as a unit or as consisting of twelve parts. If the former, the sum of the composite man amounted to the mystic number 13; if the latter, to the equally sacred number 24, or an upper and a lower dodecade.

As the mother of generations, the moon presided over vapors and humidity—the mist of the middle world. It is not to be inferred that the ancients
actually believed that human souls pass to the moon but rather that they verge
towards a lunar state, becoming as it were reflectors of *nous* as the moon is
radiant with the reflected light of the sun. When it casts off the animal soul
and returns to its radiant source, *nous* must escape upward through seven
gates; for the animal soul is a coat of many colors (seven auras), each of its
divisions being under the dominion of a planet. Here again we have recourse

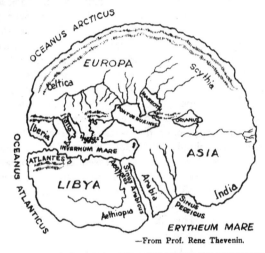

—From Prof. Rene Thevenin.

MAP OF THE WORLD FROM THE TIME OF HERODOTUS

*The resemblance between this figure and the human brain is very marked. Libya becomes
the cerebellum, Europe the top brain, and Asia the forebrain. The seas are suggestive of
the ventricular system.*

to an old ritual. "The grand doctrine of Gnosticism was this:" writes C. W.
King, "The soul on being released from the body (its prison-house and place
of torment) has to pass through the regions of the Seven Powers; which it
cannot do unless impregnated beforehand with *knowledge:* otherwise it is
seized upon and swallowed by the dragon-formed Ruler of this world, Satan
Ophiomorphos, and voided forth through his tail upon earth again. * * *
But should it [the soul] be filled with *knowledge,* it eludes the Seven Powers,
and tramples upon the head of Sabaoth . . . and mounts up unto the eighth
heaven, the abode of Barbelo, the Universal Mother, and who according to
the Pistis-Sophia is the celestial Mother of the Saviour."

According to Valentinus, the planets are the lords of death. Their
machinations weave the tangled web of destiny and, like spiders, they spin
threads which bind the *nous* to the inferior world. The host of planetary
powers, like industrious Lilliputs tie the cosmic Gulliver down. Is it not more

than a mere coincidence that two peoples as distantly removed as the Egyptians and the Tibetans should each possess a "Book of the Dead"? These writings are rituals devoted to the release of the soul from the net of the snarer. Known to all ancient peoples are "words of power" which, if pronounced by the soul as it passes through the seven spheres, will force the guardians to open their gates. The hierophants of Memphis and the Lord Lamas of Tashi-lhunpo were the common possessors of those plenipotent words which control the hosts of heaven. To die well is to be born with a better hope. "There are persons," writes Paracelsus, "who have been exalted to God, and who have remained in that state of exaltation, and they have not died. Their physical bodies have lost their lives, but without being conscious of it, without sensation, without any disease, and without suffering, and their bodies became transformed, and disappeared in such a manner that nobody knew what became of them, and yet they remained on the earth. But their spirits and heavenly bodies, having neither corporeal form, shape, nor colour, were exalted to heaven, like Enoch and Elias of old." When the philosophers affirm that there are "men whom death has forgotten," they make no statement unreasonable in the light of scientific premise. "We should live longer than we do," declares Sir Oliver Lodge. He adds: "Death does not seem essential to an organism. We are secreting poisons, but if they are taken away and our bodies kept clean, there is no reason we should die." The secret, then, of eternal life is to keep bodies clean. What is cleanliness? Is it not the purification of mind and soul and not mere bodily hygiene? The Chaldean hierophants who, according to tradition, lived to exceed a thousand years and then disappeared to their gods, may not be fables after all. The intellect that could build the Pyramid could also grasp the mystery of immortality. He who has stilled within himself the conflict of the ages need not die, but may triumphantly ascend into the splendid presence of truth. To prolong, however, merely the phenomenal aspect of life, without this internal conquest of environment, is actually to forge new fetters for the soul. All life must ebb and flow with the periodic phenomena of birth and death until the rational consciousness becomes established in wisdom and has assimilated both beginning and end. Man, aspiring to immortal heights, however, must not trust himself to Icarian wings. Enmeshed in animal matter and bereft of sense by the noxious fumes which rise from earth, the animal soul becomes "unable and unwilling" to depart from a physical state. Only by the disciplines of the Mysteries is the soul awakened from its lethargy and stimulated to achieve self-liberation.

As the result of perfected virtues and powers, the adept may attain to philosophic immortality; or, more correctly, to a rational extension of life, for the Absolute alone is truly immortal. We have demonstrated that immortality and death are not incompatible but may exist together, in that death does not necessarily interfere with the continuity of consciousness. Though his body has returned to the dust, Plato still lives. Socrates drank the hemlock with no regret, strong in the realization that body is but an incident in the duration of intelligence. The wise seek release not from the phenomenon of death, but from bondage to ignorance, for ignorance is the most grievous affliction of the soul. "There is no death for the sage," declares Eliphas Levi, "death is a phantom, made horrible by the weakness and ignorance of the vulgar. Change is the sign of motion, and motion reveals life; if the corpse itself were dead, its decomposition would be impossible; all its constituent molecules are living and working out their liberation. Yet you dream that the spirit is set free first so that it may cease to live! You believe that thought and love can die when the grossest matter is imperishable! If change must be called death, we die and are reborn daily, because daily our forms change. Fear therefore to soil or rend your garments, but do not fear to lay them by when the hour of sleep approaches."

The brain is that part of the cerebrospinal axis, or central nervous system, which is contained within the cranial cavity. The four principal parts of the brain recognized by anatomists are: (1) the *cerebrum,* which fills the upper and greater part of the cranial cavity and is divided by a great longitudinal fissure into the right and left cerebral hemispheres, which are thrown into numerous folds called convolutions; (2) the *cerebellum* (the diminutive of *cerebrum*), sometimes called the little brain or the after-brain, which is situated in the occipital fossæ at the rear of the head and generally regarded as the seat of the motor nerves; (3) the *pons varolii,* which lies almost in the center of the cranium and rests upon the upper part of the basilar process and body of the sphenoid bone, the large wing-shaped bone that lies behind the face; (4) the *medulla oblongata,* which is the enlarged upper end of the spinal cord, extending from the upper part of the Atlas vertebrae of the spine to the lower border of the pons varolii. In addition to the parts already enumerated there are the ventricles, glands, and plexuses, each with its own peculiar significance and correspondent in the organs and members of the lower body. The vaulted chambers, passageways, and labyrinths of the brain so excited the admiration of the ancients that they were moved to write thereon *cum copia verborum* in their efforts to establish analogies between these parts and every portion of the universe.

"In the first place, then, the gods bound the two divine circulations of the soul in a spherical body, in imitation of the circular figure of the universe; and this part of the body is what we now denominate the head; a most divine member, and the sovereign ruler of our whole corporeal composition, through the decree of the gods, who considered that it would participate of all possible motions." (See THE TIMAEUS.)

The average weight of the brain, not including the skull, is 48 ounces in males and 44 ounces in females, and the brain accounts for 98 per cent of the weight of the entire nervous system.

The pia mater (that delicate membrane which invests the brain and spinal cord, forming as it were an inner garment) offers a definite clue to the anatomical *arcana* of the philosophers. Many scientific terms now in general use have been appropriated from older orders of learning, often with little understanding and less appreciation of the original meanings. *Pia*, for example, is the feminine of *pius* (pious), meaning "godly" or "devoted to Deity," while *mater* is "mother." Thus, *pia mater* is the Holy Mother, the Sophia- Achamoth of the Gnostics, containing within herself the fœtus of the Heavenly Man. *Mater*,

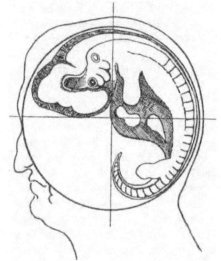

THE BRAIN IN THE FORM OF AN EMBRYO

also interpreted as the origin or the source of, when read cabalistically, indicates the brain to be the place where the gods are generated, or where piety or godliness has its seat. When the Cabalists declared the Heavenly Man to be androgynous, they stated only that which is testified to by the inner structure of man himself and by the early development of the embryo. Thus, the fœtal creature within the womb of the Holy Mother *(pia mater)* is the celestial hermaphrodite, whose parts and members may be faintly traced in even the modern terms used to identify the parts of this amazing organ which we call the brain. The *corpora quadrigemina*, four rounded eminences immediately behind the third ventricle and under the control of Saturn, are divided into an anterior and a posterior pair, of which the former is called *nates*, or buttocks, and the latter the *testes*. Not far from these quadrigeminal bodies are also the mammallary bodies—two perfectly formed little breasts. Thus, the brain reflects the androgynous condition of the Superior Man, the pineal gland and the pituitary body being the generative organs of this celestial hermaphrodite.

Madam Blavatsky states that the pineal gland corresponds with the uterus in the female and the peduncles with the Fallopian tubes. Hence, we have a creature like the Melchizedek of old, who is king and priest, male and female, capable of being its own father and mother. In some systems of symbology, this brain creature is considered as two rather than one, and they are pictured as locked within each other's embrace like twins within the womb. One of these creatures is male and the other female. They are Gemini, the Celestial Twins, Adam-Eve before the separation. They are twisted together like the Yin and the Yang of the Chinese, or the black and white dragons biting at each other, which to the Oriental mind signified the agent and patient in every department of Nature.

The brain must, therefore, be considered not as a single organ but as a whole creature, a microcosm—the original of the whole bodily structure and the seat of all the intelligences which are reflected into the bodily organs, being as Burton calls it, "the Privy Councillor and Chancellor to the heart." Curious diagrams are in existence setting forth the human spermatozoon with a minute embryonic body twisted up in the head. This figure (see page 81) may have originated from an effort to establish the correspondences in appearance between the spinal system and the sperm, for the brain (including the spinal cord) is not dissimilar in shape to the spermatozoon. The coiled up figure in the head of the sperm is an intimation of the brain man which is to follow. In each part of the anatomical structure of the brain and the terms applied thereto is contained some hint as to its occult significance. Form is an expression of force and is molded into the purpose of the impulse which engendered it. Thus, the *medulla oblongata* is very informative, Freemasonically, as can be discovered by reference to the older writers. An archaic meaning for *medulla* is "marrow," and the "marrow in the bone" or "skull" is of particular interest to the French tradition, for it is truly "the place of concealment of the murdered one." The *medulla* also signifies an essence or a summary or a compendium, the consummation of the alchemists and the "consummatum est" of the Christian Mysteries. How rich this field of research is can be very easily realized when we learn that the parts of the *medulla* are distinguished by anatomists under such extraordinary terms as the anterior and posterior *pyramids*, the *olivary* bodies, the restiform bodies, etc. It is in the *medulla*, then, that the soul experiences the Mysteries of the Pyramids. Here also is the Mount of Olives, no more significant for its Biblical allusion than for the oil which is pressed therefrom. The word *restiform* means "ropelike," for was it not on the Mount of Olives that Christ was bound with ropes and is it not in the funeral sermon of the Kadosh that the "ties" are loosened? The whole of the brain should be treated in like manner, for such analysis is indispensable to the study of man's divine nature.

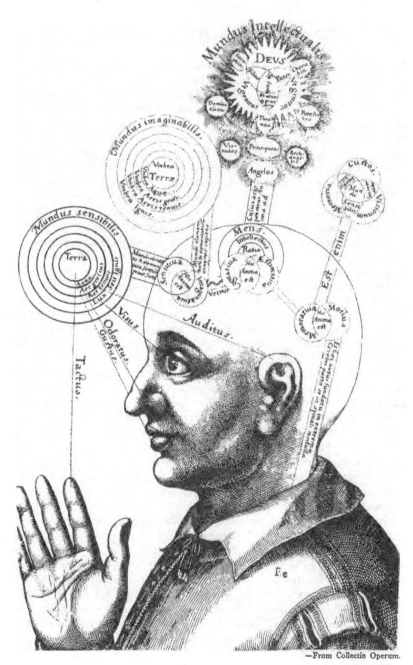

FLUDD'S DIAGRAM OF THE VENTRICULAR AND SENSORY HARMONIES

CHAPTER X

THE VENTRICLES AND THE BRAIN DEW

I N HIS work on Rosicrucian anatomy, THE MICROCOSMI HISTORIA, Robert Fludd assigns the three departments of the *Empyrean* (or mundane heaven) to the cranium of the microcosm (man). In common with Boehme, therefore, he locates the paradisiacal spheres in the head, or highest part, of the inferior Adam. Fludd calls the highest plane or division of the brain the "Radius of Deity," or the "Uncreated Light." The middle he designates the "Luminous Sphere," or the "Created Light"; and the lowest he terms the "Spiritual Sphere", or the "Empyrean". This classification the great de Fluctibus derives from the Chaldaic-Cabalistic concept of AIN SOPH. The Absolute Deity of THE ZOHAR is caused to assume definition by imposing upon it certain hypothetical qualifications. The first is Boundlessness, the second Boundless Life, and the third Boundless Light. Fludd further visualizes these spiritual aspects as abiding in certain recesses of the brain. He establishes the location of these compartments by recourse to the divisions of the cranium laid down by earlier anatomists. In his astronomical teachings, Pythagoras taught that the gods did not reside in the planetary bodies but, more correctly, in the interplanetary "intervals." (*Iamblichus.*) In accordance with this astronomical concept, mediæval disciples of Galen and Avicenna assigned no organs to the "spirits" (vital centers) in the brain, but gave them cavities (ventricles) in which to mingle their essences. From this viewpoint, the soul was likened to a vapor, gas, or even a humidity, bottled up during life in remote caverns of the body (i.e., the ventricles, arteries, etc.).

Science recognizes four ventricles in the adult human brain—the two laterals, the third, and the fourth. To paraphrase the account given by Vesalius, the lateral ventricles are placed one in the upper right and one in the upper left in relation to the center of the brain. They are somewhat wing-shaped and are shown as L and M in the plate from DE HUMANI CORPORIS FABRICA. (See page 136.) The third ventricle is in the center and below them, "about midway from the forehead and the occiput." The fourth ventricle lies in the region of the cerebellum to the rear of and below the third ventricle. If to these be added the so-called fifth ventricle, and the sixth (the latter the tiny tube in the spinal cord) and all then be regarded as symbolically enclosed within the great cavern of the skull, the seven ventricles of the occultists are revealed. "There are seven cavities in the brain," writes H. P. Blavatsky, "which during life are empty in the ordinary sense of the word. In reality, they are filled with Akasa, each cavity having its own color, according to the state of consciousness * * *. These cavities are called in occultism 'the seven harmonies,' the scale of the divine harmonies, and it is these that the visions must be reflected in if they are to remain in the brain-memory." In these cavities also the "brain stars" of Paracelsus are located, which are visible to the seer as twinkling atoms vibrating in the akasic field. The seven harmonies are reminiscent of the "singing Memnon," that lonely colossus of the Egyptian desert, which to this day utters his weird lament when the wind sweeps through the chambers of his head. St. Hildegard, of Bingen, an illumined mystic of the Middle Ages, writes thus of the mystery of the seven caves: "From the summit of the vessel of the brain to the extremity of the forehead seven equal spaces can be distinguished. Here the seven planets are designated, the uppermost planet in the highest part, the moon in front, the sun in the middle, and the other planets distributed among the other places."

For the most part, the ancients concerned themselves with only three of the brain ventricles, i.e., the laterals (considered as one), the third, and the fourth. In the earlier works of Albertus Magnus, these cavities are represented by three circles of equal size filling the entire cranium. No effort was made towards anatomical accuracy, the figure herewith reproduced being unmodifiedly diagrammatic. This is a pertinent example of the "theoretical" science of the Scholastics, whose dogmatism provoked Lord Bacon to attempt the INSTAURATION. It is the temperament of the twentieth century to take too extreme an attitude towards matters of earlier learning. We have outgrown a little, so we reject all. The recently discovered ciphers of Roger Bacon are a warning against hasty conclusions, and there is evidence that Albertus Magnus knew the true purpose of the ventricles, while we are acquainted only with their shape. In the course of time, the circular ventricles of the first authors were modified until, as in the drawing published in the first encyclopedia—a quaint old incunabula entitled REISCH'S MARGARITA PHILOSOPHICA—these caverns, or "cells," have assumed indescribable proportions and are connected by ducts, or stems. In some of his early anatomical drawings Leonardo da Vinci follows the same general concept as the Arabians, but the virtues of da Vinci's own temperament cause him to depict the ventricles as orderly and "artistic." Later, however, through dissection, he learned the correct relationship of these cavities, and the figures from his fuller knowledge, while not comparable with the exactitude of modern textbooks, are of vital importance as revealing the transition from the old to the new in the understanding of the interior structure of the brain. Da Vinci anticipated to some degree the work of Vesalius, whose monumental achievement, DE HUMANI CORPORIS FABRICA, was to bring to a close the mediæval period of theoretical anatomy. As Garrison so well notes, the FABRICA caused anatomical science to break forever with the past and throw overboard Galenical tradition. Leonardo, as his drawings prove, had the Vesalian spirit stirring within his soul, but destiny had chosen another to give the vision to a waiting world.

In his LEONARDO DA VINCI THE ANATOMIST, Professor J. Playfair McMurrich prefaces his consideration of Leonardo's conclusions concerning the interior construction of the brain with a summary of the earlier writers. He says in part: "Galen had located the intellectual faculties in the brain substance in close proximity to the ventricles, which contained the psychic pneuma, but his successors, notably Poseidonius and Numesius, transferred their seat to the ventricles themselves." Then, to paraphrase the professor,

—From Musæum Hermeticum.

THE SEVEN SPIRITS WHICH ABIDE IN THE BRAIN
The three figures seated above the cavern bear the symbols of the ventricles

Avicenna with his Arabic penchant for metaphysical subtleties added to and revised the opinions of these first authorities. Where Leonardo's observations did not agree with the earlier traditions, he promptly disregarded traditions and gave expression to his own theories as to the localization of function in the brain. In da Vinci's drawings the posterior ventricle is marked with the older legend, *memory*, "but the other two each have a double legend. To the middle ventricle, in addition to *senso commune*, there is assigned also *voluntá*, and the anterior one besides the legend *imprensiva* bears that of *intelletto*." Leonardo associated the will with the *sensus communis* in the middle ventricle "where the nerves are said 'to move the members at the good-pleasure of the will of the soul'," and the soul is located "in the judicial part (of the brain)." Da Vinci also made the extremely significant statement "that the ventricles of the brain and those of the sperm (seminal vesicles) are equally distant from those of the heart." Leonardo, then, recognized with the earlier anatomists of the initiate period, the presence in the body of three great systems of ventricles —those of the brain, those of the heart, and those of the reproductive system. The Bembine Table of Isis is supposed to represent in its divisions the three great rooms, or chambers, wherein abide the gods of the world, and the parts of the human soul. These compartments with their lesser divisions are analogous to the ventricular systems of the ancients.

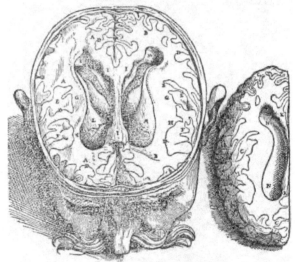

—From De Humani Corporis Fabrica.

THE LATERAL VENTRICLES OF THE BRAIN, MARKED L AND M. (After Vesalius)

Having visualized the three ventricles and their mutual relationships as these were understood in ancient times, we can better appreciate the words of Nicolai, "physician and instructor," as they have descended to us in his ANATOMIA: "On account of the three divisions of the brain, the ancient philosophers called it the temple of the spirit, for the ancients had their chambers in their temples, first the vestibulum, then the consistorium, finally the apotheca. In the first the declarations were made in law cases; in the second the statements were sifted; in the third final sentence was laid down. The ancients said that the same processes occur in the temple of the spirit, that is, the brain." Nicolai then explains the organization of thought and its orderly motion through the ventricles in an effort to show how the philosophers patterned the harmony of their external lives after the exemplar of the brain. Hippolytus, the Ante-Nicean Father, writing in the early centuries of the Christian Era, published several fragments from the arcanum of the Gnostics and other heretical sects. One of these fragments, AGAINST HERESIES, is related to our subject. He speaks first of the brain as being the dominant portion of the entire body and follows the concept of Aristotle that it remains calm and unmoved, being isolated by a narrow isthmus from the contentions of the animal nature and "containing within itself the spirit." He then observes that, when dissected, the brain reveals within itself a vaulted chamber, on either side of which are little wings which are moved gently by the motion of

—From Philosophia Naturalis.

THE VENTRICLES AS THE ABODE OF THE SOUL,
ACCORDING TO ALBERTUS MAGNUS

the spirit. There is also the significant statement that because of its shape the brain was likened by the pagan initiates to the head of a serpent. It must be remembered that when the word *spirit* is used in connection with the brain ventricles, the term does not signify the divine nature of the theologian but rather the Paracelsian *spiritus*—a life force or breath; an agent, but not necessarily the Supreme Agent. In some cases, it corresponds with the *prana* of the Hindus, or solar force, and in others with the astral light of Levi, the transcendentalist. In its ancient use, the word *soul* often signified the ego and the word *spirit* merely the emanations of force therefrom. The circulation of the *spiritus* throughout the parts and members of the soul was analogous to the circulation of the blood through the veins and arteries of the body.

To summarize the older doctrines, the brain contains in its central part four cavities of major importance. In reality, these are but one great cavity in which four rooms connected by "aqueducts" are distinguishable. According to Burton, in his ANATOMY OF MELANCHOLY, these rooms "are the receptacles of the spirits, brought hither by the arteries from the heart," there to be refined "to a more heavenly nature to perform the actions of the soul." In the graphic language of 1548, the comparative dignities of the ventricular chambers are thus described: "The foremost is the most, the second or middle-most is less, and the third or hindermost is least." According to Culpeper, imagination is seated in the anterior ventricle, memory in the posterior, and judgment in the median cavity between them. This old physician, whose name will endure to the end of science, further makes the front ventricle to be hot and dry, the central warm and moist, and the rear cold and dry. Do these ventricles, then, contain the philosophical sulphur, mercury, and salt, the ingredients of the Wise Man's Stone, which Paracelsus, in his NINE BOOKS OF THE NATURE OF THINGS, declares to signify soul, spirit, and body? Among the figures of Nicholas Flamel from THE BOOK OF ABRAHAM THE JEW is one depicting the sun and moon pouring their rays into a small central bottle. Is the third ventricle that vessel in which the "marriage" of the sun and moon takes place? Are the animal spirits in the cerebellum united with the intellectual spirits in the lateral ventricles in the central chamber, which Burton calls "the common concourse"?

Petrocellus, in describing the purposes of the three cells of the brain, declares the ability to discern good or evil is located in the middle one and that the soul is in the rear, which agrees with John Heydon, who maintains that the *anima* is in the fourth ventricle. Though following the general theory of the older writers, Robert Fludd makes each of the cavities twofold, a right and a left, in harmony with modern science. The two lateral ventricles he terms *sense* and *imagination;* the halves of the third ventricle, *cogitation* and *estimation;* and the halves of the fourth ventricle, *memory* and *motion.* In describing Fludd's diagram of the ventricular and sensory harmonies (see page 132), Grillot de Givry writes: "The celestial world, composed of God and the angels, penetrates directly into the skull, communicating with the soul; the perceptible world, composed of the four elements, communicates with the five senses. Then there is a sphere called the 'imaginable world,' corresponding to the entirely metaphysical sensations of the imagination, which are produced 'as in dreams, by non-existent objects and, consequently, by the shadows of elements.' Hence we see a system of spheres exactly following the preceding and containing 'the shadow of Earth, the shadow of Water, the shadow of gross Air, the shadow of tenuous Air, and, lastly, the shadow of Fire.' The intellectual sphere and the imaginative sphere are oddly linked by a slender, sinuous 'worm.' Last of all, the author places at the back of the skull the sphere which he calls 'memorative, or pertaining to remembrance.' And he shows it communicating with the spinal marrow." (See LE MUSEE DES SORCIERS.) Thus, the intellectual Deity is established in the midmost place, with Mercury and Mars (sense and motion) as the two extremities of the brain. The two lateral ventricles are divided by a thin, transparent, "skinlike" wall, called the *septum lucidum, or speculum.* The words *septum lucidum (septum translucidum,* according to the most modern authorities) are generally translated "translucent wall," but in their older form they can also be interpreted as "the wall of light," and the word *speculum* means "a mirror," or "that which catches reflections."

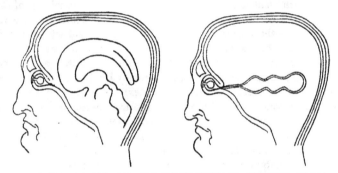

TWO DRAWINGS OF THE VENTRICULAR SYSTEM FROM
AMONG THE PAPERS OF LEONARDO DA VINCI

According to Sir Kenelm Digby, "gentleman of the bedchamber to King Charles the First," the "species and similitudes of things" have their abode in the lateral ventricles, "where they are moved and tumbled about when we think." These "molecular bodies" of notions and ideas hide themselves in the numerous concavities of the brain, until mental activity causes a "wind or forceful stream" to sweep through the caverns. This motion picks up the minute particles and causes them "to strike against" the speculum (a phenomenon which finds its analogy in the olfactory process), thus stimulating the seat of fantasy. The speculum is, then, the magic mirror, upon the surface of which "spirits" conjure up the shadows of ideas. Good Sir Digby continues his discourse by explaining how these spirits (minute bodies in suspension) "run long and perplexed journeys up and down in the brain" (from one chamber to another), to at last "smoke at liberty in the hollow ventricles." From these cavities they "reek out of the little arterial branches" (chorioid plexuses) and "being now grown heavy" (precipitated), fall downward through the fourth ventricle through the medulla oblongata into the marrow (spinal cord) of the backbone, from which they are distributed through the nerves as sensory impulses to all parts of the body.

Burton expresses the same thought when he says that the fourth "creek" (ventricle) is common to both the cerebellum and the marrow and, receiving the animal spirits from the other cavities into itself, conveys them into the spinal cord. In the cell of fantasy we gather ideas, says an old anatomist, in the central cell we think them over, and in the cell to the rear we commit them to memory. Galen defines *melancholy* as "a privation or infection of the middle cell of the head." Costa ben Luca, of Baalbek, writing in the ninth century, gives what Lynn Thorndike, Ph.D., calls in his work, A HISTORY OF MAGIC AND EXPERIMENTAL SCIENCE, "a most amusing explanation" of the processes by which memory, imagination, and reason—the three hypostases of thought—take place. In clarifying his point, this Arab refers to the third and fourth ventricles only, explaining that the recalling of anything to the memory is accomplished by the passage of a subtle essence from the anterior cavity to the posterior (i.e., from the third ventricle to the fourth). The opening (cerebral aqueduct) between these two cavities of the brain is closed by a sort of valve, which Costa ben Luca describes as "a particle of the body of the brain similar to a worm" (Robert Fludd's *Vermis?*). Occultism would identify this "worm" as a somewhat extraordinary title bestowed upon the pineal gland which, according to the esoteric tradition, is actually so placed that in the normal individual it forms a little door, closing the ventricles from each other. When this gland has been stimulated by Kundalini, it is said to "rise" and when in an erect position it is referred to as an "open door" through which a free circulation of the volatile forces in the ventricles is made possible. (See section on the *Pineal Gland* for details.) The activities of the sensory and motor nerves, then, may be regarded as a sort of Jacob's ladder up which impulses ascend to seek audience with intellect and down which descend "vapors" pregnant with despotic edicts.

There are delicate fringelike processes consisting almost entirely of blood vessels which project into the third, fourth, and lateral ventricles of the brain and are termed the *chorioid plexuses*. It is the epithelial cells of these plexuses that secrete the cerebrospinal fluid and pour it into the ventricles, from whence it flows through the numerous apertures which open into the subarachnoid spaces. Santee describes the cerebrospinal fluid which fills the various serous spaces of the central nervous system as a displaceable fluid "more like tears and sweat than lymph" in consistency. In writing of the *Brahma-randhra* as the greatest of the chambers in the brain, Dr. Rele says that this cavity is constantly secreting a fluid called "the nectar of life" or "the divine fluid," which bathes the brain and the spinal cord. The cerebrospinal fluid, then, is synonymous with the "tears of the sky God," or "the wine-weeping heavens," yes, even *lachrymae Christi*, "the tears of Christ." It is symbolically the *liquor amnii* of the brain fœtus. We cannot but be reminded of the Ganges River which rises from hidden springs in the head of Shiva, or again the sacred Jordan and the deified Nile. It should prove both interesting and instructive

to explore the mystery of this heavenly water, as its secrets have been preserved
in the writings of ancient and mediæval "adepts."

In their search for the elixir of life, the alchemists discovered the occult
properties of a certain mysterious "dew" and were moved to write thereof, but
always in a most guarded manner. In the preparation of their medicines with
which they sought to heal all the diseases and evils of the world, these philosophers made use of a crystalline "dew" gathered at night on plates of glass

De potētijs aie fenfitiue

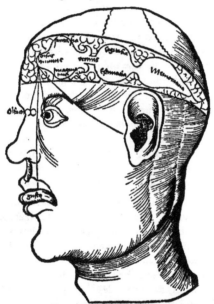

—From Reisch's Margarita Philosophica.

THE FRONT CELL OF THE HEAD AS THE SEAT OF THE SENSORY REFLEXES
according to fifteenth century anatomists.

during the major conjunctions of planets and at certain phases of the moon.
They declared that they were thus able to capture the celestial "virtues" and
apply them to the all too numerous ills of humankind. The word *dew* is traceable to the Sanskrit *Dhav*, "to flow," and the term is occasionally applied to
tears. It will be remembered that the Egyptians, and often the Greeks and
Latins, highly esteemed tears and caused them to be collected in lachrimatories,
or tear bottles. In some cases, these bottles were buried with the dead as
evidence of grief. More often, however, they were preserved for purposes of
healing or magic.

Several authors, including Mosheim and Higgins, are of the opinion that
the word *Rosicrucian* is derived from the words *Ros* and *crux*. *Ros* is a Latin

word which may be translated dew or dripping moisture or even tears without taxing the credulity. In a Gnostic ritual it is written that the rulers of the sphere (zodiac) create the soul from their own substance "out of the tears of their eyes and the sweat of their torment." The Latin form of rose is *rosa* and by a simple cabala this becomes *ros-a*. As the first of the sacred vowels the *a* is the moon, which in the Mysteries was the symbol of the brain, as already noted. In early anatomical treatises it is even mentioned that the brain moves in the skull according to the phases of the moon. So the word can be interpreted as the "dew or moisture from the brain" or, as the Rosicrucians themselves called it, "the dew in the brain." This is the "dew" from heaven described by the sages as "descending upon the tops of the mountains." In their letter to Eugenius Philalethes, the Brothers of R. C. hint at this mystery in these words: "Near the daybreak there shall be a great calm and you shall see the Day-Star arise and the dawning will appear, and you shall perceive a *great treasure*. The chief thing in it, and the most perfect, is a *certain exalted tincture*, with which the world (if it served God and were worthy of such gifts) might be tinged and turned into most pure gold." (See LUMEN DE LUMINE.) Is not this *exalted tincture* covering the mountains at dawn "the dew of the sages," which contains captured within itself the *shadow* of the whole world and the virtues of the stars? Did not the wise Paracelsus go forth just preceding dawn to *gather* the heavenly moisture which falls more thickly on the *mountains* about Hohenheim than any other part of the world?

This "dew" lost all its virtue unless it was gathered by certain means in especially purified vessels. One ancient alchemist recommended four glass plates, another linen cloths that had been made absolutely clean. The purified vessels, the clean glass plates, and the linen cloths refer, of course, to the regenerated body of the alchemist. who has gained the right to discover the *Universal Solvent* by cleansing. as it were, the inside of his own cup. The philosophers also revealed that this mysterious "dew" drips down into the heart of the redeemed (baptism), by which such a man is empowered to understand all mysteries. Therefore, the "dew" is also called truth. Hence, Emanuel Swedenborg, the uninitiated seer, refers to "dew" in one place as the truth of good, which is derived from a state of innocence and peace, and in another place as the *multiplication* of good from truth and the fructification of good by truth. By the term *multiplication* it is indicated that Swedenborg sensed the alchemical significance of that heavenly moisture which is both physical and spiritual in its esoteric interpretation.

It has already been hinted that the "dew" was to be found only in the most mountainous parts. This, of course, intimates the brain, which is the *high place* so often referred to in the sacred writings. Lest this analogy be regarded as far-fetched, let us turn to the SIPHRA DTZENIOUTHA—*The Book of the Concealed Mystery*—wherein it is said of the head of the great Universal Man that it has been formed in the likeness of the cranium, or skull

—From Anatomia Corporis Humani.

*THE VENTRICULAR CONTROL OF THE SENSORY FUNCTIONS,
ACCORDING TO JOHANN DRYANDER*

(the monad) and "is filled with the crystalline dew." (See THE ZOHAR.)
This "dew" is called the second confirmation or aspect of the Great Face. Is
not this "dew" the *lux* or light fluid, the pure *akasa*, the fiery mist, the heavenly
luminous water, the *Schamayim*, or the fiery water, the sea of crystalline before
the throne of God, the fountain from which flows the four ethereal rivers that
water the whole earth? Philo even suggests that the cherub which guards
Eden is, in reality, a cloud of divine humidity which conceals the paradisiacal
garden from the relapsed mankind even as the Rosicrucians were declared
to have concealed their sanctum—the House of the Holy Spirit—from the
profane by surrounding it with what one of their writers called "clouds" or
"mists."

A few quotations from the HA IDRA RABBA QADISHA—*The Greater Holy Assembly*—will give further hints. "And from that skull distilleth a dew upon him which is external, and filleth his head daily." It may be well to mention here that the word *cranium*, or skull, is used in THE ZOHAR to signify what the Pythagoreans would call the monad (or wholeness). It is, so to speak, the seed of the world and is referred to as a skull to symbolize its spherical shape. In the quotation just given this monad is depicted as causing its spiritual emanations to flow into the lesser cranium—the inferior universe— for it is also written, "and by that dew are sustained the holy supernal ones." If we desire to discover the nature of the supernal ones mentioned in THE ZOHAR, it is only necessary to read on a little and learn that the "dew" dripping down waters the field in which grow "the holy apple trees." It is also written that the "dew of the lights is thy dew." Are not these *lights* identical with the stars of Paracelsus, which must never be considered as heavenly bodies but powers or centers of intellection? "All that intellect can conceive of," writes the Swiss Hermes, "comes from the stars." And he adds: "The activity of the organism of man is the result of the actions of the interior constellations of stars existing in his inferior world." When the Cabalists maintain that these stars are contained within the skull of Macroprosophus, the secret is out.

The *holy apple trees* which are nourished by the heavenly "dew" cannot but be identical in significance with the golden apple trees of the Hesperides. Apollodorus assures us that the golden apples carried away by Hercules grew in the Hyperborean Atlantis. Hyperboreas was the Northern Paradise of the Greeks, the sub-polar continent, the terrestrial Eden, where also grew the symbolic apple tree of the Chaldo-Hebraic Mysteries. The importance of the golden apples which grew on Mount Atlas—the North Pole of the human body—can be more fully understood when we realize that they signify the spiritual monads, atoms or stars which abide in the superior worlds and which are the origins of the terrestrial natures suspended from them. (See ORPHEUS, by G.R.S. Mead.) These *apples* are the effulgent blossoms of Proclus, "the golden atoms" in the hearts of living things, whose reflections are set up in the ether of the brain. Here also is the mystery of the Golden Fleece guarded by the Polar Constellation of the mystic Dragon.

We have already learned that the Seven Builders seated upon their akasic thrones in the vast cranium of the Universal Man have their microcosmic correspondences in the human brain. These are the Seven Stars—the supernal ones—whose essences are carried by the "dew," even as the sidereal "humidity" carries the seven aspects of the astral light. There can be no doubt that the seven Dhyana Buddhas (two unnamed) which are described as abiding within the aura of the heart have their correspondences in the seven cavities of the brain, wherein their essences are enthroned by reflection. Thus, Mars corresponds with the cerebellum, Saturn with the corpora quadrigemina, Venus with the pineal gland, Mercury with the same gland after it has been tinctured

—From Musæum Hermeticum.

AN ALCHEMICAL REPRESENTATION OF THE VENTRICULAR SYSTEM,
ACCORDING TO F. BASILIUS VALENTINUS

The lateral and fourth ventricles are represented as two contesting swordsmen, with Mercury
as the third ventricle in equilibrium between them

with Kundalini, Jupiter with the whole cavity of the skull filled with *akasa*, the
moon with the fornix, and the sun with the *prana* in the third ventricle. Some
modern writers assign Uranus to the pituitary body and Neptune to the pineal
gland, or vice versa.

The crystalline "dew" described by St. John and the oceans above the
heavens indicated in the opening verses of Genesis are not without their physiological correspondences in the human body. The Ocean of Eternity and the
Milky Way—are these not again hints as to the crystalline "dew" of the
adepts? There is confirmation again in the Oriental philosophies. The seventh
chakra—the *sahasrara*, or highest brain chakra— is frequently spoken of as a
lotus tank in Hindu mystical books. (See T. Subba Row.) "The 'sweet-
sounding water' of this tank," continues the eminent scholar, "is described as
amrita, or nectar." An entirely new line of research is opened up. The *amrita*,
or the "water of immortality," was obtained, according to the Vedas, from the
churning of the great ocean. The word means literally, "deathless." Here is
the elixir of life of the alchemists. It was also called the sacred soma juice,
the drink of initiation, the true formula of which, like the prescriptions of the
alchemists, is supposed to have been lost. "Plainly speaking," writes H. P.
Blavatsky, in LUCIFER, "soma is the fruit of the Tree of Knowledge." Soma
is also a symbol of the moon, and esoterically the moon is the ruler of the mind
even as the sun is the ruler of the spirit. To return to the *sahasrara* chakra, it

is written in the ARUNOPNISHAD that in this chakra "is a golden cup sur-rounded by bright rays, the abode of happiness." Here, then, is the Sangrail, the sacred chalice guarded by the knights in the domed castle on the heights of Christian Spain. Here is the esoteric significance of the communion cup, for does not even Max Müller say that the soma juice "has the same signi-ficance in Veda and Avasta sacrifices as the juice of the grape had in the worship of Bacchus"? The wine of Bacchus became the wine of Christ, the blood of the Logos, which is pictured flowing from the Paschal Lamb in seven streams.

Ambrosia was the drink of the gods on high Olympus. It was the all-sustaining beverage of the immortals, and as the cup of Ganymede is now perpetuated in the water vessel of the constellation of Aquarius. Like the waters of life referred to by the Holy Nazarene, those who drank thereof thirsted no more. Can we doubt that all these mysterious hints point to some occult truth of profound significance which, for the most part, has escaped the attention of modern symbolists? In the Gothic rites before mentioned the neophyte consummated his initiation by drinking the heavenly mead from a bowl fashioned out of a human skull. Similar skull bowls are among the sacred paraphernalia of the Tibetan Mysteries. Does not this ritual possess a signi-ficance more profound than merely the outer ceremony? The Rosicrucian rose rising out of the skull restates the formula once more—the "dew" and the brain. We move gradually amidst the mass of symbols and one of the most convincing links in the chain of analogies comes from an unexpected source—the EDDAS. In describing the World Tree—Yggdrasil—as explained in a later chapter of this work, it is clearly revealed that the entire symbol was devised to interpret not only the universe but also the human body. In the upper branches of the tree, at a point analogous to the brain, are depicted five animals—*heidrun,* Odin's goat, which supplies the heavenly mead, and four stags, *dain, dvalin, duneyr,* and *durathor,* from whose horns, according to the legend, honey "dew" drops down upon the earth. The branches of the tree are the same as those referred to in THE ZOHAR, in which the birds (angels) have their nests (plexuses).

Denuded of its symbolism and applied to the microcosm, all these allegories point to a secret in occult anatomy. The activity of the human brain, which we have already seen to be filled and surrounded by a subtle humidity, causes an akasic precipitation, a brain "dew," which is more of a luminous ether than a liquid. This "dew," however, is more tangible than a gas, and as the manna is said to have fallen from heaven, so this "dew" of thought trickles down between the two hemispheres of the cerebrum and finally fills the third ventricle, which is the reservoir, so to speak, of this heavenly water. This "dew" carries in suspension, or as the alchemists might say, is "tinctured" by the mental activity of the seven brain stars which form the northern constellation of man.

It is this water which is contained within the celestial microcosmic "Dipper," which is called by the Hindus the constellation of the Seven Rishis of the Pole.

We have another clue in the practice of primitive peoples of anointing the head with oil and fat and allowing it to run down over the body. Sir E. A. Wallis-Budge, in his OSIRIS AND THE EGYPTIAN RESURRECTION, describes how certain natives tie to their heads lumps of fat or substances saturated with oil or filled with grease, "which melted down through the hair of his head and ran down over his hair or wig, and penetrated to his shoulders and body." Having reached the third ventricle and being caught therein, the "dew" must act in conformity with the symbolism involved. It must be *caught* by the wise man in the cup of the Mysteries. We must, therefore, search for the sacred vessel, the lachrimatory, which is to hold the tears of the brain, produced as is told in the MAHABHARATA by the churning of the Suras and Asuras. The search is not an extended one. We have already learned that among the symbolic names for the pituitary body is the Holy Grail. Thus, the brain "dew" is collected, for it flows or seeps from the third ventricle into the pituitary body through a tiny tube, the infundibulum. In his description of the posterior lobe of this gland, Gray writes that it "is developed by an outgrowth from the embryonic brain and during foetal life contains a cavity which communicates through the infundibulum with the cavity of the third ventricle." It is believed that this channel is closed in the adult, but occultism knows this to be erroneous. After this point, the distribution of the "dew" through the body is made possible by the fact that the pituitary gland is, so to speak, the key of the bodily harmony. Of the secretions of the pituitary body, Dr. Herman H. Rubin writes: "From the anterior portion of the gland a secretion passes directly into the blood stream—from the posterior a fluid called pituitrin joins the spinal fluid that bathes the nervous system. Pituitrin is a *complex and most marvellous substance.*" (Italics mine, M.P.H.) Thus it seems that through the brain "dew" the Governors of the body convey their will and purpose to the several departments thereof. There can be no direct connection between spirit and matter. The former must work upon the latter through an intermediary, a fact well established through the philosophy of Emanationism. Water—either the physical fluid or its occult analogue, ether—must always be the medium through which the impulses of the superphysical life centers communicate with the lower personality and distribute their energies throughout the corporeal body. Paracelsus thus sums up the mystery: "The whole of the Microcosm is potentially contained in the *Liquor Vitae,* a nerve fluid—in which is contained the nature, quality, character and essence of beings."

PVLSVS.

Seu

NOVA ET ARCANA

PVLSVVM
HISTORIA, E SACRO
FONTE RADICALITER
EXTRACTA, NEC NON MEDI-
CORVM ETHNICORVM DICTIS

& authoritate comprobata.

Hoc Est,

PORTIONIS TERTIÆ PARS TERTIA,

DE PVLSVVM SCIENTIA

Authore ROBERTO FLVD

Armigero , & in Medicina Doctore Oxoniensi

TITLE PAGE TO FLUDD'S TREATISE ON THE PULSE

CHAPTER XI

THE HEART, THE SEAT OF LIFE

HE HEART is described anatomically as a hollow muscular organ of *conical* form, about five inches in length, three and one-half inches in breadth, and two and one-half inches in thickness. It varies somewhat in weight, being from 10 to 12 ounces in the male and from 8 to 10 ounces in the female. The organ is placed obliquely in the chest, with its apex directed forward, downward and to the left, and is divided by a longitudinal muscular septum and a transverse constriction into four cavities, of which the two upper are called auricles (early authorities refer to them as ears) and the two lower ventricles. The heart may be considered as a double organ, of which the right side is devoted to the circulation of the blood through the lungs and the left side to its distribution by the aorta and its subdivisions throughout the entire body. Of the pulse point in the heart, Dr. Charles W. Chapman writes in THE HEART AND ITS DISEASES: "The *sino-auricular node* is a small mass of specialized tissue, situated at the junction of the superior vena cava with the right auricle, and immediately below the endocardium. This node is the seat of the origin of the heart beat and has been called the pacemaker. It is considered that it receives fibres from the vagus and sympathetic nerves."

To briefly summarize the arterial circulation, the dark venous blood, returning through the veins, enters the right auricle of the heart by the superior and inferior *vena cava* and the coronary sinus. From the right auricle the blood passes into the right ventricle and thence through the pulmonary artery to the lungs. It then returns to the left side of the heart through the pulmonary veins, entering by way of the left auricle. From the left auricle it passes to the left ventricle, to flow out to every extremity of the body through the aorta and its innumerable branches. Paracelsus comments on the occult significance of this circulation of the blood. "The human blood contains an airy, fiery spirit, and this spirit has its center in the heart, where it is most condensed and from which it radiates, and the radiating rays return to the heart." Paracelsus then establishes the universal correspondence. "Thus the world has its fiery spirit pervading the atmosphere, and its center is called the sun, and the influences radiating from the sun return to that center."

Macrobius tells us that in its original state the soul is spherical, by which he signifies not only its form but that it partakes in every respect of the attributes of the Ptolemaic, or universal, sphere, consisting of the zodiac and the seven planetary and five elemental planes. He further writes that in its progress downward into generation the soul becomes "elongated" gradually to assume the appearance of a cone. According to G. R. S. Mead, in his commentaries on the Hermetic fragments, a pine cone rather than a geometrical cone is to be inferred. If this be true and there be within man "an organ patterned after the world soul," as affirmed by the Gnostics, may not this description indicate the heart, which is referred to by Gray, in his ANATOMY, DESCRIPTIVE AND SURGICAL, as of "conical form," and by Morris, in his HUMAN ANATOMY, as a "fairly regular truncated cone."

After examining the Scriptures and discovering such quotations as were relevant to the mystery, Tertullian affirms the presence in the soul of a directing faculty; in other words, "a supreme principle of intelligence and vitality (for where there is intelligence there must be vitality), and that it resides in that most precious part of our body, to which God especially looks." The great Ante-Nicean Father then concludes: "You must not suppose with Heraclitus that this sovereign faculty of which we are treating is moved by some external force; nor with Marcion, that it floats about through the whole body; nor with Plato, that it is enclosed in the head; nor with Zenophanes, that it culminates in the crown of the head; nor that it reposes in the brain, according to the opinion of Hippocrates; nor around the basis of the brain, as Heraphilus thought; nor in the membranes thereof, as Strato and Erasistratus said; nor in the space between the eyebrows, as Strato, the physician, held; nor within the enclosure of the breast, according to Epicurus; but rather as the Egyptians have always taught, especially such of them as were accounted the expounders of sacred truths; in accordance, too, with that verse of Orpheus and Empedocles: *Namque homini sanguis circumcordialis est sensus,* (Man has his (supreme) sensation in the blood around the heart)." St. Chrysostom adds his testimony by definitely stating that "the heart has preeminence over all the members of our body, and that the supreme power over our whole life is entrusted to it."

In the philosophical systems of the ancient Chinese the five elements of which the bodily structure is composed are symbolized as five kings, or souls, each of which is seated in one of the five major organs of the body. Of these kings that which is established in the heart is the chief of all. (See CHINESE GHOULS AND GOBLINS, by J. Willoughby-Meade.) Pliny informs us that the Egyptians regarded the heart as the "great vital principle," and Diodorus is authority for the significant statement that in the process of embalming their dead the Egyptians did not remove the heart with other viscera. The brain, however, they ingeniously removed through the nostrils. (See Wilkinson's MANNERS AND CUSTOMS OF THE ANCIENT EGYPTIANS.) In the Tantric writings of the Hindus, the heart is referred to as "a small lotus of eight petals," the seat of Brahma, or the center of spiritual consciousness in man. On this subject, the KHANDOGYA-UPANISHAD is most informative. "There is this city of Brahman (the body) and in it the palace, the small lotus (of the heart) and in it that small ether. Now what exists within that small ether, that is to be sought for, that is to be understood. . . . 'As large as this ether (of space) is, so large is that ether within the heart. Both heaven and earth are contained within it, both fire and air, both sun and moon, both lightning and stars, and whatever there is of Him (the Self) here in the world and whatever is not (i. e. whatever has been or will be), all that is contained within it.'" The UPANI-SHAD then continues by explaining that though the body ages, the Brahman, or ether, within it does not age, and that by the death of the body this ether is not spilled. It is this ether, or Brahman, that is the true Self, free from ignorance and change and partaking of the qualities of Reality.

In his commentary on the KATHA-UPANISHAD, the great Vedantist adept, Sankaracharya, observes that the Atman, the Lord of the past and of the future, should be meditated upon "as a light of the size of the thumb in the cavity of the heart." Paracelsus, the Trismegistus of Switzerland, describes the "Dweller in the heart," as a bluish, flamelike body, "equal in size to the last joint of a man's thumb." While in Constantinople, Paracelsus had been instructed in this mystery by the Arabians, who had performed vivisection and who had recorded in their scientific books that "if a certain point in the heart of a living animal be touched with the finger, the heat is so great that a blister will result." The early files of THE PLATONIST magazine contain several refer-ences to these Arabian experiments. Jacob Boehme, the illumined shoemaker, called by H. P. Blavatsky "the nursling of the angels," though unschooled in the sciences of the ancients, was led by inspiration to the realization of the supremacy of the heart among the organs; for in one place he writes that "the spirit moveth upon the heart in the bosom of the heart." Again, com-menting upon the seat of the spirit, he adds: "The heart is its original; it is the inward fire of the heart, in the inward blood of the heart."

The "Deity who is manifesting himself in the activities of the universe always dwells in the heart of man as the supreme soul," says an ancient UPANISHAD quoted by Rhabindranath Tagore in SADHANA. Boehme represents this mystery by a figure which appears in an early German edition of his LIBRI APOLOGETICI, wherein is depicted a heart containing the *Tetragrammaton*, or four-lettered Cabalistic name of God, arranged in the form of the Pytha-gorean *tetractys*. Thus the ten beatific powers or principles—the outer decad of the internal man which, according to occult philosophy, have their rooms within the heart and its aura—are revealed through an appropriate symbol. The writings of the great Jesuit Father, Loyola, are also illustrated with most significant figures relating to the heart mystery. The most important inter-preters of Jacob Boehme were Johann Gichtel and William Law, who attempted to illustrate the obscure doctrines of the Seidenburg seer by strange diagrams, which for lack of explanation are, for the most part, more perplexing than the original text. Both these commentators show the heart as the center of the microcosm and draw upon and trace over it a blazing sun. The 1764 English edition of Boehme's writings contains the manikin plates erroneously ascribed to William Law. The first of these, designated Table I, is of special significance. A dotted line, called "the thread of life," has its origin in the sign of Aries upon the outermost layer of the figure, and as the parts of the manikin are lifted up, the thread winds through the bodies of the seven planets (which the author calls "veils" or "coverings") and enters the human heart through a sunburst. The most significant part follows. The line continues on within the heart through four other "veils," which are designated fire, tincture, majesty, and the ternary, to end finally in the fifth unnumbered element, where the line has its finish in the sperm-shaped whorl containing the four Hebrew letters of the Sacred Name, IHVH (Jehovah). This order is perfectly harmonious with the speculations of the later Cabalists, who designated the Sephira Tiphereth (the sun) as the heart of the Sephirothic Adam— the Lesser Countenance of THE ZOHAR. Burton defines the heart as "the seat and fountain of life, of heat, of spirits, of pulse, and respiration; the Sun of our Body, the King and sole commander of it: the seat and Organ of all passions and affections."

In an extremely rare work, GEHEIME FIGUREN DER ROSENKREUZER, appears the symbolical heart set forth herewith. In the center is the blazing sun, the Vedantic Atman, and to the alchemist the philosophic "sabbath," or sphere of rest surrounded by the circles of the elements numbered from 1 to 5, the fifth being the ether, or akasa, the fifth essence (or quintessence) containing the divine punctum, the point or vortex of God. This heart splendidly reveals the previously considered symbolism of Boehme, the five divisions of the elements being in accord with the Brahman tradition of the five heads of Brahma, the fifth and highest of which is invisible. In this Rosicrucian figure even the zodiac is included, from which we must infer that all the parts and members of the outer man—the corporeal Adam, or the curious figure shown in the almanac—are situated in the heart and derive their existence from "Him who dwells therein." Well does Paracelsus maintain that the "heart is the seed of the microcosm." The body is in the heart as the oak is in the acorn. The heart is the sacred island, the first of the seven continents, and within it dwell the "children of the fire mist," whose reflections are later to be set up in the organs and functions of the outer body.

Before his symbolic "fall" downward (or, more correctly, outward) into the objective, or bodily, state, according to the old Rabbinical traditions, man dwelt in an Edenic, or internal, world; his state and nature being that of the third, or Yetziratic, Adam of THE ZOHAR—the one whose reflection became the external man. While he abode in this interior sphere man possessed an Edenic, or ethereal body, androgynous and incorruptible. From the old Hebrew legends the Neo-Hermetists evolved a curious symbolism, for all its strangeness quaintly appropriate. To them the heart was analogous to the interior body, while the organs and members surrounding the heart were viewed as the exterior body. Thus, the heart became the Garden of Eden— a place of beauty and felicity. The small area within it, now called the pulse point, was recognized as the little interior Paradise, which mediæval theologians located in the "eastern part" of Eden. The anatomical analogies are evident. The Garden of the Lord was located upon a mountain, which corresponds to the diaphragm and is in the midst of the body. Within it are the springs which, becoming rivers (the arteries), pour forth the living waters (the blood) for the preservation of the land (the whole physical body). Unredeemed mortals can no longer converse with the Lord who walks in the Garden or whose light shines in the dark recesses of the heart. Man has been banished from the sphere of his subjective existence and must reattain it by those

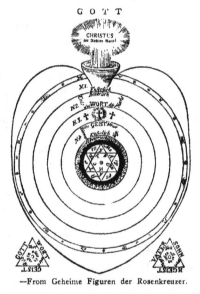

—From Geheime Figuren der Rosenkreuzer.

THE UNIVERSE WITHIN THE HUMAN HEART

mysteries of the spirit inferred by the thought that he who would discover God must enter into the dark closet and worship Him in secret.

When the UPANISHAD says that heaven and earth are contained within the ether of the heart, it but confirms these words of the mediæval adept who concealed his identity under the pseudonym of Benedictus Figulus: "In the heart of man is the true Iliastic Necrocosmic heaven. Yes, the heart of man itself is the true heaven of immortal being, out of which the soul has never yet come." When we learn from another philosopher of the Middle Ages that the higher aspect of the human soul did not actually descend into matter at the time of the Fall but remains in Paradise awaiting the redemption of the body from mortal sin, it becomes evident from their symbols and formulæ that the Hermetists and the Rosicrucians must have been aware of the fact that the "kingdom of heaven within" referred to the heart mystery. "Astronomy (a term used to signify the study of the astral world rather than the stars) is the upper part of philosophy," writes Paracelsus, "by which the soul of the microcosm may become known. Philosophy deals with the elements of earth and water, belonging to man's constitution. Astronomy deals with his air and fire. There is a heaven and earth in man as there is in the microcosm, and in that heaven there are all the celestial influences, whose visible representations we see in the sky, such as the planets and stars, the Milky Way, the zodiac, and so forth, nor more or less; for the microcosm is an exact counterpart of the macrocosm in every respect except its external form." This does not mean that the occultist claims that the physical heart as an organ by its dissection would reveal the presence of internal stars or planets, but rather that the heart is but the outer vestment of a spiritual organ in which all these statements are mystically true.

Man is the living temple of God and the heart is the Holy of Holies of that temple. It is not only the palace of the microcosmic king but also the Mystery Temple. It is the inner room, the sanctuary, the adytum, the very oracular vent in which moves the Deity. In the ancient temples of initiation there were rooms which were regarded as the very abode of the divinities and none could enter without periods of special purification and prayer. In a few cases it was believed that the god who dwelt in such a chamber was a corporeal being, but more often he was invisible, abiding in the air or ether and only manifesting himself through the hierophant of his order. Von Hammer describes certain Baphometic idols, with triple faces and their bodies covered with eyes, ears, and planetary symbols. The figures are girded with serpents and stand in deformed and distorted attitudes. Von Hammer identifies them with the "Old Man" supposedly worshipped by the Knights Templars. The adytum of the Samothracian temple is reported to have contained the aged Cabirian dwarf, who on one occasion was seen seated upon the altar as a dimly perceptible astral shape surrounded by a flame of electric blue. Are not these but figures of the little "man in the heart" who was no larger than the "thumb"? The temple was the symbol of a spiritual universe in the midst of a material one. It was the heart of the cultural life of the community, supporting the well-being of man as the heart supports the physical body. We should not, therefore, be amazed to discover the heart to be the original temple from which religious edifices of the world have been patterned. In his discourse to his son Tatian, Hermes refers to Deity as having "formed the heart like a pyramid." The significance of this statement cannot be overestimated; it is the clue to the mystery of the "House of the Hidden Places," somewhere in the chambers of which dwelt the mysterious hierophant "robed in blue and gold," whom "no man hath ever seen," but who is referred to as "the Master of the Hidden House."

H. P. Blavatsky writes that "occultists know every minute portion of the heart and have a name for each. They call them by the names of the gods, as Brahma's hall, Vishnu's hall, and so forth. They correspond to the parts of the brain." In THE BOOK OF THE MASTER, by W. Marsham Adams, is found a curious confirmation and amplification of this statement. In describing a temple of the Egyptian goddess Hathor, he notes: "The 'Hall of the Golden Rays' was the title of one of the great halls. The Chamber of Gold, the Chamber of Frankincense, the Chamber of Birth, the Place of the Altar, the Dwelling of the Golden One, the Chamber of Flames, and the Throne Room of Ra, are among the hieroglyphic titles attached to the various portions of the temple." Do not these names rather suggest occult anatomy? Is not the "Hall of Golden Rays" the spinal canal and are not the seven chambers (which the Tantric philosophers would call the "chakras") identical with the seven compartments of the saptaparna, the cave where the Arhats of Buddha received their initiation? The eminent Oriental scholar, T. Subba Row, declares that the five chambers of construction above the King's Chamber in the Great Pyramid are symbolic of the five Dhyana Buddhas of the Mahayana Buddhistic system. If the Pyramid be a temple of the Heart Mystery, which is certainly indicated both by its form and position, then the Dhyana Buddhas have their microcosmic thrones in the aura of the heart.

Commenting on the FIRST ALCIBIADES of Plato, Proclus asserts that the soul, in her search for wisdom, "proceeds into her interior recesses, and into the adytum, as it were, of the soul (where) she perceives . . . the genus of the gods and the unities of things." This statement is in harmony with the ambiguous method of Greek writers who were so bound by their obligations to the Mystery Schools that they could but hint at great spiritual truths. Enough is revealed, however, to show that the Greeks were aware that the heart was the source of life and that the several aspects of life—the centers of consciousness called the "gods"—could have no other dwelling than the heart. The Greeks drank deeply at the fountain of Egyptian learning and we must remember that in the papyri of the Egyptians the heart was always figured as the urn of the spirit, and it was from this urn that the spirit spoke in the ceremony of the psychostasia, or the weighing of the conscience. Something like this symbol is also met with among the traditions of Islam, for certain Dervishes wear kulahs, or caps, which are vase-shaped to symbolize the vessel of golden light in which God kept the soul of Mohammed. It will also be remembered that God purified Mohammed in his childhood by sending the angel Gabriel, who took Mohammed's heart out of his body, cleansed it of the black sin of Adam, and then restored it to him. If the Caaba be the heart of Islam, is not the black stone set in its wall of identical meaning with the drop of black sin within the heart of every unredeemed mortal?

The heart is not only the temple of God in the microcosm; it is also the Holy City, the Jerusalem of the Jews and Christians, the Mecca of Islam, and the Benares of the pious Hindus. Among the organs of the body the heart is the chief and king, and of the divinities in man, the highest is enthroned therein. For that reason, Sankaracharya, in his commentary on the Vedanta Sutras, calls him that abides in the heart "Lord of the city of Brahma." T. Subba Row, writing on the subject of pilgrimages to sacred places for the securing of *Moksha*, or liberation from ignorance, after correlating the seven holy cities (the seven churches of the Apocalypse) with the seven chakras, continues: "Benares corresponds with the heart in the human body, in the center of which the *Anahata* chakra is located. . . . The state of ecstasy is realized when consciousness is centered in the germ of *Pragna*, which is located in this chakra." Though the Tantric system differs somewhat from the above (see Sir John Woodroffe), the spirit of the Brahmanic symbolism is unchanged. THE ZOHAR is rich in thoughts on this subject. With the Cabalist, Jerusalem is not only called the Holy City, but it is also described "as the temple or tabernacle below," the "house in the center of all."

Recognizing the "king" mentioned in THE ZOHAR to be the Atman, or the spirit hidden in the very depths of the heart—that is to say, in its most subtle element—it becomes easy to interpret the words of THE ZOHAR: "Who enters to the king can enter only from the Holy City, from whence alone the Road lies to the king, from here the way is prepared." One cannot fail to be reminded of Mohammed's night journey to heaven described in the Apocrypha of Islam. The Prophet is first carried to Jerusalem (the heart) by Alborak. Standing upon Mount Moriah (the most sacred point in the heart), Mohammed beholds a ladder falling from heaven, up which he climbs into the indescribable glory of the Eternal God. Like the vision of St. John on the Isle of Patmos, Mohammed's night journey to heaven signifies the symbolic death.

Turning again to our correspondences in Eastern occultism, when the time of death arrives, the spirit withdraws its radiations from the parts and extremities of the body to heart. "Whereupon the point of the heart becomes luminous; from this fact it has become luminous, the soul departs." We learn furthermore from the sixth Khanda of the KHANDOGYA-UPANISHAD that "there are a hundred and one arteries of the heart; one of them penetrates the crown of the head; moving upward by it a man reaches the immortal; the others serve for departing in different directions, yea, in different directions." Thus the 101st artery goes directly to that point in the head where the door of Brahma is located. The souls of ordinary men depart through the one hundred Nadis (arteries), but the soul of the adept alone departs through the higher one. Our text, therefore, tells us that while the external perceptions of the adept are failing, "he is going to the sun, for the sun is the door of the world." By the "sun" should be understood in this case *Brahma-randhra*, which is indeed the little door in the wall of heaven.

One other correspondence is of interest. Valentinus, the Gnostic, writing of the heart, says that it "seems to receive somewhat the same treatment as an

—From Collectio Operum.

ROBERT FLUDD, PHYSICIAN AND PHILOSOPHER

inn (or caravansery) which has holes and gaps made in its walls, and is frequently filled with dung, men living filthily in it and taking no care of the place as being someone else's property. Thus, it is that the heart so long as it has no care taken of it, is ever unclean and the abode of dæmons. . . . But when the Alone Good Father hath regard unto it, it is sanctified and shineth with light; and he who possesses such a heart is so blessed that 'he shall see God.' " Here Valentinus re-emphasizes the earlier statement of Proclus of the spirits, or dæmons, in the heart; for as all five of the worlds exist within this organ, so the creators of these worlds also reside therein, the heart being moved by either divine or infernal spirits according to the soul development of the individual.

"Even if the head be severed from the body," writes H. P. Blavatsky, "the heart will continue to beat for thirty minutes. It will beat for some hours if wrapped in cotton wool and put in a warm place. The spot in the heart which is the last of all to die is the seat of life, the center of all, Brahma, the first spot that lives in the fœtus, and the last that dies. This spot contains potential mind, life, energy, and will. During life it radiates prismatic colors, fiery and opalescent." The aura of the heart (or, more correctly, of the flame which is in the heart) consists of a complete spectrum, revealing that all the seven principles which conspire to precipitate the objective man have their thrones, or monadic existence, in the greater monad of this aura, itself a miniature and reflection of that greater aura which surrounds the entire body and which is man's undifferentiated spiritual existence. According to the Instruction, there are seven brains in the heart and also seven hearts in the brain. The seven heart brains are the intelligences of the vital organs, for the "Seven Spirits before the throne" of the Atman do not actually leave the "face" of their Lord but it is rather their reflections that go forth, as in the case of the Planetary Lords of the solar system. The Seven Logoi are all in the sun and to understand how their reflections precipitate the worlds one should study the Cabala, wherein is described how the Sephiroth—or the ten qualities of God—are reflected downward through all the departments of being to establish orders of life in each department. It is explicitly stated in THE ZOHAR that the principles do not themselves descend, only their shadows being cast upon the inferior substances.

Descartes likened the heart to a hollow cavern. In fact, he attempted to explain the "motion" of the blood by declaring that at the bottom of the organ was a "hot stone," and the blood coming in contact therewith, was transformed into a smoke or steam, which by virtue of its volatile nature insinuated itself into the smallest branches of the arterial system. Reaching the extremities of the body, this gas or steam lost its heat and was condensed again to flow back through the veins to the heart. Descartes had imbibed the wisdom of Galen and the Arabs, but was not able to completely understand

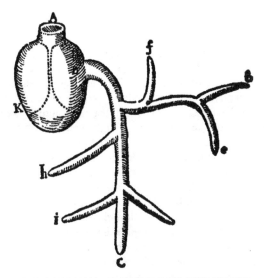

A DIAGRAMMATIC FIGURE OF THE HEART

the mystery of the "hot stone" in the heart. His fault lay in his effort to apply literally that which was intended to convey a metaphysical reality. Sir Kenelm Digby, a pioneer thinker in scientific matters, in his treatise ON THE BODY AND SOUL, comments upon the theories of Descartes and Harvey. After affirming the heart to be the "first part generated in the human being" and that the "most virtuous parts" thereof serve "as a shop or hot forge to mold spirits in," the learned Knight goes on to describe some experiments made by him with the heart of a snake. He chose a viper for the experiment, noting that not only will the heart of this reptile, if kept in a warm, moist place, beat for 24 hours after it has been removed from the body, but if after it has ceased motion it be carefully moistened with tepid water, the action will commence again. Also according to his experiments, if the heart be cut into several pieces, the separate parts will continue to exhibit life for a considerable period. *"Primum vivens, ultimum moriens,* it lives first, and dies last in all creatures," writes Burton. If, however, any spirituous substance, such as wine, was brought in contact with the heart of the viper or the parts thereof, it immediately ceased to beat. One cannot but be reminded at this point of the statement of Heraclitus to the effect that souls are bound to bodies by moisture and that any structure possessing a humid vehicle may through this moisture bind a soul or energy to itself. Having refuted the errors of all his predecessors, Sir Digby then advances the strange theory of his own, namely, that the action of the heart is caused by gravity, derived, in turn, from the gravity of the earth, closing his speculations

thereon by referring to the heart as a "furnace" or "cauldron" in which the
blood is "boiled" and "spiritualized."

Mohammed received his first enlightenment in the cave on Mount Hira.
It has already been noted that the word cave has occasionally been used to
signify the heart. The most secret rituals of ancient initiation were performed
in subterranean crypts, which were called "caverns of the Mysteries." In the
Gothic rites, the final ceremony in which the new initiate was invested with
the insignia of his order took place in a high, vaulted, cavernous chamber in
the presence of the luminous statue of Balder the Beautiful—the Nordic
Christ. In the midst of this vaulted compartment grew a tree of gold which
bore jewels for blossoms and fruit. This is the tree of the Seven Logoi, the
roots of which are in Eternity and the branches in Time. This golden tree
was the seven-branched candlestick of the Tabernacle Mysteries of the Israel-
ites. Josephus tells us that this candlestick represented the planets, so it is
taking no liberty with tradition to interpret the lamps burning on the candlestick
as typifying the Seven Glorious Ones who are the light of the world (microcosm). Here also are the Seven Sleepers of Ephesus and the cave-dwelling
Rishis of India—the seven original beings who in the mythology of Central
America were the cave-born progenitors of the races.

In one of the Hermetic fragments, Hermes says that the Father sowed
lives into the sphere of the world and "shut them up as in a cave." In his
essay ON THE CAVE OF THE NYMPHS, Porphyry quotes Eubulus as authority
that "Zoroaster was the first who consecrated, in the neighboring mountains of
Persia, a spontaneously produced cave, florid and having fountains," and in a
later place is described as having the zodiacal symbols about its walls. Here
again is the Rosicrucian heart previously mentioned, with the signs of the
zodiac about its dark wall. When the elements and climates are intimated, the
Greek description corresponds exactly with the veils and elemental compartments set forth by Boehme. "Let, therefore," concludes Porphyry, "this
present cavern be consecrated to souls, and among the more partial powers, to
nymphs (souls in generation), that preside over streams and fountains."

In ANACALYPSIS, Godfrey Higgins inquires into the mystery of the Mercavah, which is interpreted by Maimonides as the chariot of Ezekiel. The
Cabalists were most reticent in discussing the mystery of the Mercavah,
declaring that only to those who had found God in their "hearts" was it
permissible even to read aloud the names of the chapters concerned with the
subject. Higgins ventured in where angels fear to tread. By analyzing the
word, he discovered that it can be interpreted as a cave or circular vault sacred
to Om. We believe the Heart Mystery to be definitely indicated by the entire
vision of the Mercavah. In every way this would be consistent with the
Rabbinical symbolism, for the heavenly throne is often described as "being in
the midst of the world," and the radiant figure in the Mercavah is the Lord of

the World enthroned in the midst of the four elements and above them. In at least one of its interpretations, the Mercavah is the lower quaternary in man—the vehicle of the soul—even as in the alchemical symbolism the four elements are the *vahan,* or carrier, of the fifth (ether).

"The principal part in the human body, namely, the heart," writes Moses Maimonides in his GUIDE FOR THE PERPLEXED, "is in constant motion, and is the source of every motion noticed in the body; it rules over the other members, and communicates to them through its own pulsations the force required for their functions. The outermost sphere [Primum Mobile] by its motion rules in a similar way over all other parts of the universe, and supplies all things with their special properties. Every motion in the universe has thus its origin in the motion of that sphere; and the soul of every animate being derives its origin from the soul of that same sphere." The heart is an epitome of the whole body. It, therefore, consists of an inner, middle, and outer part corresponding to the three great cavities of the body—cerebral, thoracic, and abdominal—as well as to the three main divisions into mind, spirit, and body. In the heart, says the Secret Work, is the only manifested God. The two higher aspects of Divinity—Atman (consciousness) and Buddhi (intelligence) —are utterly invisible and beyond the limitations of generation. "The 'First Born'," says THE SECRET DOCTRINE, "are the LIFE, the heart and pulse." To some degree, therefore, the "being in the heart" is Shiva, the third and lowest aspect of Brahma—force, or mind. Shiva is the Lord of the pulse, the only direct manifestation of spirit in matter. The pulse has often been referred to as the heavenly breath and certain esoteric systems of time calculation are based upon the duration of the pulse beat. It is the rhythm of the Infinite. The pulse point also has been properly termed the drum of Shiva—the drum that beats the doom of every man. It is of this mystery that Sankaracharya writes when he says: "Unless Shiva be united to Shakti, he cannot produce even the flutter of well-being." In Israel's Holy of Holies could be heard the soft flutter of angels' wings, the whisper and the rustling of the curtains, and in the midst the flame of the Covenant—God in His world. The heart, then, is not only the seat of the emotions so-called, but also high Olympus, for it is said that the mountain of the gods rises above the four elements until its peak is in ether. And there in the utter tranquillity of the fifth element the gods reside. This ether is not the ether of science but that "small ether" wherein is concealed a spirit so vast that the universe can scarcely contain it.

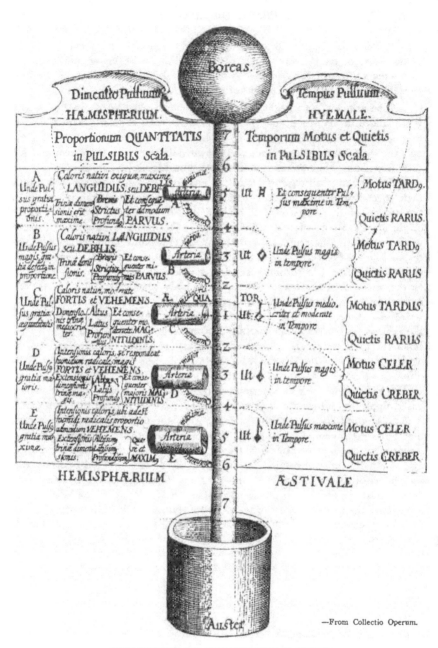

THE SYSTEM OF THE UNIVERSAL PULSE

—From Collectio Operum.

CHAPTER XII

THE BLOOD, THE UNIVERSAL PROTEUS

HE HUMAN blood is a thickish, opaque fluid, bright red or scarlet when it flows from the arteries and dark red or purple when it flows from the veins. When examined under the microscope, it is seen to consist of many minute bodies, or corpuscles, floating in a clear liquid. These corpuscles are of two kinds—colored and colorless—and the liquid in which they are held in suspension is called the *liquor sanguinis*. According to Klein, there is a large preponderance of red corpuscles. They may even run 1,200 to 1. The red, or colored, corpuscles when examined under the microscope, are circular discs, each with a slight central depression. Their size varies, but their average diameter is 1/3200 of an inch. The white corpuscles are rather larger than the red, being approximately 1/2000 of an inch in diameter. When entirely without motion, they are spheroidal, but in locomotion push out pseudopodia. The white corpuscles are a type of true animal cell. They have no limiting membrane, but consist of a mass of transparent albuminous substance called protoplasm containing one or more nuclei. "When blood is exposed to the vacuum of the air pump, about half its volume is given off in the form of gases"—carbonic acid, nitrogen, and oxygen. (See Gray's ANATOMY.)

In addition to meaning "blood," the Latin *sanguis* also implies family, race, descent, stock, and relation. *Sanguis Bacchius*, "the blood of Bacchus," also signifies wine. Here, then, we might say is the origin of the Eucharist—pagan and Christian. Higgins was persuaded that the *Eucharistia*—the sacrifice of bread and wine—was the most universal of all ancient religious rites. By breaking up the word *Eucharistia* into *EuCaRiSTia*, he derives therefrom the definition, "the good deity Ceres." Higgins then explains that the cluster of grapes was the emblem of wisdom or knowledge—"the fruit of the tree of knowledge, of the elm, the first letter of the alphabet, which bore on its trunk all the tree of letters, of the Vedas, in which were concealed all sacred knowledge." This, then, is the origin of the body and blood ceremony, the Communion of the Gnostics and of the primitive Church. "And, in allusion to this, Jesus is made to say 'I will drink no more of the fruit of the vine until that day that I drink it new in the kingdom of God,' that is, I shall no more give you lessons, or join you in the search of wisdom; no more initiate you into the divine mysteries . . . till we meet in a future life, in my Father's kingdom; till we are all reunited to our eternal Father, absorbed into the *To On*." (See ANACALYPSIS.) The analogy can be carried still further, for Jesus who called himself "the vine" and referred to the cup of the Last Supper as containing

His blood, was born in Bethlehem, from *Beth-Lamed,* "the house of bread." Bread was the support of the inferior, or material, man. In this symbolism the bread supports the physical and wine the spiritual body—bread and wine, body and soul.

The priests of the sun at Heliopolis, according to Plutarch, carried no wine into their temples, regarding it as indecent for those who are devoted to the service of the divinities to indulge in intoxicants while under the immediate inspection of their lord. Even the kings, being themselves of the priestcraft, writes Hecatæus, had their wine administered to them in amounts prescribed by the sacred books and only that in late times. In the earlier periods of the Empire, they drank no wine at all, but occasionally used it as a libation to the gods by pouring it over their altars to signify the blood of those enemies who formerly fought against them. "For they look upon the vine to have first sprung out of the earth, after it was fattened with the carcasses of those who fell in the wars against the Gods. And this, say they, is the reason why drinking its juice in great quantities makes men mad and beside themselves, filling them as it were with the blood of their own ancestors. These things are thus related by Eudoxus in the second book of his *Geographical History,* as he had them from the priests themselves." (See ISIS AND OSIRIS.)

In referring to the knowledge possessed by the Gnostics regarding the circulation of the blood, G. R. S. Mead writes: "In the human body are *at least* two 'Trees,' the nervous and vascular systems. The former has its roots above in the cerebrum, the latter has its roots in the heart. Among the trunks and branches run currents of 'nervous ether' and 'life' respectively." (See SIMON MAGUS.) Again H. P. Blavatsky says: "Speaking of the Mystic Trees, the Gokard, the source of all medicines, is said to grow out of the earth, whereas the White Haoma, 'which will furnish man with immortality at the time of the resurrection, is spoken of as being in the Ocean, or the sea with the wide shores,' esoterically Space. And, we might add, that the one grows with its roots in the earth, the other with its roots in heaven, twin-trees, one the reflection of the other, and both within every man. From all of which we may perceive that perhaps the superstition is not so absurd, for 'the water or sap in the plants circulates like the waters of the earth, or like the blessings which the righteous utter, which come back to themselves,' and as 'blood' is under the same law, therefore it follows that the Mazdean Initiates knew both of the 'circulation of the blood' and, more important still, of the cyclic and Karmic law." (See LUCIFER.)

For some time mystics have affirmed that blood was a vapor rather than a fluid. Science does not fully sustain this opinion, which may be traced to van Helmont, who declares without qualification that "the arterial spirit of our life is of the nature of a gas." He further describes this arterial spirit as a vital air and a sharp saltish vapor which has its origin in the arterial blood. Lord

Bulwer-Lytton makes his character, Margrave, to say: "The mediæval empirics were great discoverers." (See A STRANGE STORY.) There may be more to all this than at first appears. "In the blood is the life" pronounced the ancient prophets, and this "most peculiar essence" (Goethe) is in truth the mirror of the microcosm, to borrow a phrase from van Helmont. The vital principle of which the blood is the precipitation or embodiment is not to be understood as the soul in its rational aspect but rather only in its animating sense.

"Spirit is a most subtle vapor," says Burton, "which is expressed from the blood, and the instrument of the soul, to perform all his actions; a common tie or medium betwixt the body and the soul, as some will have it; or as Paracelsus, a fourth soul of itself. Melanchthon holds the fountain of these spirits to be the heart, begotten there; and afterward conveyed to the brain, they take another nature to them. Of these spirits there be three kinds, according to the three principal parts: Brain, heart, liver; natural, vital, animal. The natural are begotten in the liver, and thence dispersed through the veins, to perform those natural actions. The vital spirits are made in the heart of the natural, which by the arteries are transported to all the other parts. If these spirits cease, then life ceaseth, as in a syncope or swooning. The animal spirits formed of the vital, brought up to the brain, and diffused by the nerves, to the subordinate members, give sense and motion to them all." (See ANATOMY OF MELANCHOLY.)

Let us pause for a moment over the word *nephesh*, a term loosely used in the Bible, usually to signify the breath of life but much more completely defined in the literature of the Cabalists. From THE ZOHAR we learn that man as a composite soul derives his qualities from the four worlds. From the highest sphere (Atziluth) he derives his spiritual principle, from the second sphere (Briah) his reasoning part, from the third sphere (Yetzirah) his emotions, and from the fourth and lowest sphere (Assiah) the nephesh—the substance of his physical existence. Nephesh—the breath and also the pulse—dwells in a vital medium described as a smoky vapor abiding in the cavity of the heart and is dispersed from thence throughout the whole body. "And since this vital medium is the habitation for nephesh, it is necessary for it to be very similar to that nephesh," that is, sufficiently like it in quality to be diffused through it. That the nephesh may be distributed to all the extremities of the body "it is needful that the vital medium be extended and drawn out to the likeness of the image of man." As the nephesh, or breath, is tenuous, its medium must also be tenuous. This tenuous medium is the blood "detained in the arteries of the heart, which are the vital arteries having a pulse." The arteries, therefore, are destined for the irrigation of this fleshly garden. The vital medium remains in man until death, but the nephesh, or breath, which it carries upon it, may escape in sleep and be borne away "to render an account in the presence of its Creator" (the ego). The vital medium (the blood) "preserves the human economy," and as the blood is the vehicle of the breath, so the breath is the vehicle of motion, motion of thought, and thought of the "Image" (the life). (See THE ZOHAR, *Tractatus de Anima.*) Cabalistically, then, the blood is an electric fluid carrying suspended within itself the breath, here used to signify a life-giving principle. The new theory that the heart is not actually the source of the physical circulation of the blood is susceptible of demonstration, for the blood has its life and motion from within itself—that is, from the nephesh, which is the breath of the Elohim.

The word *Lucifer* is compounded from the Latin words *Lux* and *ferre*, meaning "a bearer or carrier of light,' and is a Mystery name for the blood. Lucifer's flaming garments also derived their color from this mysterious fluid. Light here has the same meaning as nephesh, or the breath; that is, it is the radiant agent pulsating in waves of force through the arterial system. "Blood and Adam are synonymous," declares Gerald Massey, who thereupon enters into a detailed discussion of the subject. Among other things, he notes that the "blood soul" was one of the deepest mysteries of the Egyptians and that in Egypt the divine descent was through the blood mother. The seventh, or highest, soul was the blood soul. The secret is concealed under such figures as Adam, the man from the red dirt; Atum, the red creator; Isis, the red heifer; Horus, the red-complexioned calf; Neith, the vulture, the bird of blood; and the pelican nursing her seven young from the blood of her breast. (See ANCIENT EGYPT, THE LIGHT OF THE WORLD.) Blood is the most powerful of magical agents, for as Paracelsus writes, one is enabled with its fumes to call forth any spirit desired, for utilizing the emanations or effluvia of the blood the discarnate entity can build itself an appearance, a body visible if not real. He who possesses the blood controls the man. For this reason the necromancers signed their pacts with this divine fluid and employed it in the practice of their infernal rites. The mystery of the blood is sevenfold, for this subtle fluid consists of seven distinct agents, as yet known only partly to science, each of which is a powerful instrument of magic. "Homer makes Ulysses to envoke the ghosts of the departed by offering to them the life-blood of sacrificed animals. 'Then from the abyss, eager their thirst to slake, Came swarming up the spirits of the Dead.' (ODYSSEY). Connected with the same notion was the practice of strewing roses over the graves of departed friends, for as Servius explains it, the red color of the flower represented blood, and thereby served as a substitute for the living victim." (King.)

We have incorporated into the following description of the blood from Madam Blavatsky's papers certain commentary material derived from other sources. "The circulation of Life, Prana, through the body is by way of the blood. It is the vital principle in us; Pranic rather than Prana, and is closely allied to Kama, penetrated by Prana, which is Universal on this plane. [By Kama penetrated by Prana is signified desire permeated with vitality— that is, martial forces impregnated by the solar, or vital, agent.] When

Kama leaves the blood, it congeals, so that the blood may be regarded as Kama-Rupa, 'the form of Kama,' in a sense. [That is, the vehicle of desire, or the animal propensities. Kama-Rupa is the animal soul.] While Kama is the essence of the blood, its red corpuscles are drops of electrical fluid, the perspiration oozing out of every cell and the various organs, and caused to exude by electrical action. They are the progeny of the Fohatic Principle. [Fohat is force as the mediator between thought and motion. The term embraces the whole field of electrical phenomena and the nature of Fohat is revealed through electro-dynamics, especially the affinity which electricity exhibits for poles.] The Spleen does not manufacture the white corpuscles of the blood, for, as said, it is really the vehicle of the Ethereal Double. But these white corpuscles—which are the devourers, the scavengers of the body— are oozed out of the Linga-Sharira (Ethereal) and are of the same essence as itself. They come from the Spleen, not because the Spleen manufactures them, but because they are oozed out of the Etheric Double which lies curled up in the Spleen. They are the sweat-born of Chhaya [the astral image]. The blood thus serves as a physical vehicle for Kama, Prana, and the Linga-Sharira, and the student will understand why it plays so large a part in the animal economy. [The heat is derived from Kama, the volatile elements from the sun, and the congealing qualities from the Linga-Sharira—that is, the moon.] From the Spleen—enriched by the life elements from Prana, the corpuscles of the Linga-Sharira serving as the vehicle of these Pranic elements, the devourers, that build up and destroy the human body—it travels all over the body, distributing these Pranic carriers. The red corpuscles represent the Fohatic energy in the body, closely allied to Kama and Prana, while the very essence of the blood is Kama, present in every part of the body." [Kama is fire in its superphysical sense but still in its destructive aspect. Thus, the secret writings tell us that Kama must be killed out or else the body will be ultimately consumed thereby.]

To science, blood "is the fluid medium from which all the tissues of the body are nourished." (See Kirke's HANDBOOK OF PHYSIOLOGY.) Materialistic learning can go no farther than to recognize blood as life in a fluidic state. That it has functions other than nutritive, however, is more or less evident. In his "Theory of Descent," Haeckel concludes that in the process of grouping forms into categories the true relationships between the elements of these categories are relationships in blood rather than in form. In other words, when science attempts to diagram the streams or systems of life, the inevitable result is a treelike arrangement with numerous branches, and this tree is definitely and undeniably an arterial tree—that is, the tree serves as a symbol of the distribution of blood. This is perfectly in harmony with THE ZOHAR, which describes how the Macroprosophus (the Great Countenance) produced mankind in the form of a vine which spread its tendrils over the entire face of

Nature. In the CODEX NAZARAEUS, the Lord of Life, Javar Zivo, is denominated "the First Vine." It is from him that the seven vines, not only the races of the earth but also the species, had their origin. Gerald Massey took no liberty with fact when he declared Adam to be the blood man. He is more than that; he is the archetype of humanity actually flowing into humanity. From him was taken forth the "rib" (rebe, "the vine"), In other words, from Adam were separated the races. The man became mankind. Although division took place within Adam, we shall see that he was not divided but rather diffused through his progeny. So it may be said of Adam that as the father he lives in the sons. This is the key to ancestral worship, one of the earliest religions of mankind. The history of blood is the history of man. Blood is the vehicle of special and racial continuity. Evolution, from a phenomenal standpoint, is the "upward" and "forward" motion of blood through bodies. Blood consciousness is the philosophical premise underlying the scientific theory of natural salvation.

In ANCIENT EGYPT THE LIGHT OF THE WORLD are to be found several other references unsuspectingly relevant to our problem. We learn that, according to the old accounts, men were formed from the remains of a former race, these remains vivified by the blood of the gods. "When there were no human beings upon the earth certain of the lower powers solicited help from the supreme gods in the work of creation, or of a rebeginning. They were instructed to collect the remains of the former race and these will be vivified by the blood of the gods." The tradition then describes how the creator god, who corresponds to Atum, or Adam, produces a bone from a burial place and on this the gods drop the blood drawn from their own bodies. Here is a similar account to that of Zeus, who fashioned the race of men from the ashes of the Titans and the blood of Bacchus. The cult of the "saving blood" is old, indeed. Stripped of its veil of allegory, the Egyptian myth sets forth a primitive condition when the earth was "en-creatured" with bloodless beings. These were the "cold-blooded of the past" referred to in THE SECRET DOCTRINE —the original animals. "Kama-Rupa eventually breaks up and goes into animals. All red-blooded animals come from man. The cold-blooded are from the matter of the past." The burial place represents the closing period of the old order, the end of an ancient world. From this was taken the bone (the form), for the planets are the bones of the gods. The drops of blood are the Kama-Rupic lives, the principles of heat and desire which were set up in the cold animals. These were the seeds of blood; they prepared the way for consciousness; they were the vahans of the gods. All this is clearly revealed in the mysteries of embryology. With blood comes the animal soul and the first stirrings of selfhood. "The groundwork for the formation of the blood," writes Dr. Rudolph Steiner, "with all its attendant system of blood-vessels, appears very late in the development of the embroyo, and from this natural science has rightly concluded that the formation of blood occurred late in the evolution of the universe. . . . Not until the human embryo has repeated in itself all the earlier stages of human growth, thus attaining to the condition in which the world was before the formation of blood, is it ready to perform this crowning act of evolution—the transmuting and uplifting of all that had gone before into the 'very special fluid' which we call blood."

The consciousness of man was released through the blood—that is, the action of the blood resulted in certain modifications of the bodily fabric. These modifications were of the nature of refinements, affording greater opportunity for the expression of the subtle impulses from the soul. Consciousness moved from the simple to the complex, as demonstrated by Herbert Spencer. Man moved the focus of his awareness from heredity to environment—from inward to outward perception. His first blood consciousness was entirely subjective— that is, the blood lived in him. Gradually this has changed and now man lives in the blood. The first state would now be termed a subconscious existence, the second a conscious existence. The first mankind possessed a subconscious- ness in which was combined apects of both clairvoyance and mediumship. Nearly all aboriginal peoples, even though surviving at the present time, wor- ship elemental spirits and have consciousness in a borderland between the living and the dead. It has even been said of the Atlanteans that they were under the rulership of an invisible king called the Great Dragon. The sympathetic nervous system is far older than the cerebrospinal and was the organ of ancestral consciousness—that is, of the blood record. Long before the individ- ualization of man into his present state of intellectual isolation, there was a natural separation into tribes and races. These tribes and races were the vessels of a common consciousness; each had its own blood record and in that record it lived and moved and had its being.

It is difficult for man to properly estimate such a form of consciousness, yet it has descended to us under that sorely abused phrase, "the subconscious mind." Imagine the condition of being utterly incapable of dissociating your- self from your own ancestry—that is, having your father living in you and his father in him. Your memory would include a knowledge of all that had been achieved by your progenitors, and your own place would be simply that of an environmental opportunity for the fulfillment of racial impulse. You would be living continually in the dreams of the past and the dreams of the past would be working themselves out in you. Thus there would be no clear line of demarkation between yourself and the rest of your tribe. Of course, if analyzed with true occult perception, it would be apparent that the ancestor did not actually live in his descendants; for as a spiritual entity one creature cannot actually live in another. It was his memory that lived on, pictures of him and his purposes—living pictures carried in the blood. This panorama goes on like the flickering shadows of a motion picture, and the man himself,

perceiving these pictures, would be incapable either of recognizing their unreal-
ity or dissociating his own consciousness from the panorama. Intermarriage
between tribes being unknown, there was no escape from these pictures nor
were new pictures introduced.   This explains the clairvoyance of ancient
nations and is also the reason for the mythological period at the beginning of
each civilization.   Each race carries a certain record of superphysical and
subjective phenomena through its blood stream, and it is these memories which
constitute the age of fable.   In the beginning were the gods, the demigods,
the heroes, and the patriarachs.   They cannot be forgotten; they are locked
within the blood record—the subconscious mind—a tangle of impulses which
the mad hatters who call themselves psychologists will find great difficulty in
unraveling.
    Environment asserted itself over heredity when intermarriage between
families and tribes broke the continuity of the ancestral blood record. "The
birth of logical thought," writes Dr. Steiner, "the birth of the intellect, was
simultaneous with the advent of exogamy." Further on he summarizes the
whole problem. "Thus, in an unmixed blood is expressed the power of the
ancestral life, and in a mixed blood the power of personal experience." (See
THE OCCULT SIGNIFICANCE OF BLOOD.)   The cerebrospinal nervous system is
the seat of the individual reactions in man and also the medium for his contact
with the extraneous world.   As the balance of emphasis was shifted to
externals, the ancestral memory faded from his conscious awareness to assert
itself only when by some means the cerebral system was placed in temporary
abeyance.   Dreams may be fragments of the ancestral consciousness, and the
sphere in which they occur is certainly under the dominion of the same sympathetic forces which were once the carriers of the ancestral impulses.   The
composite blood of the present man, containing within it the strains from many
ancient sources, has resulted in the cosmopolitan quality of the modern mind.
Released from bondage to these phantoms of the blood stream, the thought is
turned to the assimilation of knowledge derived from the phenomenal universe.
It does not necessarily follow, however, that the blood has ceased to exert an
influence; for in its present state—that is, emancipated from ancestral influence
—it has formed into a new chemistry and is a suitable carrier for the impulses
of the ego.   The blood has become the instrument of *self*-expression and as
such carries within its subtle body the dictums of the intellectual *genius*.   As
the blood once revealed the past, so now it foretells the future; for within it
are set up the vibrations and patterns by which the future estate of man is to
be determined.   The blood is now a medium by which external phenomenal
circumstances are carried inward to be incorporated into consciousness, and by
which the consciousness, in its turn, flows outward to determine and direct the
activity of the personality.   The sympathetic cords—the threads of the
ancestral record—are also being developed into a positive instrument and will
finally become the favored instrument of consciousness.   The inner, or soul,

stimulation will come through the sympathetic system. The soul ganglia that once bound man will ultimately liberate him. Man first passes from a sub-conscious unity to a semi-conscious diversity, and then from the same semi-conscious diversity to a conscious unity.

We can now interpret certain of the ancient Mysteries which, recognizing the peculiar office of the blood, converted this fluid to serve their purposes. Consider modern Freemasonry, an institution preserving so much of the ancient arcana. "I have suggested the derivation of the Masonic name," writes Gerald Massey, "from the Egyptian *Sen*=son, for blood and brotherhood. . . . *Ma-sen*=Mason, would denote the true brotherhood, and as *Sen* is also blood, the true brotherhood as the blood-brotherhood would be the Masons in the mystical or occult sense. Red is the color of *Ma* or Truth personified, and *Sen* is blood." Members of the Masonic fraternity are sometimes referred to as "Brothers of the Mystic Tie." What is this tie? The answer is to be found among the Egyptians, for the Tet-tie, now generally presumed to have been a buckle, was the ancient symbol for the blood of Isis, i. e. the blood of the widow. The mystic tie is, then, the blood tie—the tie of the blood soul, the blood drawn by the point of the compass. By the mingling of the most sacred of all elements in the ceremony of blood brotherhood, the blood soul was communicated and all who possessed it were as one man. That is, they had one soul—the blood soul, which was above all others. The man who wronged his blood brother wronged himself, his soul, and his ancestors. Such was the ancient belief.

In the Mysteries, the blood tie was used as a method of transmitting knowledge. The unspeakable wisdom, the unpronounceable word, and other secrets which could not be commmunicated but which "if spoken, vanished away," were entrusted to the blood. In his GOLDEN BOUGH, Frazier describes the primitive rite among cannibalistic peoples of drinking the blood of heroic warriors in order to gain strength therefrom. The hierophants of Egypt and Greece passed on the cleansing of blood; that is, they went through a ceremony of mingling blood. Each man made a small incision in his arm and the wounds were bound together for a short period that the blood might flow between. The result was a sympathetic bond which continued until death, for each man possessed within himself a small part of the "soul" of the other. The conditions requisite for telepathic communication, mental exchange of ideas, or communication at a great distance were thus established. The true apostolic succession is a blood succession, the perpetuation of a purpose or an idea through the blood. In the early Christian rites, Christ is described as performing the blood testament—symbolically through the wine of the Last Supper and actually through the wound made by the centurion, Longinus. Through these processes the disciples are presumed to have received the blood succession—the ancestral record. Christ lived in them because His blood was in them. This they could communicate to those who would receive it—that is, "become one of the brethren" or receive the seal of blood. If we accept the old rites as the true key to the situation, those only are Christians who have received the blood of Christ. This is symbolically set forth in the sacrament of Communion, in which the body and the blood of Christ are redistributed to the faithful. The blood descent was also recognized as the foundation of temporal monarchies. The first divine or semi-divine rulers lived on in their legitimate descendants, in that way preserving the "divine right" of kings.

If the subconscious mind be regarded as an aspect of the ancestral blood record, producing a negative stimulation of the brain centers by agitating the threads of the sympathetic cord, an answer will be found for many different questions in the field of psychological research. Of the picture consciousness carried in the blood, four aspects may be differentiated: (1) The fractured ancestral continuity. We say "fractured" because it has been broken up into a kaleidoscopic mass of incomplete pictures by the intermingling of racial bloods. These come through to the objective awareness as the meaningless, rushing, tumbling phantoms of sleep. (2) The etheric breath-blood record; that is, the immediate mental, emotional, and physical environments photographed into the blood as the first step towards its assimilation into the self-consciousness of the individual. Certain of the more vivid of these blood impressions may impinge themselves upon the sympathetic system during sleep, producing that form of dream which is a living over of the incidents of the immediate or even more remote past. As the blood record contains a faithful picture of man's moral and æsthetic attitudes and qualities, and as these escape in sleep from the domination of the conscious soul, it is apparent that the blood also supplies the substance for such research as that carried on by Freud and Jung. (3) Ideas are primarily geometrical symbols or figures, called by the Tibetans *mandalas*—wheels or patterns—and in some cases the blood record may impress itself negatively upon the brain centers in symbolic forms, geometrical or otherwise. These forms may clothe themselves in familiar "thought appearances," playing out dream pantomines which have a meaning other than the apparent one. (4) Clairvoyant and prophetic aspects of the blood record are also worthy of note. The sensitive nature of the vital agent in the blood permits it to respond to the mental and emotional vibrations of other people, thus sometimes producing an uncanny realization of the thoughts and motives of persons either near or distant. This is especially true if some strong sympathy or antipathy exists. As the blood carries a partly developed archetype of future conditions within itself and is *en rapport* with the patterns which Nature is setting up in the external world, under certain moods man can almost violently anticipate impending change either for good or ill. Cases are on record where persons receiving blood transfusions have for a time retained dim memories of episodes in the life of the individual from whom the blood was derived. These should be sufficiently intriguing to result in major "rediscoveries" in the field of subjective mentality.

In harmony with the theory underlying all scriptural writings, the Bible—both the Old and New Testaments—is susceptible of both an anatomical and a physiological interpretation. It is not amiss to emphasize the possible scientific importance of Biblical traditions. It is evident that the human body is both the temple of God and the Holy City. Having some comprehension of the mystery of blood, we can now understand what is meant when it is written in REVELATION that the Holy City (the composite man) is not lighted by the sun by day nor the moon by night, but rather by the light of the Lord (the Lamb)—the blood light, the nephesh, the internal luminance of the soul. In discussing the miracles of Jesus, by which we understand the mysteries of the Solar Agent of the alchemists, Dr. George Carey shows that the original meaning of the word *Galilee* was "a circle of water, or fluid—the circulatory system." In the same way the word *Cana* signifies "a dividing place, the lungs or reeds, the tissues and cells of the lungs." To the biochemist, then, the first miracle of Jesus (i. e. of the divine man) is that of changing water into wine at the marriage feast of Cana. This is another interpretation of the old mystery, for the first duty of the ego was the "creation of blood." In other words, the transmutation of the cold fluids of the earlier creation into the warm humid carrier of transcendental impulse.

We must now turn with regret from that portion of the CODEX MAGIAE which is concerned with the mystery of blood. As we close the pages of the old tradition, our eyes fall upon the words of Abbe Alphonse Louis Constant (Eliphas Levi), the last of the sorcerers: "Blood is the first incarnation of the universal fluid; it is the materialized *vital light*. Its birth is the most marvelous of all nature's marvels; it lives only by perpetually transforming itself, for it is the universal Proteus. The blood issues from principles where there was none of it before, and it becomes flesh, bones, hair, nails . . . tears, and perspiration. It can be allied neither to corruption nor death; when life is gone it begins decomposing; if you know how to reanimate it, to infuse into it life by a new magnetism of its globules, life will return to it again. The universal substance, with its double motion, is the great arcanum of being; blood is the great arcanum of life."

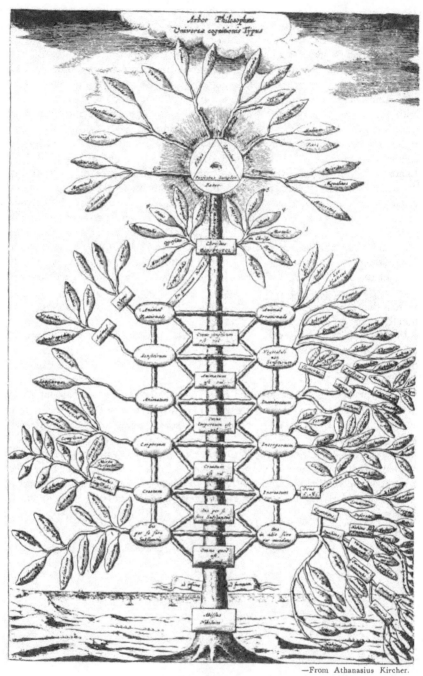

—From Athanasius Kircher.

THE SPINAL COLUMN AS THE PHILOSOPHIC TREE

CHAPTER XIII

THE SPINAL COLUMN AND THE WORLD TREE

HE SPINE is a flexible column consisting of 33 segments or vertebrae (from *vertere*, "to turn.") The bones composing it are divided into five groups, which have received their names from the positions occupied by them, viz.: (1) *cervical*, 7 in number; (2) *dorsal*, or *thoracic*, 12 in number (one for each rib); (3) *lumbar*, 5 in number; (4) *sacral* (five segments which in the adult are united into one bone); and (5) *coccygeal* (four small segments of bone, the most rudimentary parts of the spinal column). The vertebrae are described as "piled one upon the other, forming a strong pillar for the support of the cranium and trunk," and the whole column may be considered as a hollow cylinder, one of its chief purposes being the protection of the spinal cord. This ladder of bones played a most important part in the religious symbolism of the ancients, where it is often referred to as a winding road or stairway (the strait and narrow way), sometimes as a serpent, and again as a wand or sceptre. "Like the backbone of a vina, or harp, the long tract of bone, with many joints, that stretches along the trunk up to the head of a human being is called the Meru-Danda (spinal column)." (See UTTARA-GITA.) The number 33 is highly significant, for David reigned 33 years in Jerusalem, the lifetime of Christ was 33 years, 33 degrees are recognized in the ritualisms of Freemasonry, and the number 33 was the cryptic signature of Sir Francis Bacon.

In referring to the Tat pillar of the Egyptians as the backbone of the god Ptah and later of Osiris, Gerald Massey says: "The backbone was a figure of the pole; it is at one time the backbone of Sut, at another the backbone of Anup, at another of Ptah or Osiris—the backbone being a natural type of sustaining power. . . . The figure is referred to in the Magic Papyrus as the long backbone of Ptah, the Nemma. 'O Nemma of the great face, of the long backbone, of the deformed legs! O long column which commences in (both) the upper and the lower heaven. O lord of the great body which reposes in Annu,' the place of the column or pole, now doubled in Amenta *(Magic Papyrus)*." (See ANCIENT EGYPT, THE LIGHT OF THE WORLD.) Is not the Tat "doubled in Amenta" the double spinal column of the coming sixth root race of men, of whom it has been written that the ganglia of the sympathetic chain will be linked, forming a second spinal cord, which will finally merge with the first in the production of the ultimate type of physical body? Here is the mystery of the double pole, the two poles in one body. According to the Cabalists, Adam and Eve were fashioned together back to back—two beings with one spine. They were separated by the will of the Demiurge, but in the perfection of the body this mystery will be consummated by the blending of the two poles in the ultimate union of the cerebrospinal and sympathetic nerves. The double-headed phœnix is the symbol of this accomplishment, as is also the two-faced king of the alchemists. "The spinal column," writes H. P. Blavatsky, "is called Brahmananda, the rod or stick of Brahma, and it is this which is symbolized by the bamboo rod carried by ascetics, the seven knotted wand of the Yogi, the seven knots of the seven Nadi along the spinal cord. The Yogis beyond the Himalayas, who assemble regularly at Lake Mansararahara, carry a triple knotted bamboo stick, are called Tridandas. The three knots signify the three vital airs that play in the spinal column, symbolized also by the triple Brahmanical thread."

In a person of average size the spinal cord is about eighteen inches in length, weighs approximately one ounce, and terminates opposite the first lumbar vertebra in a slender filament of gray substance which is continued a considerable distance into the *filum terminale*. Up to the third month, in the fœtus, the cord extends to the bottom of the sacral canal, after which time the encroachment of the bones forces it to recede. The cord does not fill the canal, and with its investing membranes is isolated from the walls by areolar tissue and a plexus of veins. The upper end of the spinal cord, passing through the *foramen magnum* (the large opening in the occipital bone of the skull— "the hole in the floor"), ends in the *medulla oblongata*. Santee calls the *medulla spinalis* (spinal cord) the central axis of the nervous system. Each half of the spinal cord is divided by fissures into four columns: An anterior, posterior, lateral, and posterior median column.

The sixth ventricle of Western science runs longitudinally through the center of the spinal cord. It originates in the ventricles of the brain and, descending the length of the cord, is presumed to end, according to the Tantric mystics, opposite the *sacro-coccygeal* ganglion—the *Muladhara* plexus, or chakra. Krausei describes the sixth ventricle as follows: "It is just visible to the naked eye, but it extends throughout the cord and expands above into the fourth ventricle. In the *conus medullaris* it is also dilated, forming the *ventriculus terminalis*." Most Oriental writers agree that the sixth ventricle is identical with the *Sushumna,* the chief of the Nadis, or tubes of the body, as taught in Hatha and Raja Yoga. According to the UTTARA-GITA, the Sushumna is a fine nerve, a golden tube through which move the vital airs of the microcosm and from which all the *Jnana-Nadis* (sensory nerves) take their birth. T. Subba Row defines this "nerve of wisdom" as a sort of vein of magnetic electricity and adds that Sushumna is recognized as the chief of the Nadis because in the case of an adept or Yogi the soul at death departs through this tube. (See page 204 on the pneumogastric nerve for an analysis of this theory.) He also defines the Sushumna as "the seat of the circulation of the soul."

The Norse Ask, the Hesiodic ash-tree, from which issued the men of the generation of bronze, the *Tzite-tree* of the *Popol-Vuh,* out of which the

Mexican third race of men was created are all, according to H. P. Blavatsky, symbols of man himself. Their fruits are the perfections of natures and the serpent which dwells in the branches of each tree is "the conscious *Manas*, the connecting link between spirit and matter, heaven and earth." (See THE SECRET DOCTRINE.) These are quite evidently the symbolic trees referred to in Genesis, for the arterial system with its numerous branches is certainly a "tree of life," and the nervous system with its infinite ramifications, with its roots in the brain, is with equal certainty the "tree of the knowledge of good and evil." From an examination of the human spine it is not difficult to recognize therein the simile to the World Tree as set forth in the BHAGAVAD-GITA: "They say the imperishable Ashvattha is with root above and branches below, of which the sacred hymns are the leaves. Who knows this, is a knower of Knowledge. Upwards and downwards stretch its branches, expanded by the three Potencies; the sense-objects are its sprouts. Downwards, too, its roots are stretched, constraining to action in the world of men. Here neither its form is comprehended, nor its end, nor beginning, nor its support." Here, then, is the mysterious tree of the Cabalists with its triple trunk, its roots in heaven (the cranium of Adam) and its branches descending through the four worlds. The central trunk of this tree is termed *Mildness* and corresponds with the *Sushumna* of the Yogins. The right and left trunks —*Mercy* and *Severity*—are the *Ida* and *Pingala*, the black and the white serpents; and the whole tree is figured with its branches distributed throughout the body of the crowned supernal Adam.

Recognizing the evident analogy between the spinal column and the tree, it will be useful to briefly summarize some of the earlier "tree" myths. The World Tree of the Hindus is the Ashvattha already mentioned. Its main branches represent the major divisions of the mundane sphere and its leaves are "the mantras of the Vedas." The latter are symbolical of the superphysical elements which are essential to the maintenance of the universe, and also of the vibrations pulsating at the nerve ends. Among the Tibetans, the great World Tree is called *Zampun*, and of its three roots one extends to heaven, another to hell, while the third remains in the median distance between and extends to the eastern corner of the world. Here, again, is an intimation of the three principal *Nadis* of the Tantric system. *Gogard* is the Hellenic tree of life. According to one account, it was a sacred oak, and amidst its magnificent foliage dwelt a serpent which no one was capable of dislodging. Windischmann writes: "Homa is the first of the trees planted by Ahura-Mazda in the fountain of life. He who drinks of its juice never dies. According to the Bundehesh, the Gogard or Gaokerena tree bears the Homa, which gives health and generative power, and imparts life at the resurrection. The Homa plant does not decay, bears no fruit, resembles the vine, is knotty, and has leaves like jessamin, yellow and white. . . . From this it appears that the

White Homa or the Tree Gokard is the Tree of Life which grew in Paradise."
(See TREE AND SERPENT WORSHIP.)

Is not this description of the knotted vinelike branches of the Homa plant reminiscent of the gangliated cords of the nervous system? In the VEDAS, the *Kalpadruma,* a cloud tree of immense size is mentioned. This grew on the steep of a mountain and the shadow that it cast produced the phenomenon of day and night prior to the creation of the sun and moon. In the RIG-VEDA, Brahma as the Creator is described in the form of a vast tree which overspreads the whole world and the gods are depicted as branches of this tree. The Bodhi tree under which Gautama Buddha received his illumination is described as covered with divine flowers and gleaming with every kind of precious stone. To its smallest leaves this most sacred pipal tree is described in the allegories as formed of gems more resplendent than the peacock's tail. The Egyptians also possessed a tree allegory, for in their sacred writings is described a jewel-bearing tree which is placed to the East of the world, up which the god Horus climbs to produce the phenomenon of sunrise. In the Chinese mythology seven miraculous trees once flourished in the Kuen-Lun mountains. The greatest of these, which was of jade, bore fruit that conferred immortality—the golden apples of the Hesperides. The Arabians represented the zodiac in the form of a tree and figured the stars as its fruit. Thus, there were twelve branches, and as the sun in its annual course entered each sign, it ripened the fruit thereof, from which circumstance was derived the fable of the Apocalyptic tree that bore twelve manner of fruit and yielded its fruit every month.

In the Scandinavian rites there is the star-bearing World Tree—Yggdrasil—upon which Odin hung himself for nine months that he might secure wisdom. "The *Edda,*" writes H. P. Blavatsky, "makes our visible universe spring from beneath the luxuriant branches of the mundane tree—the Yggdrasil, the tree with the *three* roots. * * * The care of the mundane tree is intrusted to three maidens (the Norns or Parcæ), Urdhr, Verdandi, and Skuld—or the Present, the Past, and the Future. Every morning, while fixing the term of human life, they draw water from the Urdar-fountain, and sprinkle with it the roots of the mundane tree, that it may live. The exhalations of the ash, Yggdrasil, condense, and falling down upon our earth call into existence and exchange of form every portion of the inanimate matter. This tree is the symbol of the *universal* Life, organic as well as inorganic; its emanations represent the spirit which vivifies every form of creation; and of its three roots, one extends to heaven, the second to the dwelling of the magicians—giants, inhabitants of the lofty mountains—and at the third, under which is the spring Hvergelmir, gnaws the monster Nidhogg, who constantly leads mankind into evil."

The Finnish people also have their World Tree which they term the tree of eternal well-being, and its fruits confer "the delight that never ceases." In his translation of an early Babylonian fragment, A. H. Sayce describes the great tree which grew up from the center of the earth and had its roots in the very depths of being. The roots of the tree were of crystal, its seat was the central place of the earth, and its foliage was the couch of Zikum, the Sky Mother. "Into the heart of its holy house, which spread its shade like a forest, hath no man entered. * * * In the midst of it was Tammuz. There is the shrine of the two gods." The possibility of interpreting these myths in terms of anatomy and physiology is unlimited. There is the war of the trees. The tree of the soul, growing up from the heart as described by Jacob Boehme, and

THE WORLD TREE IN THE HUMAN BODY

bearing the fruit of immortality, destroys the great world tree of illusion with its snaky branches. The jewels upon the branches of the tree represent the mandalas and chakras. The cords of the sympathetic system carry jewels for fruit, for the etheric vortices (chakras) are the blossoms of precious stones, seven of which grew upon the world tree of the Gothic rites and also upon the chemical tree of the mediæval alchemists and Rosicrucians. To the Yogi, there is no mystery about the tree which bestows "the delight that never ceases," for he knows those who can master its mysteries achieve to immortality.

Captain Wilford, in his articles on THE ISLES OF THE WEST, which appeared in the early volumes of THE ASIATIC RESEARCHES, declared that he had discovered among the writings of the Cabalists evidence that the early initiates among the Jews regarded Mount Moriah as a type of the World Mountain— the Hindu Meru, or Saokant. He even asserts that Moriah, like these sacred mountains, was placed in the midst of the Seven Continents and was the highest of them—a form of the Axis, or Polar, Mountain. In the occult anatomy of man, the Polar Mountain is usually identified with the brain. "We have seen," writes one Oriental, "that Meru-Danda is the same as the spinal cord, and as Mount Meru—analogically Mount Saokant—is placed at the North Pole of the earth, we may reasonably seek for this sacred mountain in the human constitution at the very top of the spinal column." (See ZOROASTRIANISM.) Thus, in the midst of the "little world" (the human body) rises the "high place" (the head), wherein is located the sanctuary of the rationality, where sits the intellect as the administrator of divine law.

The adepts of the old world were bound together by the common knowledge of certain great truths. To these Masters have been communicated the true significance of the Mountain of the Mysteries, upon whose summit stands the temple of the divine government surrounded by a hierarchy of enlightened and perfected initiates and attended by beings of other worlds. According to Eastern tradition, this temple stands upon the highest point of the earth directly under the Pole Star and, like the Caaba at Mecca, is the shadow cast upon the earth by the everlasting house of the gods in the heavens above. How well this mystery is revealed in the vision of Hiouen-Thsang, who beheld a mighty pillar of pure light rising up from the earth, its lower end resting upon the dark body of matter and its capital supporting the ridge-pole of Shamballah. The polar axis of the earth is the Great Spine. The Lord of the planet dwells in the core thereof (the heart) surrounded by twelve concentric strata, in each of which abides the ambassador of a celestial state as regent. The Being who controls the activities of the planet holds court in the fabled Shamballah, the Heavenly City that exists in the superphysical strata of the earth, held up by the mysterious lotus blossom of the Pole. From the sacred Shamballah come forth the edicts of progress and purpose. Here, according to the legends of Tibet, are determined those major policies by which the direction of earthly march is decided. The Regent of Shamballah is the Mind of the earth, and as the nerves of the human body convey the impulses from the brain to all the parts and members, so the Great Prince is served by a host of horsemen who, receiving his instructions, hasten to carry them to all parts of the world. These horsemen signify, in part at least, the adepts and initiates through whom the Mind of the world controls its outer body. Black magic is always represented by an inversion or perversion of power. So the black Shamballah is regarded as standing at the lower end of the great axis—the South Pole—pointing away from the North Star, the jewel which shows the way of cosmic order. Of course, the North Star, whose position is revealed by the Seven Rishis, or Wise Men of the Great Dipper, is again only a symbolic term to represent a divine principle, for the true meaning of the North Star is as yet beyond the comprehension of men.

It is our purpose to suggest an interpretation of this allegory in the terms of the microcosm, or the body of man. Shamballah signifies the brain as the positive pole of the consciousness of the human spirit. Thus, the intellectual monad (the Thinker) is the regent, or prince, of the body, to whom is given dominion over all the functions and purposes of the outer life. At the northern, or upper, end of the spine, which is the axis of the body, is the seat of the intellectual regent of life, enthroned amidst the twelve convolutions of the brain, who are his spirits, ministers, and *Suras*. The four imperishable continents over which he rules are the seed atoms, or monads, of the four bodies which produce from themselves the sequence of personalities. As Atlas bears the heavens upon his shoulders, so the spine is the mysterious column which supports the ridge-pole of Shamballah. A gentleman of scientific propensities, in discussing recently the problem of electricity, declared that he regarded the brain as a transformer or transmitter of the vital electricity of life. This is in perfect harmony with the ancient traditions, for the regent of Shamballah is not king but the ambassador or transmitter of the king. The supreme ruler holds court only in the innermost recesses of the heart, where is the seat of the subjective life.

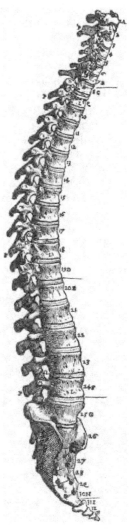

A very interesting sidelight upon the thought of rulership can be gathered from the traditions of the caravan routes. All caravans are under the control of three heads: first is the master of the caravan, who is the inclusive ruler of the whole enterprise; then there is a second official, who is called the master of march. The moment the caravan begins its traveling for the day, the master of the march comes into authority and remains sole dictator of its course until the encampment is made for the night. The third officer is called the master of rest and refreshment and he has undisputed sway during all the periods of encampment. Interpreted in terms of the body, the master of the caravan signifies the heart, for it is the overseer of the whole. The master of the march is the brain, which has dominion over all the activities of the life; and the master of rest and refreshment is the generative system, or physical nature manifesting its recuperative power. As dictator of means, the master of march has undisputed sway over the daily activities of the soul. For this reason, to the average person the regent of activity is the true ruler, but only to the initiated is it evident that the mind simply follows the patterns set down by the unseen One—the heart-dweller.

THE SPINAL COLUMN
(After Vesalius)

We cannot pass over unnoted the experiments of Anton Mesmer in animal electricity and magnetism. "Mesmer rediscovered and did not invent the secret science of Nature. That first, unique and elementary substance to which he testifies in his APHORISMS was known to Hermes and Pythagoras. It was celebrated by Synesius in his HYMNS, and he had found it among the Platonic reminiscences of the Alexandrian School." (See LA CLEF DES GRANDS MYSTERES.) The Thessalian sorceresses were adepts in mesmerism and hypnotism, and the eldest of the Chaldean initiates practiced suggestive therapy five millenia before Dr. Benjamin Franklin was appointed chairman of a committee for its investigation. The Druids considered the mistletoe sacred because the priests of this cult believed that this parasitic plant fell to the earth in the form of lightning bolts and that wherever a tree was struck by lightning the seeds of the mistletoe were placed within its bark. The actual reason for the high veneration of this parasite was that it served as a powerful medium for the collection of the "cosmic fire" circulating through the ether. The priests valued the medicinal properties of the mistletoe because of its close connection with this astral light. Concerning this, Eliphas Levi writes in his HISTORY OF MAGIC: "The Druids were priests and physicians, curing by magnetism and charging amulets with their fluidic influence. Their universal remedies were mistletoe and serpents' eggs, because these substances attract the astral light in a special manner. The solemnity with which mistletoe was cut down drew upon this plant the popular confidence and rendered it powerfully magnetic. * * * The progress of magnetism will some day reveal to us the absorbing properties of mistletoe. We shall then understand the secret of those spongy growths which draw the unused virtues of plants and become surcharged with tinctures and savors. Mushrooms, truffles, gall on trees and the different kinds of mistletoe will be employed with understanding by a medical science, which will be new because it is old."

Certain plants, minerals, and animals have been held sacred among all the nations of the earth because of their sensitiveness to the astral fire. The cat, sacred to the city of Bubastis in Egypt, is an example of a peculiarly magnetized animal. Anyone stroking a cat's fur in a dark room can see the electrical emanations in the form of green phosphorescent light. In the temples of Bast, sacred to the cat-goddess, three-colored cats were viewed with unusual veneration, as was any member of the feline family whose eyes were of different colors. Lodestone and radium in the mineral kingdom and various parasitic growths in the plant kingdom, also the mandrake and ginseng, are susceptible to the cosmic fire. The magicians of the Middle Ages surrounded themselves with certain animals, such as bats, cats, snakes, and monkeys because they were able to borrow the power of the astral light from these creatures and appropriate it to their own uses. For the same reason, the Egyptians and certain of the Greeks kept cats in the temples and serpents were always in evidence at the oracle of Delphi. The auric body of a snake is one of the most remarkable sights that the clairvoyant will ever see, and the secrets concealed within its aura demonstrate why the serpent is the symbol of wisdom among so many nations.

It is erroneous to attribute even the rediscovery of the magnetic theory to either Father Hehl or Mesmer, for both Paracelsus and Descartes had anticipated this rediscovery and the former had actually employed magnetism for healing purposes. "There are qualities in a magnet not known to every ignoramus," announced the gentle Theophrastus, "and one of these qualities is that the magnet * * * attracts all martial humours that are in the human system." He then describes his magnet as having a front, or north pole, and a back, or south pole, the former of which attracts and the latter repels. Paracelsus declared the magnet to be useful in all inflammations, fluxes, ulcerations, and in diseases of the bowels and uterus, whether the malignancy be internal or external. By his magnets Paracelsus could control the martial part of the aura, expanding it or contracting it according to whether the positive or negative magnetic pole was applied to the area involved. It is, indeed, regrettable that the experiments of Baron Reichenbach in the field of magnets and magnetism have been so completely ignored by scientific men. Especially is this true in the field of healing, for we may say of the physicians of this day what Paracelsus said of the "leeches" of the early sixteenth century: "They have every day occasion to see magnets publicly and privately, and yet they continue to act as if no magnets were in existence."

There is a tenacious tradition to the effect that the celebrated Comte de St.-Germain, that grand master of all the magical arts, instructed Mesmer in the details of magnetic procedure. Irrespective, however, whether Paracelsus or St.-Germain was his mentor, this cannot detract from the laurels of occult science, since both were adepts in theurgy. Dr. Bell, surnamed "the Ingenious," an early practitioner in animal magnetism, thus describes the premises upon which the science was built: "There is a universal fluid which fills all space. Every body is endowed with a certain quantity of electric fluid. There exists an attraction, or sympathy and antipathy, between animated bodies. The universal currents of the universal fluid, are the cause and existence of bodies. One may accelerate those currents in a body, and produce crises and somnambulism, which is done by acting reciprocally upon one another, by increasing the currents going across their interstices or pores, *in consequence of the absolute will of the operator.* * * *The reciprocal action of all these bodies is operated upon by the *insensible perspiration,* or vapor, flowing in and out, as you see in a real loadstone or in an artificial magnet, *forming an outside atmosphere;* it also produces currents in a more or less direct manner, according to the analogy of bodies." [Italics mine, M.P.H.] What is magic but the directing of the Great Magnetic Agent by the will of the enlightened adept? Every mesmerist is a magician, every magnet a magical wand. Shades of those skilled in the Theopœa, you are vindicated!

Kircher, Paracelsus, Fludd, Descartes, Mesmer, etc., had not long experimented with the "Magnes" before they realized that all natural bodies have poles. These poles are magnetic rather than physical, however, although there is evidence of a natural tendency in form to group itself along these poles, as in the case of the human spinal cord and column. George Adams, another early research worker in the field of magnetism, wrote: "In some future period it may be discovered that most bodies are possessed of a polarity." It was also noted that the magnetic fluids passed out in greater abundance from the extremities of the body, and it gradually followed that the human body was divided into a sort of northern and southern hemisphere, as well as an eastern

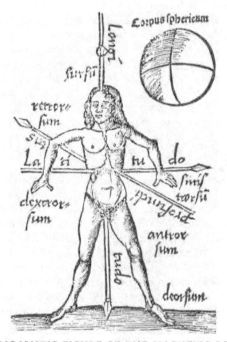

A CABALISTIC FIGURE OF THE MAGNETIC POLES

and western hemisphere. Here again man corresponds to the Macrocosm; for, like the world, he is surrounded and penetrated by magnetic currents, which from their direction and quality are determinators of order and function. We reproduce a quaint old figure from REISCH'S MARGARITA PHILOSOPHICA. At first appearance, it seems to be a "wound" man, but upon more detailed investigation it appears to represent the magnetic poles in the human body. The vertical spear carries the legend "Longitude," the horizontal "Latitude," while the third spear evidently reveals the ecliptic. Lest any doubt remain as to the implication intended, the body of the sphere appears in the upper right-hand corner, quartered by a meridian of longitude intersecting the equator. As the magnetic pole of the earth does not agree with the occult pole, so the magnetic pole of the human body does not parallel the spinal column, but has an inclination which can only be discovered through an analysis of the aura. Man, like Nature, has his seasons and his changes, his longitudes and his latitudes; and through an understanding of his magnetic field, physicians could treat successfully many ailments now beyond their power.

Several attempts have been made to correspond the vertebrae of the spine with the planets and zodiacal signs. It has not proved wholly satisfactory, however, to simply begin at the skull and follow down the vertebrae in the order of the planets and constellations. A certain degree of accuracy seems to exist in the idea, but exceptions are too numerous to be ignored. The horizontal division of the spine into three general areas—cervical, dorsal, and lumbar—offers a clue. The 7 cervicals plus the 12 dorsals plus the 5 lumbars equal 24, a most occult and significant number. In the chapter on the brain, (see page 126) we called attention to the numbers associated with the three departments of man's constitution. We found the spiritual man to correspond with 12, the sidereal (or astral) man with 7, and the physical (or elemental) man with 5. These three numbers correspond exactly with the divisions of the spine, excluding the sacrum and coccyx. The thoracic cavity corresponds with the spiritual man, also with the heavenly world; the cranial with the sidereal man and the astral world; the abdominal with the material man and the physical world. These analogies have already been traced in the section on man and the three worlds. (See page 47.) It is, therefore, in perfect harmony with the old traditions to assign the 12 dorsals, or thoracic vertebrae, to the zodiacal signs; the first dorsal with Aries, the second with Taurus, etc. The 7 cervicals correspond to the planets; the first cervical to Saturn, the second to Jupiter, the third to Mars, the fourth to the sun, the fifth to Venus, the sixth to Mercury, and the seventh to the moon. Saturn, the highest vertebra, therefore supports heaven (Ouranos). The five elements, descending from ether, are analogous to the lumbar vertebrae. Ether is the first, fire the second, air the third, water the fourth, and earth the fifth. In some systems the fire and air are reversed. The head above is the Empyrean—Abstract Cause. The sacrum and coccyx below are the subterranean spheres of the damned or lost souls, and the spine itself is the pillar set up in Egypt which is to endure as a monument to the gods and as the main support of the microcosm.

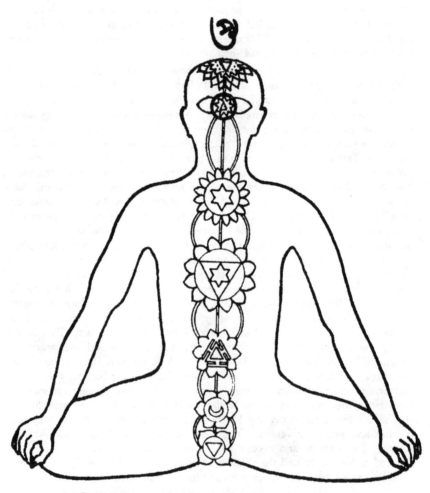

THE CHAKRAS, ACCORDING TO TANTRIC PHILOSOPHY

CHAPTER XIV

KUNDALINI AND THE SYMPATHETIC NERVOUS SYSTEM

HE sympathetic nervous system, the soul ganglia of the ancients, is a series of ganglia connected by intervening cords and extends on each side of the vertebral column from the skull above to the coccyx below. "The sympathetic cords take their rise from a sacred spot above the *medulla oblongata* called the *tridena* by the Hindus. * * * From this same spot start the Ida and Pingala, an upper junction of the sympathetic and cerebrospinal axis being thus formed." (See H. P. Blavatsky.) The sympathetic nervous system consists of three great gangliated plexuses or aggregations of nerves and ganglia—the cardaic, solar, and hypogastric—which are situated in front of the spine in the thoracic, abdominal, and pelvic cavities respectively. There are also smaller ganglia, in all to the number of twenty-four, which correspond very nearly in number to the vertebrae against which they lie. At the lower end the two cords of the sympathetic system converge as they enter the pelvis and, uniting form a single ganglion which is in front of the coccyx. "The sympathetic system is connected with the Linga Sharira, the Prana, and Kama, more than with Manas. It is played on by the Tantrikas, who call it Shiva's vina (lute) or Kali's vine, and is used in Hatha Yoga. Its most important plexus, the solar, is the brain of the stomach, and emotions are felt there, owing to the correspondence with Kama. So psychic clairvoyant perceptions often act at this region, as in the reading of letters, psychometrizing substances, etc." (H. P. Blavatsky in E. S. Ins.)

In the ARUNOPNISHAD are described the important plexuses along the sympathetic cords, which are called *chakras,* or wheels of force. The chakras are all actually within the physical body, but have not been found by dissection because the forms ascribed to them by Oriental occulists are largely symbolic. Disciples of the higher Mysteries have been warned from the beginning not to attempt the development of these centers according to Hatha Yoga. They are but parts of the illusional universe, and reality no more exists in them than in any other part of the bodily state. In this brief work no attempt will be made to give a detailed analysis of the Yoga and Tantric theories, since between the various Oriental professors of these doctrines there are unbridgeable gulfs of opinion. Probably the most authentic works available on the subject in English are from the pen of Sir John Woodroffe (Arthur Avalon). Some pandits insist that the chakras are along the spine, others that they are in the brain only; again some say that Ida and Pingala are within the spinal cord, others that they are the right and left sympathetic cords. According to some, Kundalini rises in the Sushumna (sixth ventricle), while others maintain that it moves through the pneumogastric nerve. Nor have the different schools themselves come to any complete agreement regarding the number of the chakras, some recognizing five, others six, and still others seven; and particularly with respect to those located in the brain, the hazy analogies to the organs identified by modern science only leave the present confusion worse confounded.

Accompanying this chapter is a drawing of the seven spinal chakras. In this picture the symbolic form of the chakras has been carefully preserved, special emphasis being placed upon the correct number of petals. In the secret teachings to each of these petals is assigned a letter of the Sanskrit alphabet. The Yogi is apparently suspended in the air, for the power of sight which would enable one to see the chakras would take no cognizance of the physical earth upon which he is sitting. The plate is, of course, diagrammatic and must not be considered too literally. Study carefully the flower-like centers upon the spinal column. Through the center of the seven flowers passes the tube, Sushumna, on the left of which is the tube called Ida and on the right the tube called Pingala. According to the ancient Brahmans, the Lord of the human race is keyed to the musical note *fa* and His vibration runs through the Sushumna. Madam Blavatsky speaks of the Ida and Pingala as the sharp and flat of this central tone. The two latter tubes are profoundly influenced by the nostrils on their respective sides. The Ida, which is "resplendent like the moon," and Pingala, which is "resplendent like the sun," cross at the base of the skull and both rise out of the four-petalled lotus at the base of the spine. The Ida, Sushumna, and Pingala together are the chief of the Nadis, the Sushumna, "effulgent like the sun, moon, and fire," being the most important of the three. In the ordinary individual the tube of the Sushumna is closed, but by Yoga it is opened so that there is a direct connection between the sacral plexus at the base of the spine and the pineal gland in the head. "Ida and Pingala are described as playing along the curved wall of the cord containing Sushumna. They are semi-material, positive and negative. They have distinct paths of their own, otherwise they would radiate all over the body. By concentration on Ida and Pingala is generated the sacred fire. * * * Hatha Yoga says the Ida and Pingala act alternately, but if you stop both of these the hot current is forced through the Sushumna. Also without having to do with Ida and Pingala—by practicing Kumbhaka alone—the Sushumna comes into play; but a Raja Yoga, without using either of these methods, has a way of rousing the Kundalini. The means the Raja Yoga employs belong to the mysteries of initiation." (T. Subba Row.)

To paraphrase native writers, that Nadi which takes its origin from the Sahasrara (the brain) and which, growing gradually finer, descends as the central canal of the spinal column, is called the Sushumna. "There is a very delightful place (the fissure of Sylvius?) where the mouth of the Brahma nerve emits nectar. This place is the junction of the frontal lobe with the temporal lobe of the cerebral hemispheres and is the mouth of the Sushumna nerve." (Barada Kanta.) Nine sets of smaller Nadis first spring from it and "spread

towards the eyes and other organs of sense." Afterwards from between the
vertebrae of the spinal column stretch out thirty-two other sets of Nadis with
their innumerable branchlets, which are distributed throughout the body like
a network, producing the sense of touch and performing other necessary work
requisite for the maintenance of the physical body. "These Nadis are so fine
in their texture that if four hundred of them be collected and tied together,
they still cannot be seen by the naked eye; though so fine, still they are like

—From Maier's Scrutinum Chymicum.

THE HERMETIC KUNDALINI

pipes, are hollow, and in this space there exists a certain substance, like oil,
in which the Chaitanya [pure Intelligence] reflects; for this reason, the Rishis
call the Sushumna the parent of all these smaller Nadis, the Jnana-Nadi, and
consider it to be just like a *tree* with its innumerable branches covering the
whole of the human body, the root being upward—at the Sahasrara—and the
branches downward." All outward objects which are cognized by the human
senses "are reflected in the Sushumna Nadi, therefore the Rishis call this body
the 'Microcosm.' For instance, when you see the sun, moon, or stars, you do
not actually go near to them in order to see, but you see them because they are
reflected in your Sushumna Nadi." Thus, it is evident that various Nadis
spring from the Sushumna, "the receptacle of the Inner Soul of all Jivas," and
extend in all directions throughout the physical body. This system, then, is
considered as a huge reversed tree. "Tatva-Jnanins alone are able to walk on
every branch of this tree by the help of Prana-Vayu." (ZOROASTRIANISM, article
ON THE SUN WORSHIP.) "In this human body there exists seventy-two thousand

Nadis which admit of sufficient space for entrance into them of Vayu; the Yogis alone become acquainted with the true nature of these Nadis by virtue of their Yoga-Karma. Having closed up the nine portals of the body, and being acquainted with the source and nature of the Nadis that stretch up and down the seats of the several organs of sense, the Jiva, rising to the state of superior knowledge with the aid of the Life-Breath, attains Moksha." (See the UTTARA-GITA.)

Kundalini is a Sanskrit word meaning a serpentine or twisting force or gas. According to the Tantric disciplines, this force can be drawn up through the central spinal canal (Sushumna) and when in its ascent it strikes the brain, it stimulates or opens the spiritual centers of consciousness, thereby consummating the Yogi's labors toward self-mastery and illumination. Kundalini, also sometimes called "the astral serpent," is described as a power or energy in the *Muladhara*. "It has its head in the region of the navel." It is called serpent-like because of its strange curving motion. "It appears to move around and around in a circle; Ida and Pingala alternate on account of its motion." As Kundalini ascends, it enters into one spinal chakra after another and incorporates into itself the qualities of these chakras, mastering them and resulting in certain definite extensions of power and sense perception. Upon completing its ascent, it has absorbed into its own essence all the qualitative states through which it has passed, so that the chakras appear as "united into one current," like beads upon a thread or knots upon a sacred cord.

Sheba means "seven" in Hebrew, and one writer has asked the question, Does not the Queen of Sheba represent the Kundalini, the Serpent Queen of the seven chakras? The magicians of Egypt turned their rods into serpents before Pharaoh and Moses threw down his rod also, but it was transformed into a great serpent which swallowed up all the little serpents. Here is a most vivid account of the function of Kundalini. The serpents are the countless Nadis; the great serpent is the spinal fire herself, who is victorious over all the functions of the sensory nerves, so that it is scarcely an exaggeration to say that she devours them. Kundalini is the brazen serpent of Moses which he raised upon the Tau cross in the wilderness, and those who looked upon it did not die from the stings of the little serpents. The Yogi would interpret this to signify that those who would contemplate the mystery of this chief Nadi would escape from the death-dealing stings of the senses. One writer has suggested that the hypothetical eleventh Sephiroth—Daath—placed in the midst of the Sephirothic Tree, was the Cabalistic symbol of Kundalini. But is it not more probable that *Shekinah* signified this fire? "Where is the way to the Tree of Life?" asks THE ZOHAR, and answers its own question thus: "This is the great *Matroneethah* (Shekinah). She is the way to the Great Tree, the mighty Tree of Life." What is the Tree of Life unless it be the spinal column itself? That the Cabalists recognized Shekinah to be some form of electrical force is evident from their statement that the sparks from her are

purple. Kundry in *Parsifal* is also reminiscent of Kundalini and, like this serpent goddess, is dressed in the skins of snakes.

It is said that the Logos, when the time came to create the material universe,
entered into a state of deep meditation, centralizing His thought power upon
the seven flower-like centers of the seven worlds. Gradually His life force
descended from the brain (which was the great superior world) and, striking
these flowers one after the other, gave birth to the lower worlds. When at last
His spirit fire struck the lowest center, the physical world was created and
His flame was at the base of the world's spine. When the world returns to
Him again and He once more becomes supreme in consciousness, it will be
because He withdraws the life from these seven centers, beginning with the
lowest, and returns it again to the brain. It necessarily follows that the path
of evolution for all living things is to raise this fire, whose descent made every
manifestation in this lower world possible and whose "raising" brings them
into harmony once more with the superior creation.

At the base of the spine there is a tiny nerve center concerning which
little is known by science. The occultist has learned, however, that it contains
the mystery of the second crucifixion, which is supposed to have taken place
in Egypt and which has reference to the crossing of certain nerves at the base
of the spine. The sacred rattlesnake of Mexico, the feathered snake of Kukul-
Can, or Quetzalcoatl, is again the serpent spinal fire, and in this respect the
rattles, which are carefully reproduced in the carvings of this snake, become
of vital significance. Kundalini is coiled in the sacral plexus, where it rests
upon the triangular bone at the end of the sacrum. This triangular bone is
shown as an inverted triangle in the *Muladhara*, the four-petalled lotus blossom
at the base of the spine. Here Kundalini remains coiled until through certain
exercises she is caused to rise through the Sushumna to the brain, where she
awakens the activities of the third eye, the pineal gland. This third eye is the
link connecting man with the spiritual world or, to be more correct, with the
higher spiritual nature of himself. The anthropos, or *overman*, which never
descends into incarnation, was called by the Greeks the Cyclop—the giant
who had but one eye, which eye was the pineal gland, by means of which the
higher ego was capable of seeing downward into the human nature and the
human ego was capable of seeing upward into *Buddhi*, or the *overman*. Kundalini is more or less excited into rising as the result of the directionalization
of the essences moving in the Ida and Pingala. Here we have the *caduceus*
of Hermes. The two serpents coiled around the staff are Ida and Pingala.
The central staff is Sushumna, the bulb at the upper end of the rod is *Sahasrara*,
and the wings are *Ajna*—the two-petalled lotus above the bridge of the nose.
Among Eastern occultists there is some dispute as to whether the pineal gland
is actually the thousand-petalled lotus. Some affirm that it is; others that there
is a higher center in the brain to which the term should actually be applied.

"There are seven points," says Barada Kanta, "where the spinal accessory
nerves, Ida and Pingala, meet with the Sushumna nerve. Each of these points

is called a lotus." It is now in order to consider these lotuses, or chakras, from the lowest upward. Says THE ARUNOPNISHAD: "There is a chakra in which the Kundalini attains her early youth, uttering a low, deep note; a chakra in which she attains her maturity; a chakra in which she becomes fit to marry; a chakra in which she takes a husband, these and whatever happiness is conferred by her, are all due to Agni (Fire)." That division of Yoga called *Pranayama* is devoted to awakening Kundalini from her coils and causing her to rise upward through the chakras. Each of the five lower centers distributes one of the five forms of Prana, or the broken-up energy of the sun. Each of these seven chakras also has a corresponding *tattva*, or breath—a motion or condition of spiritual air. Beginning at the base of the spine and working upward, the centers are as follows:

First, *Muladhara.* A lotus of four petals and letters, connected with Saturn and which corresponds generally with the sacral plexus of modern science. This is a network of nerves lying in the pelvis in front of the concavity of the sacral bone. It is described, in part, as "bright as gold," with petals the color of the *Bignonia indica* and containing within it "the quadrangular mundane discus surrounded by eight spears, soft and yellow as the lightning." Within this discus is deposited the procreative fluid, "decorated with four hands and mounted on the seven-trunked elephant of Indra." In the center of the quadrangle is the triangular "philoprogenitive discus," within it the phallus of Shiva, and "fine as the string of the stalk of the lotus plays above this phallus the 'charmer of the Universe' (Kundalini)." As the lightning that plays in "new clouds" or as the spiral turnings of a shell, Kundalini "rests over the phallus of Shiva in three and a half circles, as does the sleeping serpent over the head of Shiva, covering with her head the entrance to the Sushumna." The goddess Dakini, with four arms and blood-red eyes, "glorious like twelve suns rising at the same time, but visible only to the pure-minded Yogi," is also seated in this chakra. Within it also is the air of Kandarpa, "which is capable of passing freely through all the members of the body." This air is described as the sovereign lord of animals "and glorious like hundreds of millions of suns." Kundalini, residing in the Muladhara, "hums like the bee inebriated with the nectar of flowers." The tattvic power of smell is associated with this chakra, and of the organs of action it controls the feet. In the Apocalyptic symbolism it is analogous to the Church of Ephesus. "By contemplation upon this chakra," writes Dr. Vasant G. Rele, "the Yogi obtains freedom from disease, knows the past and the future, and gains all psychic powers."

Second, *Svadhishthana.* A lotus of six petals and letters, connected with Jupiter, and which corresponds generally with the prostatic plexus of modern science. This plexus is continued from the lower part of the pelvic plexus. The nerves composing it are of large size and distributed to the prostatic gland, vesiculae seminales, etc. This chakra is described as being directly above the genitals. According to the Hindu writers, it is "at the root of the pudendum virile." It is red like vermillion and "bright as lightning." Within this lotus "is the white discus of Varuna (Neptune), in which is the seed," silvery like the autumnal moon, "having a crescent on its forehead and mounted on a white creature resembling an alligator." In this chakra also, "blue like a cloud, young, and wearing red cloth, is Hari, holding the four Vedas in his four hands and also Lakshmi." Within the moon-shaped mandala, or discus, is also the goddess Rakini, her color blue, "holding many weapons in her hands, ready to attack, and wearing many ornaments and apparel." Say the old Tantric writings: "He who can realize the discus of Varuna in his mind, becomes in a moment free from individual consciousness and, emerging from the darkness of folly, shines like the sun." The tattvic power of taste is associated with this chakra, and of the organs of action it controls the hands. In the Apocalyptic symbolism it is analogous to the Church of Pergamos. "By contemplation of this," writes Dr. Rele, "freedom from death and disease is obtained."

Third, *Manipura.* A lotus of ten petals and letters, connected with Mars, and which corresponds generally with the epigastric, or solar, plexus of modern science and the navel. The solar plexus supplies all the viscera in the abdominal cavity. It consists of a great network of nerves and ganglia situated behind the stomach. The semilunar ganglia of the solar plexus—two in number, one on each side—are the largest ganglia in the body. Seven plexuses are derived from the solar plexus: the phrenic plexus, the suprarenal plexus. the renal plexus, the spermatic plexus, the cœliac plexus, the superior mesenteric plexus, and the aortic plexus. This chakra is described as "blue like the clouds" and contains within it the triangular discus of fire and three fire seeds called swastika, which lie outside of the triangle. "Within this lotus the Yogi must then contemplate the four-armed god of fire, bright as the rising sun, riding on a buffalo." On his lap is a Rudra, "red like vermillion and having three eyes." The body of "the old red Rudra" is smeared with ashes. "This old Rudra is the creator and destroyer of the universe. With one hand he deals out bounty and with another intrepidity." Within this lotus is also the four-handed, black-colored goddess Lakini, "who as the Devata of this digestive center is said to be 'fond of animal food, and whose breasts are ruddy with the blood and fat which drop from Her mouth'." (See THE SERPENT POWER.) Lakini wears many ornaments, "a red cloth, and is mad." That is, she symbolizes the appetites. The tattvic power of taste is associated with this chakra, and of the organs of action it controls those of excretion. In the Apocalyptic symbolism it is analogous to the Church of Smyrna. "By contemplation of this chakra," writes Dr. Rele, "a Yogi is able to enter into another person's body; he obtains the power of transmuting metals, and of healing the sick, and also of clairvoyance."

Fourth, *Anahata.* A lotus of twelve petals and letters, connected with Venus, and which corresponds generally with the cardiac plexus of modern science. This plexus is situated at the base of the heart and is divided into a *superficial* part lying in the concavity of the arch of the aorta and a *deep* part lying between the trachea and the aorta. In the Hindu books this chakra is described as "having the brightness of the red *Bandhuka* flower. Within this flower is the smoke-colored hexagonal air ventricle." Within this is the essence of air "mounted on a black antelope; its color is smoke and it has four hands." Within this essence of air is Isha, the Master of the first three chakras, "white as a goose, dealing out bounty and courage with its two hands." Within this lotus is also the three-eyed Kalkini, "bright as lightning, wearing a necklace of bones and holding in her four hands a snare and a skull." Within the pericarp of this lotus, "bright as millions of lightnings is a three-eyed Shakti." Within this Shakti is a gold-colored Shiva, "his head like a full-blown lotus." According to Arthur Avalon, it is in this place that the Munis (saints) hear that "sound which comes without the striking of any two things together," which is the Pulse of Life. The tattvic power of smell is associated with this chakra, and of the organs of action it controls the membrum virile. In the Apocalyptic symbolism this chakra is analogous to the Church of Thyatria. "By contemplating this lotus," writes Dr. Rele, "a Yogi becomes clairvoyant and clairaudient, and is able to see adepts moving in the air, and gains the power of traveling at will to any part of the world by the exercise of his volition."

Fifth, *Vishuddha*. A lotus of sixteen petals and letters, connected with Mercury, and which corresponds generally with the pharyngeal plexus of modern science. This plexus is formed by branches of the glosso-pharyngeal, pneumogastric, and sympathetic nerves, which supply the muscles and mucus membrane of the pharynx, etc. The Hindus describe this chakra as in the guttural region, "a smoky lotus," having within it a circular ethereal region "bright as the full moon." This ether is the essence of Akasha, which is robed in white and represented as mounted on a white elephant. The Siddhis say that "within this ethereal region (which is represented as holding a snare, a hook, benediction, and intrepidity in its four hands) is a five-faced, three-eyed, ten-handed Shiva wearing a tiger skin." There is also the goddess Shakini. Her color is red and she is robed in white garments. "Within the pericarp of this lotus is a spotless disc of the moon, which is the vestibule of final emancipation." The tattvic power of hearing is associated with this chakra, and of the organs of action it controls the mouth. In the Apocalyptic symbolism it is analogous to the Church of Sardis. "By contemplating this lotus," writes Dr. Rele, "the whole body is purified of diseases and complaints, and a Yogi is able to live for one thousand years in eternal youth; in fact, he is dead to all the outer worlds and becomes absorbed in his inner life."

Sixth, *Ajna*. A lotus of two petals and letters, connected with the moon, and which corresponds generally with the cavernous plexus of the brain. This plexus is located in the skull on each side of the sella turcica of the sphenoid bone, at a point somewhat below the bridge of the nose and behind the face. According to the UTTARA-GITA, "between the eyebrows is situated a lotus

called Ajna, having two petals. . . . It is silvery like the moonbeams and is
the place of communion of Yogis. Within this cell is a six-headed goddess
named Hakini of the color of moonbeams; she holds in her four hands books,
a skull, a musical instrument, and a rosary." According to the commentary,
in this chakra is situated the mind, and in its pericarp is the "inverted triangle,
or yoni, and the phallus of Shiva, called *Itara Linga.*" This symbol of Shiva
is "bright as electricity." By it is illumined "the minds of men," and it is the
primordial symbol of the Vedas—"OM." At the extremity of this cell, "a

—From Musæum Hermeticum.

ALCHEMICAL FIGURE OF SPINE AND CHAKRAS.
Kundalini is the hidden fire of the Rosicrucians and is declared by them to be the luminous
agent by the aid of which Moses destroyed the Golden Calf.

little above the eyebrows is the seat of the intellect, above the intellect is a
crescent, above which is a dot, and near it (the dot) is a Shiva bright as the
moon." The seat of the universal infinite Spirit, Knower and Seer of all, "is
in the brain (at the mouth of the Sushumna nerve where the two brains meet,
and over it the Brahmans keep a long braid of hair)." According to the
disciplines, the Yogi "must carry his intellect to that point, where his luminosity
excels the sun, the moon, and the fire." (The sun, moon, and fire here represent Pingala, Ida, and Sushumna, which have converged.) The Ajna shines
with the glory of Dhyana (meditation). The tattvic power or quality of
thought is associated with this chakra, and of the organs of action it is occasionally identified with the mind. In the Apocalyptic symbolism it is analogous

MAN—THE GRAND SYMBOL OF THE MYSTERIES

to the Church of Philadelphia. "By contemplation of this (chakra)," writes Dr. Rele, "a Yogi gains most wonderful powers. This chakra is called the plexus of command."

Seventh, *Sahasrara*. A lotus of a "thousand petals" and connected with the sun. It is very difficult to associate this chakra with any part or organ known to Western science. Some writers have attempted to identify it with the pineal gland, others with the higher brain ventricles, and still others with nerve centers in the upper part of the cerebral hemispheres. THE SHATCHAKRA NIRUPANA describes the Sahasrara as a lotus of a thousand petals either in or pertaining to the nature of a vacuum. The lotus is lustrous and "whiter than the full moon," and "has its head turned downward." A great effulgency pervades this lotus. "Within this effulgence is a triangle bright as electricity wherein is a very secret vacuum adored by the immortals." In this vacant place dwells the great Shiva, whose form is akashic and "who is the destroyer of ignorance and illusion." There is a phase of the moon in this chakra, "like the roseate sun of the morning, possessed of sixteen attributes and as fine as the hundredth part of the string of a stalk of the lotus." Within this phase of the moon is another phase called Nirvana, "as fine as the thousandth part of the human hair and as luminous as twelve suns. Its form is crescent-like and its luminosity is not always visible. It appears and disappears from time to time." Within this "dwells the force called Nirvana, whose effulgence transcends tens of millions of suns. She is as fine as the ten millionth part of the human hair. She is the mother of the three universes and from her is incessantly flowing the nectar of life." It is within this Nirvanic force, according to the Tantrics, that Shiva is seated, "who is pure and eternal and accessible to deep meditation." Both the tattvic power and the organ of action for this chakra are spiritual and beyond analysis. In the Apocalyptic symbolism it is analogous to the Church of Laodicea. When by the disciplines of Yogi Kundalini reaches this point, the adept is said to be in "seedless Samadhi, by which he gets in tune with the Infinite and is freed from rebirth." (Dr. (Rele.)

The passage of Kundalini upward towards Sahasrara is marked by a gentle warmth. As it rises, the lower part of the body becomes cold and only the crown of the head retains warmth and pulse. This condition is also accompanied by other phenomena, but woe to the unhappy mortal who raises Kundalini prematurely to the brain! The sting of the fiery serpent is most deadly, as those know who have witnessed the results of her being raised before her time. She will burn her way to the brain and destroy the rational qualities of the mind. This spiritual, twisting force is not only an illumining agent but, like the serpent which is its symbol, can prove a deadly poison. Hints of Eastern occultism are constantly being brought to the Western world, but in too many cases disaster has resulted. When esoteric knowledge or doctrine is committed to individuals incapable of understanding and rightly using it, the forces liberated by such discipline are almost certain to result in tragedy. The warning cannot be too strongly emphasized that, while the study of the Yoga and Tantric doctrines will acquaint the student with many useful secrets concerning the mysteries of Nature and the constitution of man, the practices of these cults should be limited to those who have identified themselves utterly with East Indian systems of living and thought and who have placed themselves under the instruction of a properly qualified East Indian teacher. It is well that all should know the theories of occultism, but woe to foolish mortals who attempt esoteric practices without proper preparation, instruction, and guidance!

Disciples of the Mysteries have been warned for centuries not to attempt the development of the chakras of the sympathetic cord according to Hatha Yoga. These chakras are too closely connected with the illusional world. The real plexuses which the disciple of the higher knowledge should strive to unfold are the true soul ganglia within the brain (the master chakras). The body is a negative pole and its own positive parts are contained within the cranial cavity. As the body is controlled by the brain, so the enlightened neophyte should work with the brain, avoiding the negative poles of the brain centers located along the spine. Proper development of the seven brain discs, or spiritual interpenetrating globes, results in the awakening of the spinal flowers by an indirect process. Beware of the direct process of concentrating upon or directionalizing the internal breath towards the spinal centers. The breath of true Raja Yoga is not an air moving in the body, but is the will itself.

TRIGINTA PARI-
QUÆ A DORSALI ME
DUO CONTENTA, ORIGI-
delineatio, quæ trium subsequen-
figurarum secunda

VM NERVORVM
DULLA, DORSI OSSI-
NEM DVCVNT, NVDA
tibus Capitibus communium
numeratur.

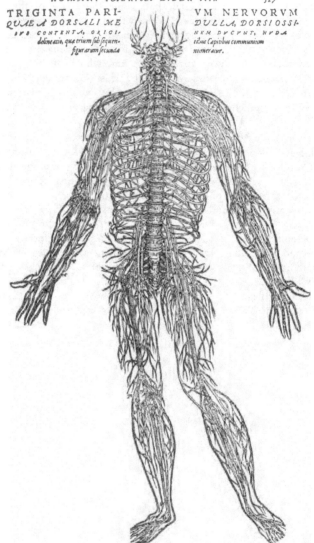

THE NERVOUS SYSTEM OF THE HUMAN BODY. (After Vesalius)

CHAPTER XV

THE SOLAR PLEXUS AND THE PNEUMOGASTRIC NERVE

N THE fourfold division of the human body, such as that made by Philolaos, the Pythagorean, the four elements are assigned to the cavities of the body in the following order: *Earth,* the generative aspect of the soul, to the pelvic cavity; *water,* the passional aspect of the soul, to the abdominal cavity; *fire,* the psycho-intellectual aspect of the soul, to the thoracic cavity; and *air,* the higher intellectual aspect of the soul, to the cranial cavity. The word *thumos*—the lower mind in Greek metaphysics—is derived from *thuein,* "to sacrifice," and is the key to the whole Christian mythos, revealing the true significance of the sacrifice of the one just man slain for the sins of the world. The fact that the word *thymus* is also derived from *thumos* should prove of interest to students of the ductless glands. Esoteric commentaries reverse the elements of fire and air, so that the psycho-intellectual man may be assigned to the cranial cavity and the spiritual, or higher intellect, to the thoracic cavity. Philolaos seats the emotions in the navel and surrounding parts, which is in harmony with Madam Blavatsky, who says there are three principal centers in man—the heart, the head, and the navel. These may again be correlated to spirit, intellect, and emotion respectively.

The solar plexus is the most important of the centers of the sympathetic system and has been called the brain of the stomach. Of the three suns in the microcosm recognized by the Cabalists, the solar plexus is the third and lowest, and in the terms of the Mysteries was the nocturnal, or infernal, luminary—the light of the underworld. Among the names given to the solar plexus, the most significant is the *celiac plexus.* The derivation of the word *celiac* is traceable to *coeliacus,* "relating to the stomach," which, in turn, is derived from *koilia,* meaning "abdomen," and *koilos,* meaning "hollow" or "heavens." Three heavens were recognized by the philosophers. The highest, or starry, was the seat of principles; the central, planetary or sidereal, was the seat of the Governors, or Builders; and the lowest, or sublunary, was the seat of the four elements referred to in mystical literature as the quaternary. The sublunary, or elemental, world, which to the sages included the whole visible creation, therefore subsisted in the abdominal cavity of the Grand Man, and over it ruled the night sun—the subterranean Zeus, the infernal Jupiter, under such names as Hades, Father Dis, and Serapis. In the curious figure of the Grand Man which appears in REISCH'S MARGARITA PHILOSOPHICA, this mystery is cabalistically set forth, for it will be noted that the figure so stands that the elements correspond with the abdominal region, and the planetary orbits with the higher parts of the body of the Grand Man. With his head he supports the heavens, while the upper part of the cranium coincides with the North Pole marked by a large star, and the soles of the feet with the South Pole similarly marked.

Paracelsus recognizes the existence of three suns, of which the first lights the spirit, the second the soul, and the third the body—and by *body*, the animal impulses as well as the organisms are inferred. As the great Swiss so wisely observed: "The body will not be warmed and lighted and the mind and spirit be left in darkness." The physical sun of our solar system is merely the reflector of spiritual and intellectual light. The Rosicrucians affirmed the existence of an intellectual sun, which illumines the sphere of reason, as well as a spiritual sun by which our divine natures are lighted. By the spiritual sun, von Welling understood God the Father; by the intellectual (or soular) sun, Christos, the Redeemer; and by the physical (or bodily) sun, Lucifer who, falling from heaven, established his kingdom in the abyss and is now "locked" within the elemental bodies which have encased his fire. Of the three great brains in the body, therefore, the solar plexus is the "brain of Kama," reflecting from its "polished surface" the rays of the emotional nature, which from this center are distributed throughout the body; and also receiving into itself psychical impressions. "Psychic clairvoyant perceptions," writes Madam Blavatsky of the solar plexus, "often act at this region, as in the reading of letters, psychometrizing substances, etc."

Among the Indians of Old Mexico, the god Tezcatlipoca occupies the position of the Gnostic Demiurge, and has been called the "Jupiter of the Nahua Pantheon." From tradition, it appears that he was originally a mortal man, a great magician or, more correctly, a sorcerer, who turned his infernal necromancies against the benevolent Quetzalcoatl and finally drove him from the land of Anahuac. The name Tezcatlipoca means "the fiery mirror." He is supposed to have carried upon his arm (or, according to some accounts, strapped over his abdomen) a great mirror or polished shield into the surface of which was reflected all the thoughts and actions of mankind. It will be remembered also that the priests of the old Persian fire mysteries carried mirrors as symbols of the etheric world and of their own clairvoyant powers. Tezcatlipoca was "the Adversary" in the Mexican Pantheon. Like the Scandinavian Loki, he plotted against the divine harmony, bringing war and destruction into a land of peaceful valleys and fertile plains. He is described as flying over the world at the head of a vast army of red demons, and any creature of earth who chanced to gaze into his mirror thereupon lost his soul. The power and action of the solar plexus are certainly suggested in this account; for Tezcatlipoca is but a symbol of Kama, the personification of those passions and desires which, loosed upon the world, destroy its peace and order, finally bringing nations as well as men to a common ruin.

In mediumship, the solar plexus functions as a sort of mirror, for upon its sensitive nerve centers are reflected pictures existing in the invisible ethers. To encourage such a condition, however, must inevitably result in retrogression;

—From Reisch's Margarita Philosophica.

THE DEMIURGE OF THE WORLD

it is to return in one sense of the word to the animal state, for the animal kingdom is governed by impulses thrown against the solar plexus and distributed therefrom through the sympathetic nerves. Having no active will of its own, the animal is incapable of combatting the Kamic impulses; consequently, it obeys them implicitly. Through his cerebrospinal nervous system, man combats these impulses with intellect and, having developed individuality, is no longer a pawn in the hand of emotion—except through choice. By thus opening himself to impulses through the solar plexus area, the medium works against his own perfection and by weakening the authority of the will, gradually loses control over his own destiny. There is a difference, then, of about two-thirds the length of the spine between the clairvoyance of the cerebrospinal system and that of mediumship through Kamic control of the sympathetic cords. It is true that the sympathetic nervous system is the vehicle of soul power, but not until Kama has been transmuted and passion has become compassion. Since the solar plexus is the brain of the inferior quaternary, emotional unbalance is generally felt in that region. Fear and excitement may cause nausea or palpitation in the epigastric area. By control of his emotional life man is released from the domination of Kamic impulses. Through unbalanced activity of the solar plexus negative psychic phenomena are often produced, which those unacquainted with the illusionary nature of the astral light may erroneously ascribe to a spiritual origin.

The tenth pair of cranial nerves which rise from the sides of the *medulla oblongata* and, descending in almost a vertical course, "give branches to the external ear, the pharynx, the larynx, the trachea, the esophagus, the heart, and the abdominal viscera" (Morris) is called the *pneumogastric*, the greatest nerve of the boly. An analysis of the word is suggestive as well as informative. The Greek word *pneuma* is generally translated "lung," but it may also be rendered "breath" with equal accuracy. The Greek *pneuma* signified to the ancient philosophers "the soul," or "the life-giving principle," or "the breath of life," etc. *Gastric* specifically means "pertaining to the stomach from the Greek *gastros*, 'stomach,' " but the thought of abdomen is also implied. Instead of *pneumogastric* being simply a compound of lung and stomach, therefore, the word has a much fuller interpretation. It is the nerve of "abdominal, or internal breath, or soul breath."

Another name for the pneumogastric nerve is the *Vagus*, because of its numerous extensions throughout the viscera. This word is also rich in intimations. *Vagus* means "vagrant" or "wandering," but it also has other less familiar renderings. Thus we learn that it signifies "flying" and "light" and "vague" and "fitful" and "uncertain." All these substantiate the older doctrines that there was in the body of man "a tube like a reed through which the spirit as a subtle and indistinguishable agent careened." (See Hippolytus' AGAINST HERESIES.) From the context of this Ante-Nicean Father's remarks it is evident that this reed is not the spinal column, for he states that the spirit is later distributed into what is called the spinal marrow. It was a common belief among earlier thinkers that the breath of man was the carrier of his life principle, and the pneumogastric nerve certainly dominates the respiratory system. The motor fibres of the Vagus, it is most important to note, extend to the "pulse-point," or pacemaker, in the heart, and its branches reach to nearly every vital organ of the body.

Prometheus, the Titan, stole the heavenly fire and brought it down to earth in the hollow stalk of the *ferula*, or giant fennel, an umbelliferous plant. For this offense against the Demiurgic power, "the Friend of Man" was crucified to the high crags of Mount Caucasus. Most commentators have identified the fennel stalk, or *narthex*, with the *thyrsus*, or Bacchic wand—the goad of the gods—and have interpreted it in the mystical anatomy of the Greeks as a symbol of the spinal cord. G. R. S. Mead, in his researches into the Orphic traditions, indicates, however, that there is a difference of opinion on this subject, declaring that "many writers assume that the narthex . . . and the thyrsus or wand, were two different things." The word *ferule* not only signifies the giant fennel, but also a rod for punishing slight offences and for driving cattle. From *narthex* we have *narthecium*, which was a vessel for holding ointments and medicines, made by hollowing out a piece of narthex-wood. It is evident, then, that the hollow reed, the "hidden or mystic goad," may signify the whole body of man, which was inflicted upon the soul as punishment for disobedience to the divine edicts (i. e., the Fall). Or, again, it may more specifically infer some special part, such as the pneumogastric nerve in the stalk of which the breath of life is contained.

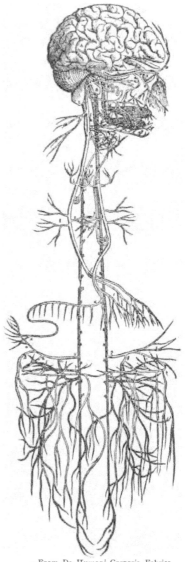

"To my mind," writes Dr. Vasant G. Rele, "Kundalini or the serpent power as it is called is the Vagus nerve of modern times, which supplies and controls all the different and vital organs through different plexuses of the sympathetic portion of the automatic system." In his belief that Kundalini moves in the right branch of the Vagus nerve the Doctor·differs from all his predecessors who have committed themselves on this intriguing subject. If the weight of his ancient Scriptures is not actually against him, the commentaries upon them by India's greatest philosophers and adepts most certainly lend no support to his opinion. Sir John Woodroffe, while admiring Dr. Rele's theory and expressing himself of the opinion that the subject is worthy of the deepest consideration, cannot see in the Vagus nerve the Kundalini, but admits the possibility that the nerve has a "function of practical importance" in Yoga. The late Dr. George Carey, whose correlations between the Bible and the human body

—From De Humani Corporis Fabrica.

THE CORDS OF THE SYMPATHETIC SYSTEM
(After Vesalius)

evidence a lifetime of patient research, sums up the importance of the pneumogastric nerve thus: "This wonderful nerve is the largest bundle of nerve fibres in the body. It is truly a Tree of Life, and its branches distribute the Holy Breath, essence, or Ghost, to lungs and solar plexus." (See GOD, MAN AND THE WORD MADE FLESH.)

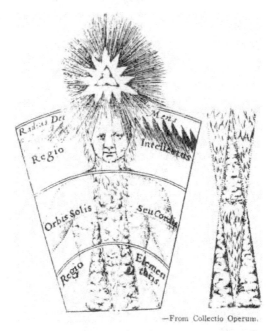

—From Collectio Operum.

EQUILIBRIUM OF THE SUPERIOR AND INFERIOR ELEMENTS THROUGH THE FOCAL POINT OF THE SOLAR PLEXUS ACCORDING TO ROBERT FLUDD

Examine with care the statements concerning the escape of the "Atman" from the body at death, as described in the section on the heart. This spiritual part with its "ethers" (powers or forces) is in juxtaposition to the pulse-point in the physical heart, which it animates and to which it communicates its rhythm. If so placed, what would be the most natural course of its egress? The KHANDOGYA-UPANISHAD describes "a very long highway," which "goes to two places, to one at the beginning and to another at the end." What is the mysterious "artery" that extends from the heart to the crown of the head, and constitutes "the royal road," the highway of the Atman? The spinal cord does not meet these requisites. Its purpose is an entirely different one. The spinal cord is the "thermometer" of the divine "Mercury," but it does not have one of its ends in the heart nor does it go directly from the seat of the Atman to the "Sun." The Vagus nerve meets every requirement as the golden tube (nerves are shown as yellow in nearly all modern textbooks on neurology) through which moves the breath of the soul. The "residue of spirits," the Logoi, or Lords of the vital organs, all retire through the branches of the pneumogastric, and in the great body of this nerve the lord of the pulse joins them and together they rush out to the "Sun." A European physician of the seventeenth century makes this contribution to the subject: "There is a nerve, one branch of which reaches from the brain to the heart, by which the senses are related to the seat of life, and this nerve is a tube through which gases, or spirits, flow upward and downward."

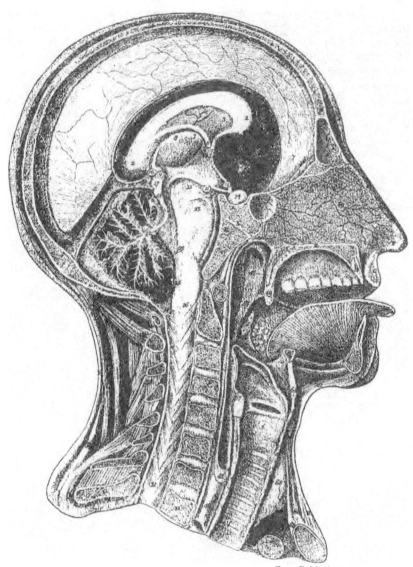

CROSS-SECTION OF THE HUMAN HEAD

In this figure the corpus callosum *is marked* (2), *the* septum lucidum (3), *the pituitary body* (14), *the pineal gland* (16), *and the quadrigeminal bodies* (17) *and* (18). *(See page 144 for further details.)*

CHAPTER XVI

THE PINEAL GLAND, THE EYE OF THE GODS

S THE pineal gland was the one most recognized and written about by the earlier adepts, it is the logical beginning of any occult discussion of the endocrine chain. The *epiphysis cerebri*, or pineal body, secures its name from its peculiar shape (the *pinus*, or pine cone) and arises in the fifth week of the human embryo as a blind sac branching off from that section of the brain which is next in front of the mid-brain—the diencephalon—which includes the area of the third ventricle and adjacent parts. The distal, or remote, portion of this sac becomes the body of the gland. The proximal portion (the point of attachment or origin) remains as the stalk. Is not this pine cone the one to which E. A. Wallis-Budge refers in his OSIRIS AND THE EGYPTIAN RESURRECTION, when in describing the entry of Ani into the presence of Osiris in the Egyptian ritual of *Coming Forth by Day* as "the so-called 'cone' on Ani's wig," for which the good Egyptologist could find no intelligent reason? Is this not also the whirring cone which was among the symbolic playthings of the child Bacchus and which Bastius describes as a small cone-shaped piece of wood around which a cord was wound so that it might be made to spin and give out a "humming noise"? (See ORPHEUS, by G. R. S. Mead.) Those acquainted with the esoteric function of the pineal gland or who have experienced the "whirring" sound attendant upon its activity will realize how apt is the analogy.

Ingrowths of connective tissue from the *pia mater*, that delicate and highly vascular membrane investing the brain and spinal cord, later divide the body of the gland into lobules. At birth the structure is comparatively large and by twelve years it has attained its full size. Here again is a possible analogy to the Bacchus myth, for the toy cone was a symbol peculiar to the childhood of the god. In other words, under normal conditions, the gland deteriorates with adolescence. Retrograde evolution, or degeneration, of the pineal body begins about the sixth or seventh year and is practically complete by puberty. It should be distinctly remembered, however, that whereas Nature has eliminated other organs and parts of the primitive man, this has remained; and realizing Nature's economy, we must recognize the gland as still contributing in some way to human functioning. According to Dr. J. F. Gudernatsch, formerly of Cornell University Medical College, "several, at least three, dorsal diverticula *(epiphyses)* develop during the second month of fetal life from the roof of the diencephalon. They are entirely rudimentary in man. The *epiphyses proper* is the most posterior one and is the only one, which, in man, differentiates to any extent. The other two are the *paraphysis* and the *parietal eye*, a rudimentary sense-organ of some reptiles." According to Haeckel, true eyes that cannot see are to be found in certain animals, deeply placed within the head, covered by thick skins and muscles.

The *thyrsus,* or sceptre of the Greek Mysteries, consisted of a staff surmounted by a pine cone and twisted about with grape and ivy leaves. The whole form of this sceptre is symbolic of the spinal cord, its Nadis and plexuses, the pineal gland, and the pneumogastric nerve, all closely related to the mysteries of regeneration. The pineal gland is described by Santee as "a cone-shaped body *(corpus pineale)* 6 mm. (0.25 in.) high and 4 mm. (0.17 in.) in diameter, joined to the roof of the third ventricle by a flattened stalk, the habenula. . . . The pineal body is situated in the floor of the transverse fissure of the cerebrum, directly below the splenium of the corpus callosum, and rests between the superior colliculi of the quadrigeminal bodies on the posterior surface of the mid-brain. It is closely invested by pia mater. The interior of the pineal body is made up of closed follicles surrounded by ingrowths of connective tissue. The follicles are filled with epithelial cells mixed with calcareous matter, the brain-sand *(acervulus cerebri).* Calcareous deposits are found also on the pineal stalk and along the chorioid plexuses. The function of the pineal body is unknown. . . . In reptiles there are two pineal bodies, an anterior and a posterior, of which the posterior remains undeveloped, but the anterior forms a rudimentary, cyclopean eye. In the Hatteria, a New Zealand lizard, it projects through the parietal foramen and presents an imperfect lens and retina and, in its long stalk, nerve fibers. The human pineal body is probably homologous with the posterior pineal body of reptiles."

The *Branchiostoma lanceolatum,* a small transparent marine animal, about two inches in length, is the only vertebrate, so far as known, which does not possess a pineal gland. In reptiles, according to Spencer, the gland is of considerable length and passes out (as noted by Santee) through an opening in the roof of the skull. In the chameleon, the gland lies under a transparent scale in the parietal foramen, and its cordlike middle structure, according to Hertwig, "bears a certain resemblance to the embryonic optic nerve. . . . Investigators who, like Rabl-Ruckhard, Ahlborn, Spencer, and others, have studied the pineal gland, are of of the opinion that *the pineal body must be considered as an unpaired parietal eye, which in many cases, for example in reptiles, appears to be tolerably well preserved, but in most vertebrates is in process of degeneration."* This learned author then affirms the probability that in reptiles the pineal gland reacts to the influence of light, but to what degree must remain *undecided.*

In his lecture on the eyes delivered at the Mayo Clinic and afterwards published by the American Optical Company, Thomas Hall Shastid, A.M., M.D., F.A.C.S., LL.D., etc., said: "Some of the amphibians had a median, or pineal, eye; an eye in the back of the head. Many of the gigantic saurians, too, of the Mesozoic time had this eye, and, in any geological museum, you can still see, in the back of the giant lizard's skull, the hole through which this strange eye formerly looked out. In ourselves the hole has boned over, and the eye has shrunk up into the so-called pineal gland. . . . The pineal eye made its first appearance in the world far back among the invertebrates. It was, indeed, an invertebrate eye (that is, one with the rods turned toward the vitreous, instead of away from it, consequently with no blind spot) but it persisted (still in the invertebrate form of eye) through some of the fishes, through the amphibians generally, through the lizards, and then began degenerating; possibly because the vertebrates had other eyes, and these were of the vertebrate (for some unguessable reason a more suitable) type." Is the occultist, then, unreasonable when he affirms that in the beginning of life upon this

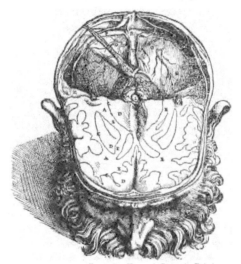

—From De Humani Corporis Fabrica.

THE PINEAL GLAND. (After Vesalius)

planet vertebrates were hermaphrodites and "objectively one-eyed"? Is it not also more reasonable to agree with occultism that this gland actually extended through the skull somewhat like an antenna as an organism of generalized sense perception than to accept the suggestions of Professor Lankester that man was originally transparent so that the inner eye could see through the walls of the head? Did the Egyptians know that reptiles present the highest development of this gland and for this reason coiled the serpent upon their foreheads where the third eye of the Orientals is placed by symbolic license? Was not the uræus the symbol of wisdom and is not the pineal gland the organ of a method of acquiring knowledge which is no longer employed in general but is a secret preserved by the elect?

As an emblem of divinity, the pineal gland would naturally be associated with royalty, for the kings were the shadows of the gods upon earth. The crown of Lower Egypt and also the *Pschent*, or crown of the Double Empire (consolidated Egypt) were surmounted by a curious antenna, feeler, or very thin curved horn, which is most reminiscent of the descriptions of the structure of the third eye that have descended from the first ages.   The *Maat*, or ostrich plume of the Law—another Egyptian symbol of truth, is quite similar to the pineal gland in shape and was worn like the feather of the American Indians as though rising from the parietal foramen. By many tribes birds are regarded as emissaries between the manidos and mankind and bird feathers worn in this fashion could easily have a double significance.   The peacock feather, with its ocellated spot, is attached to the head of the Chinese mandarin in a position somewhat similar to the pineal gland in the human head (lying backward), and as a symbol of dignity or an enlightened condition accompanying greatness may have a similar origin.

In occultism the pineal gland is regarded as a link between the objective and subjective states of consciousness; or, in exoteric terminology, the visible and invisible worlds of Nature. In the religions of the Latins it was, therefore, referred to as Janus, the two-faced god and keeper of the gates of sanctuary. This divinity was the antitype of St. Peter, who succeeded him as the warder of the heavenly portals and who carries the two keys of his office—one to the golden mystery of the spirit and the other to the silver mystery of the body. Two-faced gods are frequently spoken of in ancient records.   Hermae like the *bifrons* Janus may still be seen in old Roman villas, with the occasional and intriguing exception that one of the faces will be male and the other female—the *herm-aphroditus* again?   The female face represents the animal soul and the male the divine soul, and the whole figure is indicative of the occult structure and function of the pineal gland.   Gould, in his MYTHICAL MONSTERS, gives several examples drawn from the earliest writings of the Chinese.   Hindu mythology also abounds in polycephalous divinities, and from the far-off Tibetans we learn that one of the titles of Avalokiteshvara is *Samanta-mukha*, "he whose face looks every way."   There is an alchemical mystery also in connection with the pineal gland, for the regeneration of man is dependent upon the tincturing of this gland, which must be transmuted from base metal into gold.   Unawakened by Kundalini, the pineal gland is the vehicle of *kama-manas*—the animal mind (Aphrodite)—but when tinctured by the spiritual light, it becomes *buddhi-manas*—the divine mind (Hermes). This buddhi-manas is the Thoth of the later Egyptian Mysteries, the god of learning and letters, and (according to the extravagant statements of his priests) the source of twenty-six thousand books.

The philosophers know that the pineal gland was an organ of conscious vision long before the physical eyes *issued from the brain*, not necessarily or exclusively of such vision as we have today but rather vision of that world wherein man dwelt before his lapse into his present state. As his contact with the physical world grew more complete, the individual lost his functions upon the inner planes of life, together with his conscious connection with the

Creative Hierarchies in the universe about him. Only through discipline—effort directed by wisdom and law—can he rise again into the sphere of his spiritual completeness. It is a mistake to infer that the pineal gland *as a physical body* literally possesses all the occult virtues ascribed to it by the sages. The gland itself is not the third eye, but only the reflection of that organ—its counterpart or symbol in the material constitution. It is a relic bearing witness to an ancient faculty, and because it has endured through these eras of spiritual obscuration, promises the ultimate restoration of the function to which it bears witness. The true power of the gland is in its spiritual counterpart, even as the whole strength of man abides in his invisible nature. The true third eye cannot be seen by the ordinary vision, but is visible to the clairvoyant as a vibrant spectromatic aura surrounding the outer body of the gland and pulsating with an electrical light. "The special physical organ of perception in the brain," writes H. P. Blavatsky, "is located in the aura of the pineal gland. This aura answers in vibration to any impression, but it can only be sensed, not perceived, in the living man. During the process of thought, manifesting in consciousness, a constant vibration occurs in the light of this aura, and a clairvoyant looking at the brain of a living man may almost count, see with the spiritual eye, the seven scales, the seven shades of light, passing from the dullest to the brightest. You touch your hand; before you touch it the vibration is already in the aura of the pineal gland, and has its own shade of color. It is this aura which causes the wear and tear of the organ, by the vibrations it sets up. The brain set vibrating conveys the vibrations to the spinal cord and so to the rest of the body. Powerful vibrations of joy or sorrow may thus kill. The fires are always playing around the pineal gland but when the Kundalini illuminates them for a brief instant the whole universe is seen. Even in deep sleep the third eye opens. This is good for Manas, who profits by it, though we ourselves do not remember."

It was Descartes who saw the pineal gland as the abode of the soul or the sidereal spirit in man. He reasoned that although the *anima* was joined to every organ of the body, there must be one special part through which the divine portion exercised its functions more directly than through the rest. After concluding that neither the heart nor the brain could be as a whole that special locality, he decided through a process of elimination that it must be that little gland which, though bound to the brain, yet had an action or motion independent of it. Descartes concluded that the pineal gland could be put into a kind of swinging motion by the animal spirits which move through the concavities of the skull. We must consider him, therefore, as a powerful figure in the transition period between mediæval and modern science.

We cannot do better than to insert at this point, in Descartes' own words, the arguments by which he convinced himself that the pineal gland was the seat of the soul. The following is extracted from a very early edition of his celebrated treatise, OF MAN, and the terminology is preserved in all the quaintness of the original. "Yet is not the whole Brain the Seat of this Inward

Sense, but only some part of it; for otherwise the Optick Nerves, and the Pith of the Backbone, as being of the same substance with the Brain, would be the Residence of the Inward Sense. Now this peculiar place of the Soul's Residence is the Conarion, or Glandula Pinealis, a certain Kernel, resembling a pine-apple, placed in the midst of the Ventricles of the Brain, and surrounded with the arteries of the Plexus Chorides. The reason why we take this Kernel to be the peculiar Seat of the Soul, is because this part of the Brain is single, and one only. For whereas all the Organs of the Senses are double; there can be no Reason again, why we should not perceive two Objects instead of one; but only because above these Impressions are transmitted to a certain part of the Brain, which is single and one only, wherein both are conjoyn'd. Furthermore, it is also requisite that the part should be movable, to the end that the Soul by agitating of it immediately, might be able to send the Animal Spirits into some certain Muscles, rather than into others. And foreasmuch as this Kernel is only supported by very small Arteries that encompass it, it is certain that the least thing will put it into motion. And therefore we conclude, that this inmost part of the Brain is the Seat of the Soul, in which it exerts its operations of Understanding and Willing of whatsoever proceeds from the Body, or tends towards it."

In ascribing motion to the pineal gland, Descartes, though not an occultist, hit upon one of the most profound secrets of the ancient Mysteries. The great Descartes continues: "Accordingly the Common Sense may be described to be an Internal Sense, whereby all the Objects of the External Senses are perceived and united in the midst of the Brain, as the common Center of all Impressions. Or the Common Sense is nothing else, but the concurrence of all motions made by the Objects upon the Nerves, in the Conarion, happening at the same time that the Objects move the Senses. Neither doth the Smallness of this Kernel hinder its being the Instrument of the Common Sense; but on the contrary, those Persons are the most stupid in whom this Kernel, because of its bigness, is not so easily moved; and those the most witty and apprehensive in whom this Kernel is less, because it is so much the more easily moved: And tho' it were much less than it is, yet would it be big enough with respect to the several Points of the Ventricles, and to the Pipes of the Nerves." For centuries Descartes was ridiculed by the learned, and his mystical conclusions were of that type relegated by the great Tyndall to the field of "poesy." And now at this late day comes a "conditional" vindication of Descartes' views from a science which, all too often, suffers from an "infallibility" complex. "Recently, however, the great Frenchman's idea is gaining favor in the eye of science—that is, if we regard the soul as a department of the human intellect. [Sic!] For, apparently, the pineal gland is concerned directly, although still mysteriously, with the development of intelligence." (See HOW WE BECAME PERSONALITIES.)

Very small children but recently removed from their embryonic recapitulation of humanity's earlier struggle for existence have an extremely sensitive area about the crown of the head where the skull has not yet closed. In rare cases it never closes at all, although usually the sutures unite between the seventh and ninth years. The sensitivity of the area of the head over the third eye during childhood is usually accompanied by a phase of clairvoyance or, at least, sensitiveness. The child is still living largely in the invisible worlds and, while its physical organism is still more or less unresponsive due to its incomplete state, the child has at least a shadow of activity in those worlds with which it was once fully connected through the open gateway of the pineal gland. As the higher intellect—the *Ego* of the Latins—gradually retires into

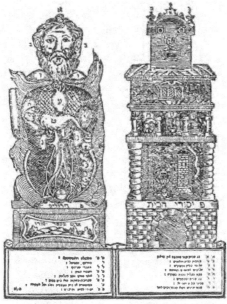

—From Cohn's Treatise on Cabalistical Medicine.

AN EARLY FIGURE SHOWING CORRESPONDENCES BETWEEN THE COM-
PARTMENTS OF THE HUMAN BODY AND THE ROOMS OF A HOUSE

the evolving physical structure, it closes the heavenly door behind it. This entry of man into his body is associated in some mysterious way with the "soul crystals" (acervulus cerebri) which form in the pineal gland.

The mystery of the third eye is very beautifully elucidated in the Scandinavian Mystery legends of the World Tree already referred to. In the Eddic tradition it is written that upon the topmost branch of Yggdrasil sat an eagle gazing out upon the universe and upon the head of the eagle, between his eyes, perched a hawk. The eagle has generally been interpreted to signify the element of air and the hawk the ether of space. But when we remember that to the Egyptians the hawk was the peculiar symbol of Horus—whose single eye unquestionably represented the pineal gland to the initiates of his order— the curious figure takes on new importance. A learned Cabalist of the last century declared that from his study of THE ZOHAR and the relation of the Tree of the Sephiroth to the human body, the first Sephira—Kether, the Crown —signified the pineal gland; and that the next two Sephiroth—Chochma and Binah, one placed on either side of it—were the two lobes of the cerebrum. Several statements appear in the Hebrew Scriptures that may be taken as indirect allusions to the pineal gland.

This little body has a tiny finger-like protuberance at one end—that farthest from the point of attachment. This protuberance is called the staff of God and corresponds to the holy spear in the Grail Mysteries. The whole gland is shaped like the evaporating vessels or retorts of the alchemists. The vibrating finger on the end of this gland is the rod of Jesse and the sceptre of the high priest. Certain exercises prescribed in the inner schools of Eastern and Western occultism, when performed by one qualified for such action, cause this finger to vibrate at an incalculable rate of speed, which results in the buzzing or droning sound in the head already mentioned. This phenomenon can be very distressing and may even have disastrous results when brought about without sufficient knowledge of occult matters. The pineal gland and the pituitary body have been called the head and the tail respectively of the Dragon of Wisdom. The psychical and occult currents moving in the brain in their ascent through the spinal cord (see chapter on *Kundalini and the Sympathetic Nervous System*) must pass through the cerebral aqueduct which is closed by the trap door of the pineal gland. When this body—the ibis of the Egyptians—"lies backwards" as it were on its haunches, it closes the opening into the fourth ventricle and forms a sort of stopper. It thus seals in the contents of the third ventricle, dividing them from the fourth. When stimulated by Kundalini, the gland stands upright, lifting itself like the head of a cobra ready to strike and, like the head of this snake, the gland increases in size and its little finger-like protuberance moves with the rapidity of a serpent's tongue. The pineal gland, having removed itself as an obstruction to the passage between the ventricles, permits the essences in the brain to mingle in a spiritual alchemy.

The "All-Seeing Eye" of the Masonic Brethren; the "Eye Single" of the Scriptures by which the body is filled with light; the "One Eye" of Odin which enabled him to know all the Mysteries; the "Eye of Horus" which at one time Typhon swallows up; the "Eye of the Lord" which, as Boehme says, "beholds all"—all these, then, are but allusions to that primitive organ which, according to the commentaries forming the basis of THE SECRET DOCTRINE, "getting gradually petrified," disappeared from view, having been drawn "deeply into the head" and buried "deeply under the hair." It is of this, then, that Proclus writes in his first book ON THE THEOLOGY OF PLATO, where he declares that the soul, having entered into the adytum, or inner recesses of her nature, perceives "the genus of the gods, and the unities of things" without the aid of her objective eyes, which are described as "closed." Is there anything unscientific, then, in affirming that the pineal gland is the third eye of the historico-mythological "men of ancient times," such as are recorded by Berossus in his fragments on the origins of the Chaldeans and of which the Greeks have record in their fables of the Cyclops? The mystic knows that the pineal gland is all that remains of the "Eye of Dangma," the inner eye of the illumined sage, the "Eye of Shiva" placed vertically upon the foreheads of the gods and Dhyanas to signify that in them the spiritual sight is not obscured. When gazing at the inscrutable face of Avalokiteshvara, be reminded by his third eye of the commentaries wherein it is written that when the inner "man" is active, the eye "swells and expands," and the Arhat is able to feel and see this activity and regulate his actions accordingly.

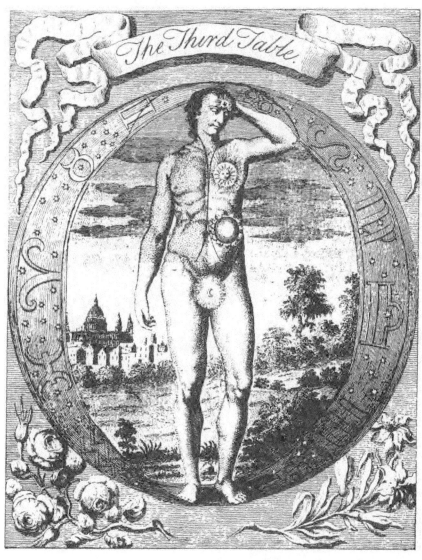

—From William Law Edition of Jacob Boehme.

THE VITAL CENTERS IN THE HUMAN BODY,
According to the figures of Jacob Boehme.

CHAPTER XVII

THE ENDOCRINE CHAIN AND BODILY EQUILIBRIUM

HE seven glands—ductless and otherwise—with which occult-ism is primarily concerned, are the pineal gland, the pituitary body, the thymus, the liver, the spleen, and the suprarenal capsules, or adrenals. These little understood bodies, at least some of which were given consideration in ancient times but were more or less ignored during the Dark Ages, have now come to be recognized as the "dictators of our destiny." Enthusiastic endocrinologists are now of the opinion that not only the harmony of the "bodily league" but also the higher aspects of man's functioning—his morals, emotions, and thoughts, his personality, individuality, and temperament—are to a great degree a matter of endocrines. Not Dr. Johnson's drop of green bile, but the glands are what put empires at hazard. Napoleon's own pituitary—and not the Duke of Wellington—brought down the eagle of the First Empire. Apropos of this, ponder the words of Samuel Wyllis Bandler: "If the world, in the near future, administers to its diplomats, to its highest officials, to its legislators, to its people the proper endocrines, especially anterior pituitary, and inhibit the adrenal cortex a little bit, there may be no more wars." (See THE ENDOCRINES.)

The opinions of occultism relative to the significance of the pineal gland are treated of in detail in the section devoted to that subject. Therefore, at this point only a few general matters will be considered. "It is almost with a shudder," writes Dr. Fred E. Wynne, "that one recalls the legend of the Cyclops! Was this tradition based on some monstrosity, perhaps some race afflicted with a hideous atavism; human in form, gigantic in stature, blundering about the earth with the undeveloped brain and the pineal eye of the inverte-brate? Fortunately, there is only Homer's imagination to suggest such a nightmare, so horrible a declension from the ordered progress of evolution." (See DUCTLESS AND OTHER GLANDS.) We fear that the good Doctor's optimism is unfounded. Unfortunately, blind Homer is not the only narrator of "giants" —one-eyed or otherwise. Monsters that would have driven endocrinologists to distraction are recorded in the early writings of nearly all civilized nations. A sarcophagus of giants was found in the year 1858 on the site of the ancient City of Carthage. Philostratus, an old pagan writer, wrote of a skeleton 22 cubits long and another of 12 cubits, both seen by himself. The Abbé Pegues, in THE VOLCANOES OF GREECE, declares that "in the neighborhood of the volcanoes of the isle of Thera, giants with enormous skulls were found laid out under colossal stones." (See THE SECRET DOCTRINE.) Since the development of the recent revolutionary theories concerning glands, science is faced with a many-horned dilemma. No longer is anything improbable in the ancient accounts of "monsters." The probability of an unsynchronized activity of the glands during the first *ages* of human life lends credence to the long ridiculed "fables" of the elder historians. It might be both interesting and illuminating for men of scientific bent to reconstruct man as he was before retrograde evolution set in in so many parts of the endocrine chain. There is a fair measure of probability that the result of their labors would prove astonishingly similar to the descriptions of the men of the pre-Adamite races which have descended to us in occult tradition.

Early in the twentieth century a boy was brought to the clinic of the great German neurologist, Von Hochwert, whose condition stirred up all manner of speculation. Apparently this was a normal boy twelve or thirteen years of age. But his parents declared that he was only five years old, and later these statements were confirmed absolutely. A few months before, this boy had begun to grow rapidly. . . . His intellectual development also—the things which he talked about and what he appeared to think about, indicated the thoughts and speculations of maturity. His voice was deep and he had long since ceased to play with the toys of childhood. Yet he was only five years old." A few weeks after his admission to the clinic, the child died and the autopsy revealed that he had been suffering from a tumor of the pineal gland. "There is also reason to believe that the pineal gland has something to do with the development of intellect." (See HOW WE BECOME PERSONALI-TIES by Edward Huntington Williams, M. D.) Does not this statement substantiate the esoteric doctrine that the pineal gland "is the chief and fore-most organ of spirituality in the human brain, the seat of genius"? (E. S. Ins.) The derangement due to the tumor of this gland resulted in a premature matur-ity. Is it not amazing that the malfunctioning of this tiny organ alone should metamorphose a child into an adult; and is it not more amazing still that a part of the body so potent should be regarded as a mere vestige of a rudi-mentary eye? This single example—without other corroborative evidence, which, however, is abundant—is sufficient to link this gland with the whole field of intellectual development. It is noteworthy that the diseased state of the gland not only resulted in bodily maturity but that the mind also increased. The tumor prevented the gland from controlling the flow of *Manas*, and certainly demonstrates the accuracy of the occult contention that the pineal body is the link between the field of man's subjective intellect and his objective thought.

The pituitary body (hypophysis cerebri) is a small ovoid, somewhat flattened vascular mass which rests in the sella turcica of the sphenoid bone, and is connected with the third ventricle of the brain by the infundibulum. The sella turcica is described as "a skull within a skull," and one author has noted that Nature must have regarded the pituitary body as of vital importance, for no other part of the body has received such protection. The gland consists of two very clearly marked lobes separated by fibrous lamina. The anterior is the largest and is somewhat oblong and concave behind (kidney-shaped), and receives into its concavity the smaller and rounder posterior lobe. According to Gray, the anterior lobe "is developed from the ectoderm of the buccal cavity, and resembles to a considerable extent, in microscopic structure, the thyroid body." The closed vesicles of the pituitary body, "lined with columnar epithelium (in part ciliated), contain a viscid, jelly-like material (pituita), which suggested the old name for the body." (See Santee.) "The posterior lobe," continues Gray, "is developed by an outgrowth from the embryonic brain, and during foetal life contains a cavity which communicates through the infundibulum with the cavity of the third ventricle." It is believed that the pituitary plays an important part in the hibernation of animals. "The anterior portion is especially concerned with the growth of the frame, of muscle and development of the brain. The posterior portion is closely concerned with the development of the sexual organs, of special muscular structures, and of certain features of the process called 'metabolism.'" (See HOW WE BECOME PERSONALITIES by Edward Huntington Williams, M. D.)

It has been noted that the pituitary body contains an internal secretion which seems to stimulate the growth of connective tissue and play an essential part in sexual development. We know also that the pituitary if over active, produces giantism and has a peculiar affinity to the bones and muscles. A subnormal supply of pituitrin produces a general bodily deterioration, reaching in its effects even to the hair and teeth. Among the blessings bestowed by a healthy pituitary are good blood pressure, healthy sex tone, initiative, zest for study, work, sustained interest in occupation, and endurance of youth. Herman H. Rubin, M.D., also comments upon the relationship between this gland and the sensory perceptions, the vitality and the transformation of energy into forms necessary for the bodily maintanance. (See YOUR MYSTERIOUS GLANDS.)

The pituitary, which has been called the gland of persistent effort, was apparently known to the initiated priests of antiquity, who associated it with the feminine aspect in symbolism. It stood as the *yoni* in its relationship to the pineal gland, which was the primitive phallus. In the legends of the Egyptian Isis, the Hindu Radha, and the Christian Virgin Mary the functions of this gland are intimated. The pituitary body is the "barometer" of the whole ductless gland chain, the first to reveal disorder in the endocrine system. In the Egyptian Mysteries, the pituitary body was the initiator, for as we shall see, it "raised the candidate"—the pineal gland. In the Egyptian mythos, Isis in her aspect as the pituitary body conjures Ra, the supreme deity of the sun, (here symbolic of the pineal gland) to disclose his sacred name—the word of power—which he is finally forced to do. In certain East Indian metaphysical systems the pituitary body is called *manas-antaskarana,* "the bridge of mind."

When stimulated by the disciplines of occult philosophy, the pituitary body begins to glow with a faint roseate hue. Little rippling rings of light emanate from it to gradually fade out a short distance from the gland itself.

If the stimulation be continued, the emanating rings about the gland grow stronger and a distinct pulse beat is apparent in the flow of the forces. The emanations are not equally distributed, the circles gradually elongating into elliptics, with the body of the gland at the small end. The elliptic extends back from the gland on the side adjacent to the third ventricle and reaches out in graceful parabolas to the pineal gland. As the stream of force becomes more powerful, the luminosity lights the interior of the ventricles, approaching ever closer to the slumbering eye of Shiva. At last tingeing the form of the gland itself with a golden red light, it gently coaxes the pineal gland into animation. Under the benign warmth and radiance of the pituitary fire, the "divine eye" thrills, flickers, and finally opens. Madam Blavatsky thus describes the process: "The arc (of the Pituitary Gland) mounts upward more and more toward the Pineal Gland, until finally the current, striking it, just as when the electric current strikes some solid object, the dormant organ is awakened and set all aglowing with the Akasic Fire. This is the psycho-physiological illustration of two organs on the physical plane, which are the concrete symbols of and represent respectively, the metaphysical concepts called Manas and Buddhi. The latter, in order to be conscious on this plane, needs the more differentiated fire of Manas: *but once the sixth sense has awakened the seventh,* the light which radiates from it illuminates the fields of infinitude; for a brief space of time, man becomes omniscient; the Past and the Future, Space and Time, disappear and become for him the present." (See E. S. Ins.)

The thyroid gland, now dignified as the "keystone of the endocrine arch," is a horseshoe-shaped body placed in the throat just below the Adam's apple. It has two lateral lobes, one on each side of the windpipe, connected below by a transverse portion called the isthmus. In giving its description, one author says that it is at the base of the neck, astride the windpipe. It is roughly H-shaped, with the cross-bar of the H representing the isthmus, or transverse connecting piece. It is very difficult to give the size or dimensions of the gland, but its length may be regarded as from two to three inches and its average weight about an ounce. The gland is larger and heavier in the female than in the male, and decreases in size with advancing years. Atrophy is especially noticeable in the pyramidal lobes. "Its first appearance," writes Dr. Fred E. Wynne, "is in extremely primitive organisms known as 'protochordates' "—the first creatures to possess gill clefts, a central nervous system, and a rudimentary backbone. The thyroid gland "still goes on producing the mucus materials used by our far back protochordate ancestor for entangling food particles; though the substance is no longer, owing to the disappearance of the duct, discharged into the pharynx." See Kerr's TEXTBOOK ON EMBRY-OLOGY.)

It is believed that in the lower forms of life the thyroid was a sex gland and was a link between the sex glands and the brain—the lower quaternary and the higher triad respectively in the human body. "The thyroid," writes

Dr. M. W. Kapp, "is the gland that produces land animals and is very important in the evolution of forms, and also progression. The feeding of a thyroid to a Newt transforms it into a salamander—a land breathing animal." The thyroid is occasionally referred to as the vanity gland, because functional disorders in it have a tendency to produce disproportion in the parts of the body and destroy the pleasing aspects of the personality. The thyroid has received more attention than the other glands because of the frequency of goitre and the unsightliness of this affliction. This gland has a tendency to "regulate the speed of living," and as it loses tone, the appearances of age manifest themselves in all parts of the body. Located, as it is, in what Plato calls the isthmus between the body and the head, the thyroid is the mediator between the emotions and the thoughts, and the common denominator of the animal and intellectual life.

The thymus gland is a small body of glandular tissue of very soft consistency, described as roughly pyramidal in shape and situated behind the upper part of the sternum, or breast-bone. At the time of its greatest development, which is during the adolescent period, the gland may reach a length of two inches and a weight of about one and one-quarter ounces. From this time on, the gland normally undergoes a retrogression. The thymic tissue is replaced by fat, so that in an adult the gland contains largely adipose tissue. "Riddle claims that the thymus lost its value for man and mammals when their ancestors began to incubate their eggs within their body and ceased laying them, as do birds and reptiles, with albumen and shells. That was the original function of the thymus. Pigeons whose thymus has been removed lay eggs without shells; but if fed thymus, will lay normal eggs with shells.   *   *   * And thank the thymus because its secretions made it possible for our reptilian ancestor to invent an egg that could evolve into a human ovum." (See WHY WE BEHAVE LIKE HUMAN BEINGS by George A. Dorsey.)

The thymus has been called the gland of precocity. It dominates the growth of the child up to the time of puberty. It has also been named the gland of eternal youth, for its failure to retrogress at the proper time inhibits the maturing of the body. When thymus is fed to a tadpole, it remains a tadpole and does not metamorphose into a frog. In OUR FEAR COMPLEXES by Williams and Hoag, it is stated that out of twenty executed criminals, "all had persistent thymus glands." If the thymus remains dominant, it has a tendency to prevent the normal differentiation of sex expression, resulting in the problem of "intermediate" types. The alarming increase of this equation in our social system warrants profound consideration of the part played by the ductless glands in the social life of man. "Complete absence of the thymus has been found in a large percentage of cases of idiocy, in which a post-mortem examination has been made. In one series of 400 cases there was no thymus in 75 per cent." (See DUCTLESS AND OTHER GLANDS.)

The liver is the largest gland in the body. It weighs approximately three and one-half pounds, is from ten to twelve inches in length, and occupies a great part of the right half of the cage, or basket, formed by the ribs below the diaphragm. The position of the liver varies somewhat with the ascent or descent of the diaphragm. In deep inspiration, the liver descends below the ribs, as also when the intestines are empty. But when the breath is expired, or when the intestines are distended, it is pushed upward. The liver is divided into a right and left lobe, of which the right is much the larger, the proportion being about six to one. Occultism affirms the seat of the *kama-rupa*, or desire body, to be in the greater lobe or vortex of the liver. There are also minor divisions of this gland which increase the number of the lobes to five. As a ductless gland, its most important function is i n connection with the nitrogenous and carbohydrate metabolism. Modern science views the liver as both a storehouse and a "clearing-house" of the body. Three hundred years ago, Burton called it "the shop of humours," declaring that melancholy could be caused by a chill in the liver.

There is a distinct correspondence between the liver and the cerebellum, both of which are seats of *kama*. Like the liver, the cerebellum is both the storehouse and clearing-house for the brain. "The liver and stomach," writes H. P. Blavatsky, "are the correspondences of kama in the trunk of the body, and with these must be classed the navel and the generative organs. The liver is closely connected with the spleen, as is *kama* with the etheric double, and both these have a share in generating the blood. The liver is the general, the spleen, the aide-de-camp. All that the liver does not accomplish is taken up and completed by the spleen." In the symbolism of the early Christians, the piercing of the liver of Christ by the spear of the centurion, Longinus, is identical in meaning with the story of Prometheus and the vulture set to devour his liver by the unrelenting Zeus. As the seat of the animal nature, the liver is the origin of those impulses which must torment man throughout the ages until through wisdom he can release himself from the "Garden of Desire."

The spleen is an oblong flattened mass, its form varying considerably in different individuals. It may be described as mushroom-shaped and is placed on the left side of the body opposite the liver, under the diaphragm and below the median line of the stomach. In the adult, the spleen is about five inches in length, from three to four inches in width but only about one and one-half inches in thickness, and weighs about seven ounces. "The structure of the spleen," writes Dr. Fred. E. Wynne, "and its relations with the blood-vascular system clearly suggested that its function is the manufacture and renewal of the cellular elements of the blood and the elimination of wornout elements. There is no doubt that this is its principal, if not its only, duty, a duty which is shared probably by the lymphatic glands and other lymphatic structures including the red-bone marrow." (See DUCTLESS AND OTHER GLANDS.) The umbrella-like surface of the spleen is but the outer vestment of an invisible organ intimately concerned with the distribution of the solar force throughout the parts of the body. "The vital force," writes Max Heindel, the Rosicrucian mystic, "is absorbed by the vital body through the etheric counterpart of the spleen, wherein it undergoes a curious transformation of color. It becomes pale rose hued and spreads along the nerves all over the dense body. It is to the nervous system what the force of electricity is to the telegraph system." The same author identifies the spleen as the origin of the ectoplasm which, oozing from the vital body of the medium, is used in the materialization of discarnate intelligences.

This conforms with the opinion of H. P. Blavatsky, who sees in the spleen a correspondence with the etheric double which, according to her, "lies curled up" therein. "As the ethereal body is the reservoir of life for the body, the medium and vehicle of Prana, the spleen acts as the center of Prana in the body, from which the life is pumped out and circulated. It is consequently a very delicate organ, though the physical spleen is only a cover for the real spleen." (See THE SECRET DOCTRINE, Vol. III.)

The suprarenal glands (the adrenals) are bodies roughly triangular in shape, slightly concave and sit, much like little cocked hats, upon the tops of the kidneys. In different individuals these glands vary greatly in size. The average is about one and one-half inches in length, somewhat less in width, and weighing about half an ounce. The left suprarenal is usually larger than the right and somewhat semilunar in form. In various forms of malformation, giantism, etc., the adrenals are usually oversized. The vital significance of these glands becomes apparent when we realize that their removal at any stage of life inevitably results in death. "During the long evolutionary rise to power of the human race the adrenals were man's bulwark in the survival of the fittest." (Dr. Herman H. Rubin.) The suprarenals are very closely connected with the sympathetic nervous system and "Gaskell has advanced the interesting hypothesis that these bodies, including the cells of the suprarenal medulla, were phylo-genetically once a part of the sympathetic nervous system." (See article by D. R. Hooker, M.D., in GLANDULAR THERAPY.) The blood and nerve supply to the adrenals is abundant and their internal secretions are of great importance to the circulatory and muscular systems.

The adrenals wreck vengeance upon those who harbor unhealthy mental or emotional reactions. They are glands of "cash" karma for temperamental excess. They prove beyond all doubt that normalcy of attitude is indispensable to health. "Our jealousies, hates, fears, struggles for wealth, power, position, lusts, and our superstitions all call upon the reserve supply of adrenal secretion —the fighting or energizing secretion—until the glands are exhausted and we wonder why so many die of heart disease (over heart action), Bright's disease, diabetes, tuberculosis, cancer, and other diseases of diminished resistance." (See OUR GLANDS AND OUR ENVIRONMENT by Dr. M. W. Kapp.) The adrenals are called the "fighters" of the endocrine system and, conversely, they not only bestow courage but also fear. The temperamental equilibrium of the individual is a definite help to the balance of the adrenals, and the normal functioning of these glands is reflected, in turn, in the optimism, generosity, and kindliness of the disposition. The adrenals are friendly to the pituitary and both exert a marked influence upon the brain and the sexual system.

From the fragmentary records available and the unfortunate confusion growing out of the use of arbitrary terminologies, it is somewhat difficult to concisely express the views of occultism regarding the nature and purpose of the ductless glands. Being unquestionably the "Governors" or "Directors" of the physical body, these glands are the physical counterparts of the vital organs of one of man's superphysical vehicles. Occult students have raised a point with respect to the meaning of the words "Vital Body" and "Etheric Double." From their descriptions, they cannot be considered identical. The Vital Body (or, more correctly, the Vital Principle) is associated with Prana, or the sun, and probably should be considered a force such as electricity rather than as a vehicle. Prana is *Jiva*, or the Universal Life after it has been differentiated throughout the human body. In her ESOTERIC INSTRUCTIONS, Madam Blavatsky states definitely that "the Linga Sharira is the vehicle of Prana," and in her KEY TO THEOSOPHY, she identifies the Linga Sharira with the Astral Body and calls it the "phantom body" and also the *"Double,"* by which the "Etheric Double" is certainly implied. She also calls the Linga Sharira the permanent seed for the physical body. The Linga Sharira is properly under the control of the moon, being so to speak, the reflector of Prana (the sun). Some occultists declare the whole glandular system to be under the control of the sun, by which is to be inferred that these glands are centers for the distribution of Prana, or the specialized solar force. Others maintain the glandular system to be under the domination of the moon, since it is true that in medical astrology glandular unbalance is more prevalent in those nativities in which the moon is afflicted or in which the water signs are prominent. Of course, if the Linga Sharira, or Etheric Double, be accepted as a vehicle of Prana, then we have the lunar agent (the humid Linga Sharira) as the carrier of the solar force (Prana) which would be in harmony with the old Egyptian teachings. Certainly the glands represent vortices in the departments of the vital force, and the physical structure of the glands might well partake of the Linga Sharira and the agent which they distribute partake of Prana. Thus, the body of the glands would be under the control of the moon and the agent which moves through them be under the control of the sun.

Efforts to establish the planetary correspondences to the glands have not proved entirely satisfactory. Indefiniteness and ambiguity among the older writers complicate the situation. Again, each organ containing, as it does, all other organs, results in an unsuspected diffusion of vital principles. For instance, "the real 'liver'," writes Paracelsus, "is to be found in all parts of the body," and only its head is in that organ which science calls the liver. Since the discovery of Neptune, that planet has been assigned the rulership of the pineal gland, but the peculiar workings of this minute body cause it to assume at various times the attributes of several planets. Under certain conditions, it is definitely Mercurial and was symbolized by both the planet and the element in alchemical writings.   In early Theosophical literature, its positive and negative aspects have also been represented by Venus and Mercury respectively, and in the figures of some mediæval mystics, the sign of Jupiter is inscribed over the place of the third eye.   Nor were the Hermetists inconsistent in concealing the mystery of this gland under the figure of the sun. Thus it would seem that any dogmatic statement would hardly be appropriate.

The pituitary body shares a similar plethora of correspondences.   Since the advent of Uranus into the solar family, this planet has enjoyed a preferential choice as the ruler of this gland.   The moon was assigned thereto by the ancients, the "Hermetic Marriage" being the union of the sun (pineal gland) and the moon (pituitary body) in the brain.   Those with a flair for riddles may find it profitable to ponder the adage that the sun rules by day and the moon by night, especially when it is intimated that the pituitary dominates the phenomenon of sleep.   By some, Venus is also regarded as a likely ruler of the pituitary body.   Both Saturn and Mercury have been assigned to the thyroid.   The sun is favored above the moon for rulership over the spleen.   The adrenals are generally given to Jupiter, but Mars is a contestant. The thymus claims Venus, but lunar activity is also evident there.   Mars is the sovereign of the liver, but in "practice" Jupiter has great power.   Each of the glands has several aspects of its function.   It is likely that the ductless glands are all septenaries and that modified forms of the activities of all the planets may be discovered in each of the glandular centers.

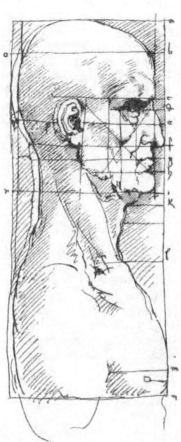

—From Del Cenacolo Di Leonardo Da Vinci Di Giuseppe Bossi.

LEONARDO DA VINCI'S CANON FOR PROPORTIONS OF HUMAN HEAD

Though Divinity seems so far removed, Its image *in* man remains as a witness *before* men. In no part of Nature is the evidence of a supreme intelligence more conclusive than in the refinement and the symmetry of human proportions. To the chemist, the human body is a laboratory; to the jurist, the embodiment of abiding law; to the musician, a summary of all symphonies; to the mathematician, crystallized geometry; to the poet, rhythm in action; to the theologian, the living temple of the living God; to the physician, the garment of life; to the architect, the trestleboard of design; to the scientist, the unsolvable enigma; to the philosopher, the image of eternal verities; to the statesman, the pattern of the commonwealth. Is it amazing, then, that the artist should delight in portraying the ever-changing moods of man; or that the architect, consciously or unconsciously, should build man's proportions into the structure he uprears?

CHAPTER XVIII

SIGHT, THE MOST EXCELLENT OF THE SENSES

O GREAT was Galen's admiration for the eyes that the brain and head were fashioned, he declared, to dignify these orbs by placing them in the highest and noblest part of the body, there to stand like sentinels upon a tower. The eyes "are next in nature unto the soul," wrote Dr. Culpeper, "for in the eyes is seen and known the disturbances and griefs, gladness and joys of the soul." He adds: "They are to the visage that which the visage is to the body; they are the face of the face; and, because they are tender, delicate, and precious, they are fenced on all sides with skins, lids, brows, and hair." The sense of sight was considered more excellent than all the rest of the senses because it did not depend upon contact with or close proximity to the object; for as one mystic rapturously exclaimed, "Sight extends even to the stars." It is said that Strabo's sight was so keen that he could discern ships and number them though they were distant 135 miles. Imprisoned within the dark recesses of the corporeal body, the soul found in the eyes the noblest instrument of its liberation. Through the eyes the soul mingles with the phenomenal universe and beholds those patterns which excite the desire for liberation and perfection.

Early writers were at a loss to adequately explain the *modus operandi* of sight. The other senses depend upon contact for their stimulation, vision alone being the exception to this rule. Seeing was evidently a more occult process and to explain it recourse must be had to metaphysics. Several solutions were advanced, all based upon the presumed necessity of some direct contact between the eye and the object seen. Emanation was the prime philosophic compromise. The sense of smell possibly suggested one explanation. The Epicureans held that all objects are constantly throwing off an invisible effluvium consisting of minute particles. These, striking against the optic nerve, stimulated sight into action by what one writer has termed a "bombardment." The matter of distant objects and the complexity of the visual panorama were the chief disadvantages of this theory. There is some truth. however, in the idea, which is incorporated in part into the conclusions of modern authorities. It is especially noteworthy that a hypothetical medium (called air, or atmosphere, by the ancients but corresponding with the much disputed "ether" of modern science) is involved as a carrier of the particles emanating from the object seen. These particles were conceived either as preserving the pattern of their original, which thus impressed its proper shape upon the eye, or else these atoms were accepted as qualitative monads—that is, each monad stimulated in the sense organ a likeness of the whole body from which it had emanated. This theory of sense stimulation agrees very closely with the doctrines of occultism as to the action of the pineal gland and the pituitary body. The former is constantly bombarded with vibrations too subtle to be registered by the external perceptions, and the latter is considerably influenced by the particles beating against the olfactory nerves.

The mystery of sight was explained in a very different way by the Stoics and their views attained wide popularity during the Middle Ages. They advanced the opinion that a virtue from the eye went forth to contact the thing seen. A sort of invisible antenna or stream of visual energy poured from the eye and, regardless of the intervening distance, enclosed within the field of its awareness the object to be cognized. This optical force was regarded as an aspect of the soul; in fact, it was even believed that the soul itself flowed out from the eye. In his COMMENTARY TO GENESIS, Ibn Ezra, the Cabalist, declares: "I will make a simile for you, from the light of the soul which comes forth from the eye." Isaac Myer, commenting on this passage, writes: "It was held by the ancient anatomists and philosophers, that in seeing, an intellectual force streamed out of the eye, which came in contact with the objects observed, and returned them to the eye." Leonardo da Vinci defends this premise against the "mathematicians" of his day who declared that the eye had no spiritual power which could extend to any distance. They maintained that such an energy would be incapable of extending itself to behold the stars without being consumed and that the strain from such an effort would exhaust the body and inevitably result in a diminution of the visual power. These objections da Vinci answers by reminding them that musk and other perfumes discharge their odor into the atmosphere, permeating a great area with very little loss to their own bulk; also that a bell, though it filled the whole countryside with its sound, is not consumed by that which it gives off in ringing. Leonardo then proceeds to advance some quaint proofs as to the virtue emanating from the eye. He explains that a snake, called the *lamia*, has a magnetism in its gaze which draws the nightingale to her death. He also notes that the wolf is credited with the power to turn men's voices hoarse with a single look; that the basilisk can destroy every living thing with its glance; that the ostrich and spider are said to hatch their eggs by looking at them; and that a fish called *linno*, found off the coast of Sardinia, sheds light from its eyes and that all fishes which come within the compass of this radiance die. Here, then, is the origin of the belief in the "Evil Eye," for the souls of wicked men, of necromancers and sorcerers, of witches, etc., poison all they look upon by the noxious forces flowing from their eyes. In DE PESTILITATE, Paracelsus describes the method of preparing poisonous mirrors impregnated with evil emanations from the moon. He continues: "If a witch desires to poison a man with her eyes, she will go to a place where she expects to meet him. When he approaches she will look into the poisoned mirror, and, then after hiding the mirror, look into his eyes, and the influence of the poison passes from the mirror into her eyes, and from her eyes into the eyes of that person."

Thomas Taylor thus summarizes the description of the visual process given by Plato in THE TIMÆUS: "With respect to sight, it must be observed that Democritus, Heraclitus, the Stoics, many of the Peripatetics and ancient geometricians, together with the Platonists, were of the opinion that vision subsists through a lucid spirit emitted from the eyes: and this spirit according to Plato and his followers, is an unburning vivific fire similar to celestial fire, from which it originally proceeds. But this fire, the illuminations of which, as we have already observed, give life to our mortal part, is abundantly collected

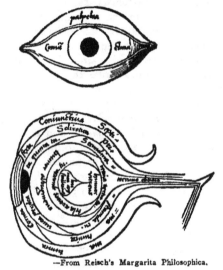

—From Reisch's Margarita Philosophica.

THE FIRST KNOWN CROSS-SECTION OF THE EYE

in the eye as in a fat diaphanous substance, whose moisture is most shining and whose membranes are tender and transparent, but yet sufficiently firm for the purpose of preserving the inherent light. But a most serene ray shines through the more solid pupil; and this ray originates internally from one nerve, but is afterwards derived through two small nerves to the two eyes. And these nerves, through the fat humours of the eyes, winding under the tunics, arrive at length at the pupils. But a light of this kind, thus preserved in the small nerves, and bursting through the narrow pupils as soon as it shines forth into rays here and there, as it commenced from one ray so it immediately returns into one, from the rays naturally uniting in one common ray: for the eyes also, on account of their lubricity, roundness, and smooth substance, are easily moved hither and thither, with an equal and similar revolution. This visual ray, however, cannot proceed externally and perceive objects at a distance, unless it is conjoined with external light proceeding conically to the eyes; and hence our ray insinuating itself into this light, and becoming strengthened by the association, continues its progression till it meets with some opposing object. But when this is the case, it either diffuses itself through the superficies of the object, or runs through it with wonderful celerity, and becomes immediately affected with the quality of the object."

In each of the foregoing theories both an active and a passive equation are involved. In the first, the object to be seen impresses itself upon the eye; in the second, the eye overwhelms and "digests" the thing seen. Seeking to reconcile these theories, the Platonists assumed the reality of both the radiation from the thing seen and the radiance of the thing seeing. To a certain degree, sight thus became a matter of chemistry. The light of the soul came forth from the eye and, after being impregnated with the particles emanating from the object of sight, returned again and communicated the impression to the soul. A seventeenth century writer thus describes this returning light as coming "impregnated with a tincture drawn from the superficies of the object it is reflected from; that is, it brings along with it several of the little atoms, * * * and they mingling themselves with the light, in company of it get into the eye, whose fabric is fit to gather and unite those species. And from the eye, their journey is but a short one to the brain."

The Neo-Platonists regarded the eye particularly as a channel for the stimulation of the soul qualities. Pythagoras taught that diseases could be healed through the eye; that is, by exposing to the sight various patterns and colors. Such figures awakened or stimulated moods and thus changed the bodily chemistry. The emotion of beauty purifies the whole corporeal fabric and thereby cures diseases which have been stimulated into manifestation through asymmetry. The contemplation of deformity stimulates deformity, and the only remedy is to superimpose a beautiful proportion over the crooked thought form and thus nullify its forces. Optical medicine was much cultivated by the philosophers. It consisted in the practice of the contemplation of beauty and filling the soul with the substance of its delight—harmony, order, and symmetry. While the bodily senses may perceive by the reflection of bodies upon their sensitized surfaces, the soul assuredly goes forth through the sense organs to mingle with the objects of its desire, namely, the qualities for which visible bodies are but outer garments.

Man began his physical evolution as a creature in which the rudimentary sense perceptions—in fact, all the parts and members—were distributed as potentialities throughout the entire body. Ultimately these potentialities will be converted into active powers and man will enjoy the extension of his sense perceptions to every part of the body, in the same manner that the sense of feeling is generalized today. A symbol of this ultimate condition was preserved in the Egyptian Mysteries by the figure of Osiris, who is often shown seated upon a throne with his body entirely covered with eyes. The Greek god Argus also was noted for his ability to see with different portions of his body. The perfect body is the sphere, and when man finally again achieves

to this shape, he will have one great center of sense perception connected to
the circumference of the body by radii, by means of which the even distribution
of awareness will be assured.   Science accepts the amoeba as illustrative of
the beginning of all animal evolution.   Life originated from the primitive protoplasm and the nucleated cell, according to Laing, and the amoeba summarizes
the scientific concept of Adam—the common ancestor of species.   The amoeba
is evidence of man's physical kinship with protoplasm, the common "earth"
from which all forms have grown and the substance out of which they have
been moulded.   Considered philosophically, the amoeba is an amazing creature

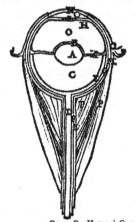

—From De Humani Corporis Fabrica.

THE STRUCTURE OF THE EYE
(After Vesalius.)

and there is about it something reminiscent of the human soul.   In the amoeba,
life seems so free of form, so little enmeshed within the limitations of matter.
The amoeba exhibits comparatively no localization of function.   It is an
organism, any part of which may serve as a leg, a stomach or an eye.   It
possesses no organs, yet metamorphoses itself into every organ necessary for
its existence.   A certain portion of it may serve as a *pseudopod*, or means of
locomotion, for one moment, and the next instant the same area will play the
role of an intestine.

When traced upward through these primitive forms of life, development
of the sense organs seems to be a movement from the simple to the complex,
from generalization to localization.   The specializing process renders the
senses more acute and establishes each faculty in such manner that its testimony will make the greatest contribution to the individual well-being.   It is
generally believed that the first eye which can be discerned makes its appearance as a tiny red spot at the anterior end of the *Euglena viridis*, a fresh water
Protozoan.   This little animal is a cyclop and its rudimentary eye serves many
purposes.   It is a general organ of sense orientation, responding to both light

and heat, and served the evolving genera of this earth when life was still but a scum upon the surface of stagnant pools. The ancients regarded the sun as the single eye of the gigantic cell of the world. In the teachings of the earlier philosophers, the eye of the soul was a single cyclopean organ in the midst of a body composed of spiritual substances somewhat analogous to an immense Protozoa. These auric substances (metaphysical protoplasm) projected various forms out of themselves—or, possibly more correctly, assumed various forms—so that the physical body of man is in reality a modification of this auric stuff. *Psycho*plasm is the basic element of the spiritual sphere, and protoplasm—its reflection in matter—is the basis of physical life.

According to a recent Dutch writer, the inward eye—that is, the visual nerve—begins first to form from the brain, and it is not until this excrescence reaches the ectoderm that the outward eye begins to be formed by bending inward. The same is true with the organ of hearing, he adds, for here also the inward part of the organ is first developed. This is a reminder to the wise that the soul, from which the sense perceptions are suspended, evolves these faculties from within itself, releasing virtues from within and not superimposing qualities from without. Growth is neither up nor down, but from within out-ward. Madam Blavatsky used the term *ideation* to signify the motion of intellect towards the circumference of body, by which it gradually tinctured matter with order, or as Plato might have said, with form.

The eye is not the source of sight, but the instrument of it. Sight is a soul quality. "Eyes do not see," wrote Swami Vivekananda. "Take away the brain centre which is in the head, the eyes will still be there, the retinae complete, and also the picture, and yet the eyes will not see. So the eyes are only a secondary instrument, not the organ of vision. The organ of vision is in the nerve centre of the brain. The two eyes will not be sufficient alone. Sometimes a man is asleep with his eyes open. The light is there and the picture is there, but a third thing is necessary; mind must be joined to the organ. The eye is the external instrument, we need also the brain centre and the agency of the mind. Carriages roll down a street and you do not hear them. Why? Because your mind has not attached itself to the organ of hearing. First, there is the instrument, then there is the organ, and third, the mind attachment to these two. The mind takes the impression farther in, and presents it to the determinative faculty—*Buddhi*—which reacts. Along with this reaction flashes the idea of egoism. Then this mixture of action and reaction is presented to the *Purusa*, the real Soul, who perceives an object in this mixture. The organs *(Indriyas)*, together with the mind *(Manas)*, the determinative faculty *(Buddhi)*, and egoism *(Ahamkara)*, form the group called the *Antahkarana* (the internal instrument). They are but various processes in the mind-stuff *(Chitta)*. * * * Naturally we see that the mind is not intelligent; yet it appears to be intelligent. Why? Because the intelligent soul is behind it. You are the only sentient being; mind is only the instrument through which you catch the external world." (See RAJA YOGA.)

Writing in the thirteenth century, Peter Hispanus declared the vital parts of the eye to be covered by seven tunics, or humorous coverings, and that these symbolized the planets. The vestments, then, form spheres like the concentric orbits of the world. The Cabalists recognized ten parts to the eye and found a correspondence between these and the globes upon the branches of the Sephirothic Tree. The ten parts of the visual apparatus are also analogous to the Pythagorean *tetractys* which consists of three concealed and seven revealed dots in the form of a triangle. "Know," says an old Cabalistic commentary, "that the eye consists of seven degrees, and that the inside one is the white

—From Maier's Scrutinum Chymicum.

THE MEASURE OF MAN ACCORDING TO ROSICRUCIAN GEOMETRY

spot." The white spot is a designation for Kether, the Crown, itself called in THE ZOHAR the eye. The eye is, therefore, a little world, the lens which is in the midst of it being an eye within an eye, a world within a world, for all the parts are patterned after the entire. The ten component parts of the eye were divided by mediæval thinkers into two groups, of which the first, consisting of three divisions, was called fluidic; and the second, consisting of seven divisions, was called solid. The three fluidic parts—the Upper Face of the Cabala—represented the Causal Trinity, or aspects of God, and were called *humors*. According to Avicenna, the *glacialis*, or icy humor, was in the center of the eye. Anterior to this was the *aqueous*, or watery humor, and posterior to it, the *vitreous*, or crystal-like humor. Samuel Carca, quoted by Isaac Myer, terms these three the crystal, the tasteless fluid (or the albugineous humor), and the sapphire. The ancients recognized the peculiar occult virtue of ice,

which captures within and upon itself forms invisible to the ordinary perceptions—as, for instance, frost pictures on window panes—and it may well have
been this mysterious quality which caused them to declare the lens of the.
eye to be ice-like. The seven tunics, or "solid shirts," of the eye are (1) the
retina, which means the net; (2) the *tunica vasculosa*, the epidermis; (3) the
tunica sclerotica, the "hard one"; (4) the *iris*, the dishlike web, or the breadlike;
(5) the *tunica uvea*, the grape-like; (6) the *tunica cornea*, the horny; and (7)
the *ligamentum ciliare*, the conjoining. (See THE QABBALAH.) These are the
seven planetary envelopes of the lens, and with the three humors, constitute
the universe of the eye.

From a consideration of the present activity of the eye it is but a step to
the anticipation of its future possibilities. Before we advance the opinions of
occultism, it is apropos to have recourse to a man of science. The same Dr.
Thomas Hall Shastid, whom we quoted in the section on the pineal gland, is
authority for the following speculations. "I even believe," he says, "that, in
the course of countless ages, the two human eyes will come closer and closer
together, the bridge of the nose will further diminish and sink (just as the
animal snout, in man's line of descent, has been doing for vast æons of time)
and, finally, man's two eyes will again become one—just one large, central,
cyclopean eye. It is likely that the merely servient (left) eye will shrink away
(as the pineal eye has already done) so that the right eye will become the
cyclopean. Certain it is that the left eye, even today, is being used less and
less continually. Man's binocular and stereoscopic visions are being destroyed.
That is the price he pays for his speech center. The great cyclopean eye,
however, will regain stereoscopic vision by developing two maculae in the one
eye, just in the fashion in which many birds have stereoscopic vision in each
eye now. Although the field of view will then be narrower than now, the eye
will probably be microscopic and telescopic; it will be exceedingly acute for
colors, for motion, and for form; and, finally, most important of all, it will
probably be able to perceive as light many forms of energy which now produce
in human eyes no sort or kind of perception."

When the good Doctor says that man in the future will probable be able
to perceive forms of energy which now produce no reaction in the human eye,
he is more than verging on the occult. Philosophy is primarily designed to
teach men how to grow by will rather than by accident. The secret schools of
the past were acquainted with disciplines by which the eye could be rendered
sensitive to these "many forms of energy." Those who accomplished this
special stimulation of the visual organ were called "clear seers," or clairvoyants.
Though occultism is tabooed in the so-called best circles of the learned, it
must be admitted that there are things which we cannot see. and there is no
reason to question that the fulfillment of the purpose of the eye is its accom-
modation to visual necessity. In other words, the thing to be seen will ultimately evoke the faculty necessary for its perception. Occultism is well
acquainted with microscopic and telescopic vision, which have been practiced

by the sages of India for thousands of years. "There are certain things," writes Albertus Magnus, "so overpowering in translucent purity that they are made so radiant that they overcome the harmony of the eye, and they can not be seen without great difficulty. There are others, too, which give forth so much illumination and translucence that they can hardly be discerned by sight because of the slightness of their composition from the transparent."

Occultism predicts ultimate dominion of a single cyclopean eye over the present visual instrument. It will not be the right eye, however, (which the ancients symbolized by the sun) nor the left eye (which they represented by the moon), but the single Hermetic eye within the brain itself. The eyes are incidental organs, their virtue dependent entirely upon the necessity for objective awareness. As man lifts himself through the refinement of his organisms, as he stimulates the inner qualities of the soul, the single eye will reopen and enable him to gaze upon those causal vistas beyond the apprehension of physical sight. Sankaracharya said the seat of the greatest clairvoyant activity is not in the eye itself but in a focal point a short distance in front of the pupils. The blind spot in the eye should be given greater consideration, for it was known to the sages that under certain conditions a positive ray was emitted therefrom. The eye is capable of seeing by two completely different processes. By the first the object is reflected into the eye; by the second, a ray of visual energy passes out through the blind spot and illumines the object to be seen. In the first process, the object is seen; in the second, man sees the object. When the object is seen, only its outer aspects are visible, as color, form, etc.; but when the intellectual ray from the eye strikes the object, it penetrates, for its action is (shall we say?) fourth-dimensional. As men see now, they behold only the shadows of objects— as it were, "through a glass darkly." But by this other perception they are enabled to gaze into the soul of things, so to say, "face to face."

DIGESTIVE INDEX

A

B

C

D

E

F

G

H

I

J

K

L

M

N

O

P

Q

R

S

T

U

Printed in the USA
CPSIA information can be obtained
at www.ICGtesting.com
CBHW021124140124
3451CB00005B/191

9 781773 239699